Security, Defence, and the Future of Europe

Michael Kaeding • Johannes Pollak
Paul Schmidt
Editors

Security, Defence, and the Future of Europe

Views from the Capitals

Editors
Michael Kaeding
Institute for Political Science
University of Duisburg-Essen
Duisburg, Nordrhein-Westfalen, Germany

Johannes Pollak
Sigmund Freud University Vienna
Wien, Austria

Paul Schmidt
Austrian Society for European Politics
Wien, Austria

ISBN 978-3-032-18278-4 ISBN 978-3-032-18279-1 (eBook)
https://doi.org/10.1007/978-3-032-18279-1

This Springer imprint is published by the registered company Springer Nature Switzerland AG
The registered company address is: Gewerbestrasse 11, 6330 Cham, Switzerland

trans-
european
policy
studies
association

Foreword

This excellent and important volume provides views on security and defence from the capitals. So let me give the view from Europe.

These contributions show that what unites us is greater than what divides us. The debate on defence is a European debate. We're clear about the threats that face us and that we must take action. Russia's invasion of Ukraine is the defining moment in all Member States, triggering universal condemnation but also security concerns. Russia is universally seen as a threat to peace.

Certainly, this is less so in some Member States farther removed from the fighting. However, it is clear to all that Putin is challenging us, with drone incursions on the eastern border and drone provocations at airports across the entire European Union (EU). He could be ready to test the North Atlantic Treaty Organisation (NATO) by 2030—or even sooner—according to intelligence service estimates. Actual Russian aggression against an EU Member State would have devastating consequences for all Member States and for the entire EU, politically, economically and militarily. If the storm comes, no one will escape the consequences.

Putin hates the EU because the massive economic and social success of the countries formerly under Soviet domination is a stark contrast with the collapse into oligarchy and corruption of Russia and the countries still under its sway. It is a constant reminder that there is a better way than the Putin way. Our power to inspire is an existential threat to the Putin regime.

Add to that the United States' (U.S.) increased focus on Asia, and it is clear to everyone that Europe must take more responsibility for its own defence. At the same time, it's also obvious that defence is primarily a responsibility for Member States. Together with NATO, they decide on defence budgets, capability needs and what they purchase for their defence. Member States operate their armed forces together with NATO.

I want to be clear about the EU's role. There will be no duplication. There is a clear division of labour, with NATO offering military power and the EU providing production power. The EU offers European added value: European laws, European funding and European coordination. This makes it possible for Member States to operate on a continental scale. Together in the EU Member States can achieve things no Member State can ever achieve alone. Delivering this European added value has been my mission as Commissioner for Defence and Space.

At the very beginning of my mandate, I said that it was my goal to have a "big bang" in defence. We now have that "big bang" in defence finances. At the historic June Summit, NATO set capability targets and agreed to increase defence spending to 3.5 % of gross domestic product (GDP) by 2035. If all Member States manage to meet their pledges, this means EUR 6.8 trillion for defence over the next 10 years.

The EU is helping Member States to meet these pledges, with unprecedented decisions on defence finances: EUR 150 billion in attractive Security Action For Europe (SAFE) loans backed by the EU budget; provision of budgetary flexibility by invoking the national escape clause of the Stability and Growth Pact. We have also proposed a five-fold increase in European defence and space spending in the next multiannual EU budget, the Multiannual Financial Framework (MFF), to EUR 131 billion from 2027 to 2035

From the numbers, it is clear that the bulk of defence spending will come from Member States. Assuming an equal division, this would mean 100 times more than from the MFF. However, here there is one danger, namely that this increase in national defence spending will only increase fragmentation of production or spending outside the EU. This is why from the Union side we encourage not only spending more but also spending better and spending European. We incentivise joint development as well as joint procurement and joint production, with a prescribed 65% minimum level of European components in our EU instruments.

In the last years we have carried out successful initiatives to scale up ammunition production (the Act in Support of Ammunition Production [ASAP]) and joint procurement (the European Defence Industry Reinforcement through Common Procurement Act). We build on these successes with our European Defence Industry Programme, which will make it possible for Member States to work together in new ways on defence production. This allows the building of pan-European defence industry projects—European Defence Projects of Common Interest—which no Member State can ever build alone, but that will protect the whole of Europe.

We also support our defence industry with proposals and initiatives to reduce red tape for industry and transform our defence industry based on Ukraine's battlefield experience, into a transformative ecosystem linking innovation, industry, testing and soldiers in the field within a constant loop. We have presented a proposal on military mobility, binding EU law to replace fragmented national rules, so troops and equipment can move in hours or days across Europe instead of months as is currently the case.

In short, we have achieved in the first year of the mandate what I call the opportunities for defence readiness. Now we must move on to the delivery phase.

Our Roadmap on Defence Readiness 2030 offers guidance for delivery, which makes it possible for Member States to fill the massive capability gaps, proposing defence industrial 'flagship' projects to protect the entire Union. These include the Drone Defence Initiative and Eastern Flank Watch, or Air Shield and the European Space Shield Initiative (ESSI) led by Member States, produced by industry, operated by NATO and Member States, supported by the EU.

In short, this is how European added value supports Member States. Here now are just a few points of general principle.

Firstly, security is a public service. We need defence to safeguard our societies, democracies and welfare states. Not investing in defence will have a much higher social cost: war.

Secondly, we need not only material defence readiness (weapons and equipment) but also institutional defence readiness to organise our defence readiness on the European continent.

It is time to build a European Defence Union. A new security architecture for Europe, which must also involve Ukraine, because there are now only two states with battle-tested armies on the European continent: Russia and Ukraine. That is why integrating Ukraine's defence industry is part of everything we do: purchasing equipment in, with and for Ukraine and learning from Ukrainian experience.

These contributions give the view from the capitals. I have given the European view and tried to provide some European added value.

As a final word: the EU is a project of peace.

Our goal in ramping up defence is not war, but to prevent war.

Our goal is to deter Russian aggression and preserve peace

Our policy is production, but our purpose is peace.

European Commissioner for Defence and Space Andrius Kubilius

Why this Book?

Since the devastating world wars of the twentieth century, which claimed millions of lives, the EU's foundational narrative of "never again" has been standing at the core of its identity. It has allowed EU Member States and their neighbours to enjoy decades of peace and prosperity. Yet, war never completely disappeared. It merely shifted elsewhere, flaring up across other world regions and, repeatedly, on the European continent itself, from the Western Balkans and Chechnya to Moldova, Georgia and Ukraine.

Si vis pacem, para bellum—if you want peace, prepare for war. Today, four years after Russia's full-scale invasion of Ukraine, Europe faces intensified hybrid attacks, disinformation campaigns, cyberattacks, acts of sabotage, assassinations and weaponised migration, while at the same time the transatlantic relationship with the U.S. stands on fragile ground. The European threat perception has changed fundamentally. Although countries still differ in their assessment of risks, a new understanding of security, deterrence and military preparedness has emerged. Since the Cold War ended, many European countries have placed their faith in diplomacy, multilateralism and trade while outsourcing hard security to the U.S. Today, the doctrine of *Wandel durch Handel* (change through trade) appears to have failed. China, Russia and even the U.S. use dependencies as a geopolitical Trojan horse to increase leverage and undermine Europe's cohesion. However, defending the rules-based international order requires a stronger European answer by recalibrating the balance between diplomacy, economic resilience and military capability. Some argue that rearmament risks militarising European societies and fuels escalation, yet recent history also shows that failing to confront aggressors early on only increases their appetite for expansion. Adjusting the balance between diplomacy and deterrence has therefore become essential.

Having long benefited from America's conventional and nuclear security umbrella, Europe is now advancing towards a European Union for Security and Defence (EUSD). This will be an integrated framework going beyond the military dimension to encompass resilience, cyber-defence, critical infrastructure protection and societal preparedness. Finnish President Sauli Niinistö's 2024 report 'Safer together: Strengthening Europe's civilian and military readiness' and the 'EU Strategic Compass implementation review' from the same year both stress that collective preparedness must span every level of society.

Accordingly, in March 2025, the European Commission and the High Representative jointly presented the 'White Paper for European Defence—'Readiness 2030'', setting out a roadmap to close critical capability gaps and consolidate a robust European defence industrial base. This paper operationalises the ReArm Europe Plan, proposing major investment in defence research and development, joint procurement of key military systems and strategic stockpiling. It also integrates the European Defence Industry Programme, endorsed by the European Council in June 2025, to accelerate production capacity for ammunition, air defence and advanced surveillance technologies.

While NATO remains Europe's cornerstone of collective defence, the EU's role as a security provider has expanded substantially. Between 2021 and 2024, Member States increased total defence expenditure by more than 30%, reaching an estimated EUR 326 billion in 2024 (around 1.9% of EU GDP). In 2025, the figure is projected to exceed EUR 350 billion, reflecting both national budgetary adjustments under the reformed Stability and Growth Pact as well as establishment of the European Defence Investment Fund. The ReArm Europe Plan and 'Readiness 2030' aim to mobilise at least EUR 800 billion in additional investment, structured around three pillars: Flexibility within fiscal rules (activating the national escape clause of the Stability and Growth Pact to provide budgetary space approaching 1.5% of GDP for defence investment); Capital market mobilisation (jointly raising up to EUR 150 billion through the SAFE initiative); together with private and institutional leverage (mobilising private capital via the European Investment Bank (EIB) group and advancing the Savings and Investments Union to channel European household savings into strategic security industries).

Meanwhile, Russia's military spending has surged by 240% since 2000 and China's by over 600%. Despite diminished financial transparency, Russia's military expenditure in 2024 is estimated at 7.2% of GDP (RUB 15.5 trillion), but with Russia's GDP being approximately one-tenth of EU GDP. By contrast, the U.S. defence budget reached nearly USD 1 trillion in 2024, about 3.4% of its GDP. In addition, during the late summer 2025 NATO Summit in The Hague, Allies committed (with the tentative exception of Spain) to investing 5% of GDP annually on core defence requirements along with defence- and security-related spending by 2035. This new arms race is not merely about EU countries spending more, therefore, but about more efficient cooperation and expenditure.

In a world where deal-making, disruption and military might have become the new normal, the EU must find a way to consolidate its political, industrial and military capacities. It must learn to act strategically. To regain geopolitical relevance, the EU and its Member States, together with neighbouring and like-minded countries, will need to leverage economic power and transform their collective posture. Building a credible EUSD will not replace NATO, but it will help Europe to sit at the global security table.

This volume offers the much-needed preparatory groundwork, as it provides insights into the different mindsets and priorities, the willingness, concerns and fears in the 27 EU Member States and 15 neighbouring countries. Short, opinionated articles outline many answers to questions that complete the European picture, explain the current challenges it faces and how these could potentially be overcome. Each country chapter ends with clear recommendations to the respective national governments and European decision-makers.

EU Security and Defence: National Contributions, Priorities and the Path Towards an EUSD

Across Europe, security and defence have moved from peripheral concerns to the very centre of political discourse. Russia's invasion of Ukraine in 2022 has transformed threat perceptions and the urgency of rearmament. Yet, the EU's capitals interpret the idea of an EUSD rather differently.

Northern and Eastern EU Member States such as Estonia, Lithuania, Finland, Poland and Denmark are now driving the agenda for stronger European defence integration. Estonia and Lithuania, facing direct Russian pressure, are investing record shares of GDP in defence (3–5%), maintaining robust conscription and calling for the EU to become a capability provider within NATO rather than a substitute. Finland and Sweden's accession to NATO has strengthened the northern flank and demonstrated that neutrality is no longer a viable long-term option. Denmark, historically one of the most transatlanticist states, has since Trump's second term turned markedly towards Europe, seeing the EU as the only dependable partner should America retreat from the continent. The same holds true for Norway and Iceland.

In Central Europe, countries such as Czechia, Slovakia and Croatia are pursuing modernisation and seeking a balance between NATO reliance and EU autonomy. Czechia, once cautious about EU defence, now supports joint U.S. systems. Croatia has raised defence spending to 2% of GDP and reintroduced conscription in 2025. However, the political wind of change and polarisation in many countries is likely to complicate European support for Ukraine still further.

Among the southern members, Italy, Spain, Portugal and Greece are advocating a pragmatic yet ambitious European approach, arguing that Mediterranean security (migration, energy, maritime and climate change) must feature alongside the Eastern threat. France continues to be the intellectual leader of European strategic autonomy, while Italy and Spain emphasise complementarity with NATO. In addition, costs for the military build-up and support for Ukraine are often at odds with budgetary possibilities and social spending.

Neutral states show more ambivalence, with Austria, Ireland, Cyprus, Malta and Switzerland remaining outside NATO. Austria insists on its neutrality, but is slowly increasing spending and participation in EU missions. The country's 2025 defence plan targets 2% of GDP by 2032, yet its armed forces still remain largely focused on disaster relief. Belgium and Luxembourg, though fully committed politically, have long used European cooperation as an excuse for under-investment; the fairy tale of a European army has masked decades of neglect. Under U.S. pressure, Belgium has finally accelerated its budget path towards 2%. Ireland feels far away from the conflict zone, while Cyprus clearly sees Turkey as its main threat.

Front-line states such as Bulgaria, Romania and Poland view the EUSD primarily as a reinforcement mechanism for NATO. Bulgaria's Black Sea exposure, combined with heavy modernisation (F-16s, Strykers, Rheinmetall joint plants), shows how smaller countries can link EU and NATO priorities. Poland, already spending well over 4%, is calling for an 'EU of defence' that strengthens deterrence, but warns against diluting NATO command.

While the United Kingdom (UK) finds itself between its 'special relationship' with the U.S. and the need for stronger defence cooperation with Europe, all European eyes seem to be set on Germany, with its plans for massive investments in its military and infrastructure.

Looking forward, the EU's capacity to 'walk the path' to an EUSD will depend on reconciling the different viewpoints. A core group (France, Germany, Poland, Italy, Spain, the Nordics) is likely to move ahead via 'coalitions of the willing' within the EU treaties. Full independence from NATO remains unrealistic, but gradual autonomy, such as joint procurement, intelligence, cyber-defence, air and space security, appears achievable. The main risk is internal division between those without budgetary room to invest, those reluctant to spend and the 'front-liners' ready to do whatever it takes. The EUSD thus emerges as a layered system of overlapping commitments.

EU Independence and the U.S. Role

Trump's second presidency has fundamentally altered European strategic thinking. The U.S. remains Europe's indispensable ally, but no longer its unquestioned protector.

In Denmark, the Greenland dispute and U.S. unpredictability turned Washington from a trusted partner to a potential medium threat level. In polls, an unprecedented 46% of Danes now see the U.S. as a threat. Hence, the Danish government is advocating European 'self-help', expanding security spending to 3% of GDP and seeking closer defence ties with northern neighbours.

Belgium offers a textbook case of dependence: the recent leap to 2% of GDP was achieved mainly to appease Washington. Political elites still regard the transatlantic link as vital, but stress that future cooperation must be "for us, not for the U.S.". Similarly, Czechia and Poland continue to rely heavily on U.S. technology (F-35s, Abrams, Patriots) yet fear American disengagement if Washington prioritises the Indo-Pacific.

By contrast, France interprets U.S. retrenchment as validation of its long-standing push for European strategic autonomy. Germany remains the pivot: still anchored in NATO, but under pressure to lead after the *Zeitenwende*, investing EUR 100 billion in rearmament and introducing voluntary military service. Berlin is stressing complementarity with its slogan "stronger Europeans, not weaker NATO".

Southern Europe follows a more nuanced line. Italy and Spain welcome U.S. backing in NATO, but support diversification of alliances in Africa and the

Mediterranean. Portugal stresses transatlantic continuity, yet also champions EU-Africa security partnerships to reduce dependence on U.S. naval power.

In Eastern and Northern Europe, particularly Estonia, Finland, Lithuania and Poland, the U.S. is still viewed as essential for deterrence. Estonian officials privately worry that a U.S.-Russia bargain 'above Ukraine's head' could endanger Baltic security. Thus, Europe must simultaneously keep the U.S. engaged ("keep America in") while building its own capabilities ("keep Europe up").

Looking ahead, most capitals foresee the U.S. as a partner, but on a transactional basis. If Europe fails to pay the price and demonstrate burden-sharing, Washington might become a competitor rather than an ally. Hence, the EUSD concept is not anti-American but insurance against U.S. unpredictability.

Financing Defence Investments

Europe's rearmament can rightly be called a fiscal revolution. Between 2022 and 2025, average EU defence spending rose from 1.3% to 1.9% of GDP; furthermore, the EU's 'White Paper on Defence Financing' and the SAFE mechanism aim to mobilise EUR 800 billion by 2035.

Germany's special fund remains the largest single investment (EUR 100 billion), yet delivery delays highlight the challenge of absorption capacity. France raised its multi-annual defence budget to EUR 413 billion for the period 2024–2030. Poland is already investing more than 4% of GDP, funding expansion through bonds and domestic industry; Estonia plans 5% of GDP by 2028, financed through new taxes and borrowing.

Among smaller states, Belgium has raised spending from EUR 7 billion to EUR 11 billion, using debt and one-off dividends from a state-owned bank. Public acceptance is lukewarm: only 17% support a higher value-added tax (VAT) to fund defence. Bulgaria reached NATO's 2% target for the first time in 2025 and uses EU funds and U.S. arms deals; the Euro adoption in 2026 and the 'escape clause' will help exclude defence from deficit rules. Croatia plans 3% by 2030, financing purchases through growth rather than social cuts. Austria aims at 2% by 2032, but remains far below average (0.8% in 2025).

Northern states combine economic resilience with strategic purpose. Denmark's increase to 3.2% of GDP was largely financed by growth, not cuts; Finland has reached 2.4%, focusing on readiness. Norway and Sweden are also investing heavily and integrating closely with EU procurement frameworks while retaining national control.

The EU's White Paper is being widely welcomed for offering flexible tools, loans, tax incentives and exclusion of defence investment from deficit ceilings, but smaller and fiscally constrained members (Belgium, Bulgaria, Portugal, Greece) call for European Defence Bonds to ensure equity. However, critics fear that such common borrowing could spark fiscal moral hazard.

Overall, the fiscal trajectory is upwards, albeit uneven. Wealthier members (Germany, Nordics, Poland) can absorb higher spending, whilst fiscally fragile states (Belgium, Portugal, Italy) are relying on EU support. The political challenge lies in more efficiency and explaining that security is a public good, not a competing budget item.

Public Opinion, Threat Perception and Awareness

Public opinion across Europe reveals striking contrasts. Using the traffic-light system based on Tu (2024) and Rousseau & Garcia-Retamero (2007), the picture is mixed, identifying particular regional patterns: 'red' peripheries with 'green' interiors.

Colour	Countries (examples)	Perception and framing
Red (high threat)	Estonia, Lithuania, Poland, Finland, Denmark (re Russia), Cyprus (re Turkey), Romania, Bulgaria (re Russia)	Adversaries possess superior capabilities; imminent aggression feared; military and civil preparedness high; adversaries openly labelled 'enemies'
Yellow (medium threat)	Czechia, Croatia, Slovakia, Germany, France, Italy, Spain, Denmark (re U.S.)	Adversaries seen as capable but not immediate; partial preparedness; hybrid and cyber threats dominate discourse
Green (low threat)	Austria, Ireland, Malta, Switzerland, Portugal	Military aggression seen as implausible; neutrality, diplomacy, or distance from conflict reinforce complacency

Source: Own compilation based on chapters

Baltic and Nordic countries (Estonia, Lithuania, Finland, Denmark) show a 'red' level of threat. Estonian surveys (May 2025) report 82% of respondents viewing Russia as an existential danger. Danish polls record 86% seeing Russia as an enemy, with 75% backing aid to Ukraine. Central Europe sits between 'yellow' and 'red': Czechia's threat perception is a 'yellow-red hybrid', with strong institutional preparedness, but declining public enthusiasm for supporting Ukraine (circa 40%). Southeastern Europe displays mixed signals: Bulgaria rates Russia 'red', regarding migration and 'yellow' for cyber threats. Croatia identifies Russia as the main external challenge, yet only 'yellow' for direct threat, focusing instead on Western Balkan instability. Western Europe trends towards 'green': Belgium's low perceived risk ('green') is indicative of its reluctance to fund defence; whilst Austria's neutrality yields 'green' complacency. Southern Europe (Italy, Spain, Portugal) is generally 'yellow-green': threats are seen as diffuse (terrorism, energy, migration) rather than military. Cyprus remains 'red' due to Turkey's occupation and hybrid warfare.

Public understanding of security interdependence remains limited. Countries with historical trauma (Estonia, Poland, Finland) show high awareness and readiness; societies with long peace traditions (Austria, Ireland) underestimate threats. Far-right and populist parties exploit this divide, portraying rearmament as leading to escalation. Austria's far-right party slogan, "Neutrality protects us", illustrates this. Some governments attempt to 'translate' the urgency, but again approaches differ: Denmark links defence to gender equality (female conscription); Czechia and Belgium frame spending as protection against cyber and energy attacks; Bulgaria and Poland highlight national industry benefits—overall, a patchwork of interpretations that mitigates against the creation of a truly common European strategic culture.

Systems of Military Service Vary Widely

Across Europe, systems of military service vary widely, reflecting differing strategic cultures, constitutional traditions and threat perceptions. A number of states maintain compulsory service, though the details differ considerably. Finland continues to operate a robust conscription model for men, with around 75% of each cohort called up and service lasting between 165 and 347 days. Women may also volunteer. Lithuania reintroduced conscription in 2015, requiring service from young men while again women are allowed to volunteer. Cyprus mandates military service for all males over 18, currently set at 14 months. Austria also retains compulsory service, with strong public support for maintaining and even extending the current six-month term. Turkey also preserves compulsory military service for men as a core element of national defence.

Other states have recently revived conscription: Croatia reinstated mandatory service in 2025 for men, with voluntary service for women, providing two months of basic training and a monthly net salary of around EUR 1100; conscientious objectors may complete unpaid civilian service instead.

In contrast, a number of countries have abolished conscription and rely entirely on voluntary recruitment. Spain professionalised its armed forces in 2001 and retains an all-volunteer model without any political debate about returning to conscription. Romania has had voluntary service since 2007, though debates persist on whether to reintroduce compulsory service due to shrinking reserves; however, public opinion still leans towards voluntary forms of participation. North Macedonia abolished mandatory service in 2006 and maintains a professional, voluntary force, although its legal framework would allow reintroduction in emergencies. Bulgaria ended compulsory service in 2008 and now fields a professional army of nearly 27,000 personnel.

Various European states operate hybrid or selective systems. Norway applies gender-neutral conscription, but calls up only a portion of each cohort, as does Denmark. Meanwhile, Sweden reinstated gender-neutral conscription in 2017, requiring all 18-year-olds to undergo mustering, with selected individuals obliged to complete military training. Debates about reintroducing or reforming conscription have also re-emerged in Germany, compulsory service having been suspended in 2011. Political and societal discussions about its potential return have recently intensified, resulting in Germany's decision to introduce voluntary military service after months of wrangling. The government will not reintroduce conscription, but all 18-year-old males will have to fill in a questionnaire and young men will soon have to undergo mandatory physical examinations; in the UK, recruitment challenges have sparked debate about reinstating national service, although as yet no plans exist, with conscription having ended in 1960; Montenegro continues to rely on voluntary service, but repeatedly revisits the question of whether mandatory service should be reintroduced.

Peace Talks and the EU's Role in Negotiations

Across Europe, there is broad recognition that the EU must play a more prominent diplomatic role in future peace processes between Russia and Ukraine. However, differences persist on how and when.

Eastern and Nordic states (Estonia, Poland, Lithuania, Finland) reject any premature negotiations that could reward aggression. They insist that peace must follow a Ukrainian victory and full territorial restoration. For them, EU leadership means long-term support, sanctions enforcement and accountability for war crimes.

Central and southeastern members (Czechia, Croatia, Bulgaria, Slovakia) combine firmness with pragmatism. Bulgaria's surveys show that 94% favour peace talks, reflecting a societal preference for diplomacy. Sofia advocates an EU-, NATO-, and UN-coordinated mediation once battlefield conditions permit, seeing itself as a bridge due to cultural ties with Russia. Croatia supports EU coordination, but warns that peace "must not reward the aggressor".

Western Europe (France, Germany, Italy, Spain, Portugal) stresses diplomacy. France seeks "European seats at the table", arguing that Europe must not again depend on U.S.-Russia bilateralism. Germany, while upholding Ukraine's sovereignty, prepares for a "post-war order" centred on reconstruction and deterrence. Italy and Spain emphasise humanitarian diplomacy and energy security.

Neutral and non-aligned countries (Austria, Ireland, Malta, Switzerland, Serbia, Moldova) perceive mediation as their natural niche. Austria offered to host talks, yet its credibility eroded after joining the European Sky Shield Initiative. Russia now sees Vienna as 'performatively neutral'. Switzerland's traditional mediator role endures but is questioned after its alignment with EU sanctions. Serbia and Moldova, balancing between EU integration and Russian ties, could serve as regional facilitators if neutrality were perceived as genuine. Cyprus presents a unique perspective: its own experience of occupation makes it empathetic to Ukraine yet critical of double standards. Nicosia argues that Europe's credibility requires consistent enforcement of international law, including pressure against Turkey, and that the EU must set clear red lines on territorial integrity.

In summary, most European governments envisage the EU as co-architect of eventual peace, but timing and reality divides them. The north-eastern 'security first' camp sees peace talks only after victory; the southern 'diplomacy first' camp calls for immediate preparation of negotiation frameworks. A unified EU approach, combining deterrence, reconstruction planning and credible mediation, remains aspirational, but increasingly recognised, at least in Europe, as indispensable.

To conclude, this volume enhances our understanding of Europe as a continent in strategic transition under duress. The war in Ukraine has catalysed unprecedented convergence on the need for common defence, yet European unity remains fragile.

Threat perceptions range from existential ('red') in the east and north to complacent ('green') from the west to the south. Fiscal capacities diverge widely whilst public opinion oscillates between solidarity and fatigue.

This book in our series 'The Future of Europe: Views from the Capitals' takes us through a tremendously heterogeneous and vibrant political landscape of Europe and the trajectory is clear. We must move towards an EUSD that: complements, but does not replace NATO; seeks autonomy with openness; and aspires to a distinct role in building a lasting and just peace as well as security. Europe's ability to achieve this depends on three variables: sustained public support, equitable financing together with the political courage to match rhetoric with capability and strength.

As a guidebook, students and teachers, journalists and practitioners, but also the interested public may find the short overviews, scores of questions, differences and common ground provide the means to explore more deeply the breathtaking diversity that defines, sometimes divides, but ultimately unites this continent.

We are particularly grateful to Allegra Wirmer, Project Manager at the Trans European Policy Studies Association (TEPSA), for her editorial processing and tireless efforts in making this project become a reality.

November 2025
Duisburg, Germany

Michael Kaeding
Johannes Pollak
Paul Schmidt

Contents

Contributors

Pablo del Amo Elcano Royal Institute, Madrid, Spain

Odeta Barbullushi College of Europe, Tirana, Albania

Maja Bjeloš Belgrade Centre for Security Policy, Belgrade, Serbia

Karlis Bukovskis Latvian Institute of International Affairs, Riga, Latvia

Celia Burgdorff Fondation pour la Recherche Stratégique, Paris, France

Hrvoje Butković The Institute for Development and International Relations, Zagreb, Croatia

Federico Castiglioni Istituto Affari Internazionali, Rome, Italy

Luca Cinciripini Istituto Affari Internazionali, Rome, Italy

Barry Colfer Institute of International and European Affairs, Dublin, Ireland

Alice Cunha Portuguese Institute of International Relations, Lisbon, Portugal

Dženana Đurković Faculty of Economics, University of Montenegro, Podgorica, Montenegro

Athina Fatsea ELIAMEP, Athens, Greece

Sandra Fernandes Research Center in Political Science, Braga, Portugal

Christian Frommelt University of Liechtenstein, Vaduz, Liechtenstein

Josip Glaurdić Institute of Political Science of the University of Luxembourg, Esch-sur-Alzette, Luxembourg

Iulian Groza Institute for European Policies and Reforms, Republic of Moldova

Michelle Haas Ghent Institute for International and European Studies, Ghent, Belgium

Tim Haesebrouck Ghent Institute for International and European Studies, Ghent, Belgium

Nerma Halilović-Kibrić Faculty of Criminal Justice and Security Studies at the University of Sarajevo, Sarajevo, Bosnia and Herzegovina

Mark Harwood Institute of European Studies, University of Malta, Msida, Malta

Gunilla Herolf Swedish Institute of International Affairs, Stockholm, Sweden

Tuomas Iso-Markku Finnish Institute of International Affairs, Helsinki, Finland

Danijela Jaćimović Faculty of Economics, University of Montenegro, Podgorica, Montenegro

Jelena Juvan Faculty of Social Sciences, University of Ljubljana, Slovenia

Alper Kaliber Istanbul Policy Centre at Sabancı University, Istanbul, Turkey

Boglárka Koller Institute of World Economics, Centre for Economics and Regional Studies, Budapest, Hungary

Petr Kratochvíl Institute of International Relations Prague, Prague, Czechia

Tony Lawrence International Centre for Defence and Security, Tallinn, Estonia

Raquel García Llorente Elcano Royal Institute, Madrid, Spain

Jeta Loshaj Kosovar Centre for Security Studies, Prishtina, Kosovo

Oleksiy Melnyk Razumkov Centre, Kyiv, Ukraine

Marion Messmer Chatham House, London, UK

Mihai Mogildea Institute for European Policies and Reforms, Chişinău, Republic of Moldova

Ignacio Molina Elcano Royal Institute, Madrid, Spain

Ivan Nachev New Bulgarian University, Sofia, Bulgaria

Matej Navrátil Faculty of Social and Economic Sciences, Comenius University Bratislava, Bratislava, Slovakia

Mikkel Runge Olesen Danish Institute for International Studies, Copenhagen, Denmark

Hristo Panchugov New Bulgarian University, Sofia, Bulgaria

Irena Rajchinovska Pandeva Iustinianus Primus Faculty of Law, Ss. Cyril and Methodius University, Skopje, North Macedonia

Pernille Rieker ARENA – Centre for European Studies at the University of Oslo, Oslo, Norway

Janis Sarts NATO Strategic Communications Centre of Excellence, Riga, Latvia

Frank Schimmelfennig ETH Zürich, Zurich, Switzerland

Mihai Sebe European Institute of Romania, Bucharest, Romania

Loïc Simonet Austrian Institute for International Affairs, Vienna

Irakli Sirbiladze PMC Research Centre, Tbilisi, Georgia

Mykola Sunhurovskyi Razumkov Centre, Kyiv, Ukraine

Zdeněk Sychra University of West Bohemia, Plzeň, Czechia

Funda Tekin Institute for European Politics, Berlin, Germany

Andreas Theophanous Cyprus Center for European and International Affairs, Nicosia, Cyprus

Baldur Thorhallsson Institute of International Affairs, University of Iceland, Reykjavík, Iceland

Dimitris Tsaknis European Public Law Organization, Athens, Greece

Boštjan Udovič Faculty of Social Sciences, University of Ljubljana, Slovenia

Eliza Vaş European Institute of Romania, Bucharest, Romania

Auke Venema Clingendael – the Netherlands Institute of International Relations, The Hague, Netherlands

Ramūnas Vilpišauskas Institute of International Relations and Political Science, Vilnius University, Vilnius, Lithuania

Nikola Vlahović Youth Atlantic Treaty Association of Montenegro, Podgorica, Montenegro

Marcin Zubek Institute of European Studies at the Jagiellonian University, Kraków, Poland

List of Abbreviations

ASAP	Act in Support of Ammunition Production
AI	Artificial intelligence
CFSP	Common Foreign and Security Policy
CSDP	Common Security and Defence Policy
EEA	European Economic Area
EP	European Parliament
EPP	European People's Party
ESSI	European Sky Shield Initiative
EU	European Union
EUSD	European Union for Security and Defence
GDP	Gross domestic product
ISSA	Institute of Social Studies and Analysis
JEF	Joint Expeditionary Forces
KFOR	Kosovo Force
KSF	Kosovo Security Force
MFF	Multiannual Financial Framework
NATO	North Atlantic Treaty Organisation
PESCO	Permanent Structured Cooperation
S&D	Progressive Alliance of Socialists and Democrats
QMV	Qualified Majority Voting
RS	Republika Srpska
RNS	*Revue nationale stratégique*
SPD	Social Democratic Party of Germany
UK	United Kingdom
UN	United Nations
U.S.	United States
VAT	Value-added tax

Austria: The End of the Neutrality Bubble?

Loïc Simonet

Austria continues to maintain its traditional neutrality despite rising geopolitical tensions. Its threat perception is low ('green') and Russia's invasion of Ukraine in 2022 did not trigger any major change. While increasing defence spending and supporting EU initiatives, the ruling coalition must deal with strong pressure from the far right regarding Austria's EU commitment. This ambiguous stance between European solidarity and national identity risks isolating Austria strategically and weakening its role as a mediator.

In Austria, neutrality has been an essential factor in the formation of its national political identity since the country was accorded full independence in 1955. It remains a major symbol of Austria's character. The entry of formally neutral/non-aligned Finland and Sweden into NATO in the wake of Russia's aggression towards Ukraine highlighted the singular position of the four remaining European neutral countries: Austria, Ireland, Malta and Switzerland. Cyprus sits to one side because of Turkey's occupying the northern part of the island, which prevents any *rapprochement* with NATO. Paradoxically, although Vienna is within range of Russian missiles, the return of war to Europe has not drastically altered the security perception of this mountainous country, landlocked at the very heart of the continent, without any real enemies. A poll taken in May 2022, shortly after Russia's attack, showed that only 14% of Austrians favoured abandoning neutrality, with a huge 75% opposed (74% in 2025). "Austria was neutral, is neutral, and remains neutral," former Austrian Chancellor Karl Nehammer insisted. Yet, Austria's 'I do it my way' approach risks marginalisation.

L. Simonet (✉)
Österreichisches Institut für Internationale Politik (oiip), Vienna, Austria
e-mail: loic.simonet@oiip.ac.at

M. Kaeding et al. (eds.), *Security, Defence, and the Future of Europe*,
https://doi.org/10.1007/978-3-032-18279-1_1

The "Most Problematic" EU Country for a European Defence Union

Many Austrian politicians see a stronger defence union as an alternative to NATO and easier for the public to 'digest'. Foreign Minister Beate Meinl-Reisinger (NEOS, liberal, sitting with the Renew Europe group within the European Parliament [EP]) expressed clear support for the European Commission's plans: "Europe must stand on its own feet when it comes to protection and security", she said, also emphasising that Austrian neutrality and European security are on the same level, not in contradiction. The new government installed in March 2025, led by Federal Chancellor Christian Stocker (ÖVP, conservative, sitting with the European People's Party [EPP] in the EP), decided to increase Austria's defence expenditure to 2% of GDP annually by 2032 (around 0.75% in 2024, at EUR 4.015 billion), in addition to the ongoing 'development plan 2032+' which seeks to invest around EUR 17 billion additional funds into its armed forces by the same year. The "dream of disarmament is now over," Stocker acknowledged. The Chancellor soon availed himself of the EU's proposed exceptions to debt rules—the National Escape Clause which the EU Council activated for Austria on 16 February 2026. The security and defence sector plays a significant role in Austria's economy, with 114 registered arms and defence companies (including major players such as Glock GmbH and Steyr Arms), 11,000 employees and 2% of annual European arms sales in 2024 (EUR 1,174,315,022). Although being outside NATO may be a disadvantage for Austrian defence industries, Europe's rearmament offers opportunities for domestic business.

However, the hasty process of the Rearm Europe Plan/'Readiness 2030' puts Austria in a tough spot. The country lags behind in military spending (just 0.7% of GDP in 2024, increasing to only 0.8% in 2025, so well below the EU average of around 1.5% of GDP). Until now, Austria's armed forces have looked more like a disaster relief unit than a combat-ready national defence army. An enormous investment would be required to achieve even minimal interoperability with other European armies. This is why, for Clara Sophie Cramer and Ulrike Franke in their essay on 'Ambiguous Alliance: Neutrality, Opt-outs, and European Defence' (2021), "of all the special status states, Austria appears to be the most problematic for a European Defence Union". According to these two experts at the European Council on Foreign Relations, Austria would probably not take part in any collective defence operation, regardless of its legitimacy—including participation based on the EU's mutual defence clause (Art. 42.7 of the Treaty on European Union). The country might even use its sovereign veto to prevent any European Council decision that would demand military assistance for the target of any aggression.

Despite ongoing efforts, the remaining neutral EU Member State might soon appear out of sync with most of Europe and increasingly misaligned with the demands of a more integrated and security-conscious EU. This is why the European Commission, in its preparatory paper for a Council recommendation on the economic, social, employment, structural and budgetary policies of Austria, advised the country to "reinforce overall defence spending and readiness in line with the European Council conclusions of 6 March 2025." The last U.S. *diktat* at the NATO

Hague summit in June 2025—a new 5% of GDP defence spending baseline agreed 'gun to the head' by the European allies—might further enlarge the rift between the EU's main players, such as France, Germany and Poland, and militarily speaking small members such as Austria, formerly referred to as 'frugal'. These members may be forced to bridge an even wider gap in defence spending or risk being left outside the concentric circles of defence cooperation.

The Shadow of the Far Right

Federal legislative elections on 29 September 2024 saw the far right Freedom Party of Austria (FPÖ) take first place, winning 28.8% of the vote, thereby achieving the best result in the party's history. Although the FPÖ's leader Herbert Kickl was eventually unable to secure a ruling coalition, allowing Austria's three top centrist parties in parliament to reach a government deal in February 2025, the far right's cumbersome influence significantly reduces the government's room for manoeuvre. From both military and financial perspectives, Kickl coined the ReArm Europe Plan an "irresponsible, highly dangerous twist in arms buildup and escalation spiral", emphatically calling for its rejection. In the FPÖ's view, the ReArm Europe Plan would further transform the continent into a 'United States of Europe' thereby triggering loss of sovereignty and neutrality for Austria. As shown by questions addressed by FPÖ MPs to the government, the far right will carefully scrutinise the legal structure of any so-called 'defence union' and its possible contradiction with Austria's legal framework. Pressure from the extreme right also reflects growing Euroscepticism in Austrian society: in an opinion poll conducted in September 2025 by the Österreichische Gesellschaft für Europapolitik (ÖGfE), 61% of respondents believe that Austria should remain a member of the EU, whilst 29% are in favour of leaving the EU. This ambivalence is even stronger regarding European support for Ukraine in its fight against Russia's war of aggression. A total of 46% consider it "very important" or "somewhat important" (23% each), while almost as many—43%—consider European solidarity with Kyiv to be "somewhat unimportant" (18%) or "not important at all" (25%).

"*Neutralität so leben, damit sie uns schützt!*" (Living neutrality so that it protects us!): FPÖ's slogan contradicts Beate Meinl-Reisinger's assertion that "neutrality alone does not protect us." Although the Austrian Foreign Minister, in an interview for *Die Welt* in July 2025, stated that she was open to a public debate on the country potentially giving up its neutrality and joining NATO, she is well aware that there is currently no majority either in parliament or among the population supporting such a drastic policy change.

However, there is one issue on which the FPÖ's position reflects the consensus of Austrian society. Compulsory military service is seen as a crucial element of Austria's comprehensive defence and independence. General conscription is enjoying global support within the country. According to an April 2025 Gallup survey, 70% of respondents are in favour of its preservation, an increase from the previous year's 65%. 51% would even support the extension of the current six-month military service.

In Moscow's Eyes, Austria Has Gone Over to the Dark Side

Austria offered to host Russia-Ukraine peace talks and confirmed it would host Russian President Vladimir Putin, despite the International Criminal Court's pending arrest warrant. It remains to be seen, though, whether Moscow is still eager to 'buy' what Christoph Schwarz (Austria Institut für Europa und Sicherheitspolitik) calls Austria's "performative neutrality"—a constitutional *façade* exhibiting practical alignment with Western security policy framework. After Vienna became part of the ESSI, the air defence system planned by European NATO countries, Russian Ambassador Dmitry Lyubinsky notably described Austria's military neutrality as "a political sham", citing its alignment with the "aggressive NATO bloc". Austria might now be part of the 'evil camp' in Moscow's eyes. Former Russian President and Deputy Chief of the Russian Security Council Dmitry Medvedev warned that Austria's NATO accession would undermine the "spirit of Vienna", jeopardise Austria's position as a multilateral hub and trigger Russia's retaliation. The current evolution in Austria's perception of its own neutrality, limited though it seems, may therefore significantly damage Vienna's ability to act as a credible mediator or bridge-builder in today's international environment, contrary to its renowned stance during the Cold War.

Recommendations

Austria should position itself as an EU champion by countering hybrid warfare in which Russia and others are involved, thereby demonstrating democracy's resilience. That would partially resolve the 'neutrality *versus* rearmament' conundrum and allow Austria to extend its support with different means other than purely military.

Austria needs to avoid becoming a security vacuum at the heart of Europe, particularly when infrastructure and equipment which are critical for the whole of Europe—including Ukraine—are at stake.

A non-polarised discussion entrusted to an independent commission, examining whether Austria's policy of neutrality is fitting for the times, could be very productive, as Minister Meinl-Reisinger highlighted. Such reflection has already taken place in Ireland and Switzerland, Austria's remaining neutral 'colleagues'.

Dr. Loïc Simonet joined the Austrian Institute for International Affairs (oiip) in 2021 as a Research Fellow, after many years at the Organisation for Security and Co-operation in Europe (OSCE) in Vienna. The oiip is Austria's leading research institute on international politics, at the juncture between academic and policy-oriented research. *This chapter has been drafted with support by Raffael Kögel, visiting student at the oiip.*

No Fairy Tale: Belgium's Struggle with Defence Investment

Michelle Haas and Tim Haesebrouck

Belgium has long hidden behind the fairy tale of European defence cooperation as a substitute for real investment. Now, under American pressure, it is pledging higher spending, albeit the perception of any genuine threat remains low: the traffic light still seems to be set at 'green' for most Belgians. Hence, to ensure public support, leaders must frame defence expenditure as the only viable path to safeguard Belgium's security.

Beyond the Fairy Tale of a European Army

European defence cooperation has long enjoyed wide support in Belgium. Nearly every week, politicians make impassioned pleas for deeper collaboration with European partners and even the notion of a European army continues to resonate. Yet this emphasis on cooperation has often served as a substitute for serious investment in Belgium's own armed forces. Instead of reflecting a coherent vision of how cooperation could strengthen Europe's security, it has become a fairy tale—an excuse to avoid responsibility for national defence.

A stronger Europe requires more than cooperation alone. Readiness will benefit from deeper and more efficient collaboration, but it cannot be achieved without higher national spending. One does not substitute for the other. In this sense, the 'White Paper for European Defence' strikes the right balance: combining strong financial ambition—mobilising EUR 800 billion across Member States—with targeted incentives to foster cooperation. Crucially, it avoids perpetuating the fairy tale of a European army, stressing that "Member States will always retain responsibility for their own troops, from doctrine to deployment."

M. Haas (✉) · T. Haesebrouck
Department of Political Sciences, Ghent University, Ghent, Belgium
e-mail: Michelle.Haas@UGent.be; Tim.Haesebrouck@UGent.be

M. Kaeding et al. (eds.), *Security, Defence, and the Future of Europe*,
https://doi.org/10.1007/978-3-032-18279-1_2

The current Belgian government seems to have received the message, as it has revised its goal of reaching 2% of GDP by 2025 instead of 2029. Yet the argument that spending should not increase until there is more cooperation still carries weight in the Belgian debate. While supporting specific initiatives for European cooperation is important, leaders must debunk the illusion that cooperation can replace investment. If Belgium and other free riders continue to drag their feet, the result will be new dividing lines within Europe, undermining the very cooperation they claim to support.

Not for the U.S. But for Us

The ultimate goal of increased defence spending should be to strengthen European and Belgian security, not merely to appease the U.S. Yet the timing of Belgium's decisions suggests otherwise. Mounting transatlantic tensions after Trump's second inauguration provided the final push to reach the 2% target in 2025. Pressure from Washington was also pivotal in Belgium's pledge to spend 3.5% of GDP on core military expenditures. How these targets will be met remains unclear. Public support remains fragile, as the increase is easily framed as yielding to the unpopular Trump administration. A poll by Knack in April 2025 found that 52% of respondents support a higher defence budget, yet only 17% would accept a VAT increase to finance such expenditure.

The decisive role of U.S. pressure highlights how much Belgian defence policy remains dependent on Washington. Although extreme-left political parties, which average roughly 10% of the vote, and parts of the peace movement still favour leaving NATO, most of the political elite now fear the opposite: the U.S. leaving us. The Trump administration's line, "the U.S. is committed to NATO," still echoes in Rue de la Loi, but doubts about what this commitment truly means are growing. Even the right-wing conservative Minister of Defence and Prime Minister, both traditionally staunchly pro-Transatlantic, have felt compelled to voice criticism of Trump. Nevertheless, prevailing sentiment still places the U.S. as an indispensable ally. The most recent Belgian Strategic Vision even argues that Europe should not strive for absolute independence.

The transatlantic relationship is indeed beneficial for both sides and would certainly be stronger if Europe could take better care of itself. However, as disunity over Ukraine illustrates, Europe and the U.S. do not always agree on issues vital to Europe. Dependence without alternatives leaves Europe with little leverage. European leaders are often sidelined in negotiations over Ukraine's future. "Nothing about Europe without Europe" should therefore be the minimum goal for the continent. While we should be flexible about how Europe is represented—with the EU as one player alongside coalitions of committed European states—Europe must always have a seat at the table. Without greater autonomy, Europe's voice will be heard only when Washington allows it, not because Europe commands it.

In the long run, Europe should strive for working with the U.S. when necessary, but act alone wherever possible. This is especially important since the U.S. is likely to pursue a strategy of avoiding overstretch by limiting its capabilities in Europe to give more priority to national interests, with talks of troop withdrawal potentially starting as early as 2026. Defence spending is not being increased merely "to keep the Americans in", but above all to "keep the Europeans up". Both scenarios require higher spending and this message should be communicated clearly.

"There Goes Your Pension"

Belgium now seems firmly committed to substantially increasing defence spending an important turning point after decades of underinvestment. However, the perception of defence as a budgetary drain is deeply ingrained in politics, epitomised by a social-democratic poster showing an elderly person next to an F-35 fighter jet with the caption: "There goes your pension." Combined with persistent fiscal constraints, funding new commitments has proven difficult. Belgium condemned Russia's invasion of Ukraine in 2022, but its policy response has long remained 'business as usual'. The Strategic Vision (STAR Plan) was left unrevised, the defence spending trajectory continued to target 2% by 2035 and crucial capability gaps, notably the absence of air defence, were not prioritised.

In 2025, transatlantic tensions under Trump's second term, coupled with a new government, finally pushed Belgium to break with that approach. Raising the budget from EUR 7 to EUR 11 billion (1.3% to 2% of GDP) was possible only through debt, taxes on frozen assets and an exceptional dividend from a state-owned bank. A structural financing plan is now on the agenda for 2026. Given strained public finances and a divided coalition, this will be a major challenge.

Financial proposals from the EU's White Paper provide some relief. Cheaper loans via the SAFE instrument and the national escape clause for defence spending will help, but debts must still be repaid. Given Belgium's fiscal state, EU-level borrowing—such as the EU bonds advocated by former Prime Minister Alexander De Croo—would have been a better solution.

Fiscal limits are not the only hurdle, given that public awareness of security threats remains low. For many Belgians, the traffic light still seems to be set on 'green': military action against Belgium in the near future is viewed as remote. Related to this, political parties remain reluctant to defend higher spending proactively. A week before the NATO summit in 2025, three out of five coalition partners warned of "collective hysteria" and a "social bloodbath" if the budget were raised further than 2% of GDP. Yet recent cyberattacks and drone incursions in Belgium may shift perceptions, showing that hybrid threats are not as 'grey' as once thought. The reintroduction of conscription has never been seriously considered in Belgium. Instead, a voluntary service year for young people is now in place.

Recommendations

The end goal must be a Europe that can safeguard its own security, acting with the U.S. when necessary, but without it whenever possible. To achieve this, Belgian and European leaders should emphasise that higher spending is about protecting Europe itself, not about pleasing Washington. Strategic communication is therefore essential to sustain political and public support. Moreover, EU institutions can play a stronger role in incentivising this.

They should also help ensure that contributions are shared fairly, for instance through European Defence Bonds that make investments sustainable for fiscally constrained Member States.

Finally, as adversaries increasingly seek to exploit vulnerabilities and create social disruption, the EU should coordinate more actively on hybrid threats, which are still too often treated as national rather than collective challenges. Leaving these gaps unaddressed leaves the door open for further aggression; that door must remain firmly closed.

Michelle Haas is a Ph.D. Researcher at the Ghent Institute for International and European Studies. She is also an Associate Fellow at the Egmont Royal Institute for International Relations. Her research focuses on the defence policies of European states. Before joining Ghent University, she worked as a policy officer on foreign affairs and national defence at the Belgian Federal Parliament.

Tim Haesebrouck is Assistant Professor at the Ghent Institute for International and European Studies, Ghent University. His research focuses on European defence policy, military burden sharing and military interventions. The Ghent Institute for International and European Studies is the research group of Ghent University that focuses on international politics, conducting research on inter alia geopolitics and strategy, as well as the EU and the world.

Security and Defence of the EU: What Is Bulgaria's Contribution?

Ivan Nachev and Hristo Panchugov

This chapter examines the future of EU security and defence, with a focus on Bulgaria's role as a Black Sea frontline state. It highlights the country's contributions through NATO and EU missions, its gradual modernisation efforts, as well as mixed public attitudes towards European defence integration and support for Ukraine. While Bulgaria remains committed to NATO, analysis reveals that there is growing societal support for a stronger European dimension in security. Recent surveys have revealed that over 50% of respondents support the idea of a common European security mechanism operating in parallel to NATO. In part this recognises that a strong majority ultimately agrees that ensuring Ukraine's future security is the essential precondition for any peace negotiations, which also signals a changing attitude with regard to the threat assessment within Bulgarian society. From 2022 to 2024, surveys reveal a clear ambivalence: while just over 50% of Bulgarians believe that supplying military equipment helps Ukraine defend itself, around 66% fear that such support will provoke Russia and bring the likelihood of war closer. These reasons have escalated the threat perception of the Bulgarian public according to the traffic light system to 'yellow'.

The war in Ukraine, cyber threats, migration pressures and geopolitical turbulence have effectively combined to place security and defence at the core of the EU's political agenda. Within Bulgaria, though, this conflict has stirred a rather complex dynamic. On the one hand, there has been a careful albeit slow political approach, bordering on apathy, which denies any need for modernisation, capability building and deepening cooperation in response to Russia's annexation of Crimea and invasion of eastern Ukraine. Moreover, a cold and open dismissal of any plans for a common Black Sea fleet could provide support for such a view. On the other hand, though, the realisation that Bulgaria, as an external border of both the EU and NATO, holds a strategic position, especially in the Black Sea region, has sparked a

I. Nachev (✉) · H. Panchugov
New Bulgarian University, Sofia, Bulgaria

M. Kaeding et al. (eds.), *Security, Defence, and the Future of Europe*,
https://doi.org/10.1007/978-3-032-18279-1_3

series of policy decisions that have shifted the focus towards replenishing and enhancing its military capabilities, while supporting efforts to build a new European security architecture. Accordingly, creation of an EUSD has become both a European and a national priority. However, the main political parties are trying to manoeuvre between EU interests and those of Bulgarian society, where pro-Russian sentiments still prevail.

Priorities for Action and the Path Towards an EUSD

After nearly two decades of underinvestment in defence, the war in Ukraine found Bulgaria with a significant share of its military equipment across all domains still depending on Soviet-era technology. In many instances, maintenance was carried out under licenses originally granted by Russian firms to local service providers or even outsourced directly to Russian companies. This reliance persists despite Russia having been officially designated as a strategic threat to Bulgaria's national security in recent years. The annexation of Crimea and the later conflict in eastern Ukraine sparked a new momentum. This resulted in the Bulgarian parliament approving the purchase of eight F-16C/D Block 70 fighters from the U.S. in 2019 to replace its soon to be grounded late Cold War MiG-29 s, for which maintenance and spares are no longer available. The war further incentivised Bulgaria to order a second batch of eight F-16 s in 2022, aiming for a full squadron of sixteen by the end of the decade.

Additional deals in 2022 have been struck to purchase not only over 180 Stryker vehicles (for around USD 1.5 billion), replacing Soviet BMPs and building a NATO-standard mechanised brigade, but also FGM-148 Javelins, providing modern anti-tank capabilities for the Stryker units. The first F-16 and Stryker deliveries were made in 2025, with their integration into land forces now underway.

Bulgaria's main priorities have been to strengthen its military capabilities, hence those of the EU, by developing industrial cooperation and achieving greater operational interoperability. The 2022 EU Strategic Compass had already outlined this path through joint exercises, common missions and investment in defence. For Bulgaria, the focus should be on Black Sea security, to be achieved not only by modernising its armed forces, but also by enhancing cyber defence and resilience against hybrid threats. The heavy focus on NATO and the U.S. is being re-evaluated. This somewhat strategic shift can be observed in a number of initiatives. Bulgaria's participation in the ESSI started strongly in August 2025 with the Parliamentary Defence Committee endorsing a project to purchase a modern air defence system (IRIS-T SLS) from Germany (over EUR 182.1 million), ensuring compatibility with wider European defence frameworks. Furthermore, in July 2025 France and Bulgaria signed a framework agreement for the joint purchase of air defence radar systems. Under this deal, Bulgaria will acquire seven new 3D radar systems with related services, including personnel training. These systems are key to modernising the Bulgarian Air Force and ensuring interoperability with the newly delivered F-16 fighters.

This strategic shift is also recognisable in Bulgaria's decision to enter a joint venture with German defence company Rheinmetall to build two major military industry plants: one for gunpowder production and the other for 155 mm NATO-standard artillery shells, with part of Bulgaria's investment to be financed via the EU's new SAFE mechanism. In August 2025, the Bulgarian Council of Ministers approved a draft agreement with Italy for joint construction and use of facilities in the Kabile military base to host a larger multinational battlegroup that could be expanded to brigade size, or larger.

While it is obvious that NATO remains the backbone of Bulgarian security, the move towards better strategic alignment with efforts to build the EU's strategic autonomy is clearly visible. It is unlikely that Bulgaria will see an EUSD as replacing NATO, but rather as a second pillar of European security. A realistic scenario is gradual expansion and integration of capabilities, striving for strategic autonomy, rather than building a parallel defensive system.

EU Independence and the Role of the U.S.

Whilst the U.S. remains a key guarantor of European security, European countries increasingly recognise that they cannot rely exclusively on America's security umbrella and thus need to build their own capabilities. The current Trump administration could be seen as the necessary push towards the EU's own strategic autonomy. However, contemporary security challenges require the EU to find novel ways to integrate NATO and the U.S. in developing a new security architecture, both in Europe and further afield. Beyond the war in Ukraine, a more coordinated approach is required, perhaps through an updated partnership in the Euro-Atlantic community, to face China as a strategic rival. The existing EU-NATO framework (such as Berlin Plus and Common Proposals) needs to be revisited according to new operational priorities, the EU's own increasing capacity and the expansion of NATO (to Sweden and Finland) in order to streamline decision-making, strengthen EU internal planning/command capacity and enhance interoperability. Due to Bulgaria's geopolitical location, the transatlantic link is indispensable, but 2025 surveys show an increased preference for a stronger European orientation. Other than the policies described above, societal attitudes provide favourable support for such a development, with 62% of Bulgarians believing that their country should align primarily with the EU rather than U.S. positions on security. At the same time, two of the main political parties, Citizens for European Development of Bulgaria and Movement for Rights and Freedoms—New Beginning, are trying to curry favour with President Trump, as some of their representatives have come under fire under the global Magnitsky Act. Moreover, the Bulgarian Socialist Party—the pro-Russian, traditionally anti-NATO party—is a member of the current government and participated in these decisions. The political and social climate presents an excellent opportunity for the discussed transformations.

Compulsory military service was abolished in Bulgaria on 1 January 2008 and hence the army currently comprises 26,900 professional soldiers, ranked 16th largest amongst the 32 NATO member countries. With 2.18% of GDP allocated to defence, Bulgaria is amongst the 23 top NATO countries that allocate over 2% to military expenditure. For the current year, this amounts to USD 2.3 billion, or circa BGN 3.6 billion/EUR 1.8 billion.

Finance Defence

Creating an EUSD requires significant investment. The European Commission has foreseen that hundreds of billions of euros will be needed for joint defence expenditure over the coming decade. As a result, Bulgaria has gradually raised its defence spending to reach NATO's guideline, 2% of GDP, for the first time this year. These funds come primarily from the national budget, but are supplemented by the European Defence Fund and Permanent Structured Cooperation (PESCO) projects. Currently defence spending is projected to reach 2.5% over the next 3 years. With adoption of the Euro on 1 January 2026, Bulgaria has also decided to request activation of the national escape clause, to exclude defence spending from its budget deficit. The political challenge lies in reallocating resources, since cuts in social spending are highly unpopular. European compensation mechanisms, such as more than BGN 1 billion/EUR 500 million that Bulgaria is expected to receive for its contributions to Ukraine, thus provide an important incentive to ease the burden of military spending domestically.

Public Opinion and Threat Perceptions

Public opinion in Bulgaria is divided on security issues. In 2025, 59% of Bulgarians surveyed support the idea of a common European defence policy, while around 40% are opposed. Support for military assistance to Ukraine remains low at about 49%, showing polarisation in society. However, 71% of respondents support closer cooperation in defence among EU countries and 63% approve of greater investments in defence capabilities. A striking 94% of citizens favour peace negotiations, which suggests a strong preference for diplomatic rather than military solutions.

Bulgaria perceives these threats differently. Russia is clearly viewed as a high-level 'red' category threat due to its proven military capacity, the ongoing war in Ukraine and its strong presence in the Black Sea. Migration pressures and cyberattacks fall into the 'yellow' category, being recognised as risks, but not seen as existential. Relations with EU and NATO allies remain in the 'green' category, as they are largely regarded as partners rather than adversaries. This framework reflects both the strategic anxieties of Bulgaria and the limits of public readiness to accept higher military engagement.

Bulgaria and European Security

In Bulgaria, security debates have traditionally been tied to NATO, but the European dimension is becoming increasingly relevant. Public attitudes show strong trust in Germany, France and Italy (ranging from 77% to 85%), while trust in the U.S. and Russia is lower and almost balanced, at 52% and 48% respectively. This suggests a gradual reorientation towards European centres of security and cooperation, while maintaining the transatlantic link. Even with a high level of favourable sentiments towards Russia, its aggression towards Ukraine has expanded the policy window to rebuild Bulgarian defence capabilities, increase interoperability and expand support for EU securitisation. Despite proposals from various political parties to reinstate compulsory military service, this idea has not yet gained broad public support.

On the practical side, Bulgaria participates in EU missions such as Operation Althea in Bosnia and Herzegovina, engages actively in PESCO projects on cyber security, military mobility as well as medical support and is gradually modernising its armed forces. Key challenges remain, such as limited resources, delays in modernisation and sharply polarised public opinion, which makes building a national consensus difficult.

Recommendations

The future of European security depends on balancing autonomy with the transatlantic partnership. The EU must develop its own defence capacity without creating a duplicate of NATO. Bulgaria, with its strategic position in the Black Sea and growing public support for a European defence dimension, can contribute through participation in missions, modernisation of its armed forces and active diplomacy. The central question, though, is whether the EU will maintain its unity on the issue of an EUSD, capable of protecting its citizens and values.

The EU should play a more prominent role in peace negotiations between Russia and Ukraine. At present, the conditions for direct deals are absent, as Ukraine must first consolidate its position with Western support. However, at some point in the future, the EU could serve as a mediator, provided it acts with unity in close coordination with NATO and the UN. Bulgaria offers a unique perspective on Russia, its policy influence and communication narrative. To strengthen the EU's security and defence framework, various steps are recommended.

Firstly, the EU should maintain NATO as the cornerstone of European security while simultaneously investing in its own autonomous capabilities, particularly in cyber defence, intelligence sharing and rapid deployment forces.

Secondly, Bulgaria should prioritise modernisation of its armed forces, especially naval and air capabilities in the Black Sea region, while ensuring full interoperability with EU and NATO partners.

Thirdly, Sofia should expand its participation in PESCO projects and increase coordination with regional allies such as Romania and Greece to address common security challenges.

Fourthly, Bulgarian policy-makers need to improve public communication by explaining the direct link between national security, EU membership and support for Ukraine, thus reducing polarisation in public opinion.

Finally, the EU should create financial mechanisms to compensate smaller Member States such as Bulgaria for their security contributions, ensuring burden-sharing and enhancing public support for defence spending.

Ivan Nachev is a Bulgarian political scientist at the New Bulgarian University (NBU) and an expert on the EU's political integration. His interests are in the fields of political theory and practice, European values, European integration theories, strategies and political practices. He is a member of the Bulgarian Association for Political Sciences, the Institute for Public Policies and Partnership, the European Community Studies Association and Team Europe at the European Commission. Currently he is a director at the Bulgarian school of politics.

Hristo Panchugov is a Bulgarian political scientist, Assistant Professor in the Department of Political Science at NBU and a graduate from the Central European University (Hungary). He is an expert in the field of political parties, European integration and international relations, as well as political organisations and civic education. The New Bulgarian University was established on 18 September 1991 as the first private university in Bulgaria. It is an autonomous liberal education institution dedicated to the advancement of university education, cultivation of critical and creative thinking, sensitivity to cultural difference and problem-solving. NBU has received maximum scores in three consecutive accreditations. Since 2004, NBU has been an accredited partner of the UK's Open University.

Between NATO and the EU: Croatia's Security and Defence Choices

Hrvoje Butković

Croatia has recently increased defence spending to 2% of GDP, with a plan to reach 3% by 2030. The country purchased 12 Rafale fighter jets from France and announced the acquisition of up to 50 Leopard 2A8 tanks from Germany. Mandatory military service was reintroduced in 2025 for men, with voluntary participation for women. Prime Minister Andrej Plenković supports comprehensive assistance to Ukraine, while President Zoran Milanović maintains a more cautious stance. Public opinion shows strong solidarity with Ukraine, but a moderate perception of direct threats, with NATO seen as indispensable and regional instability in the Western Balkans viewed as a parallel concern. According to the traffic light system of threat perception, in Croatia's case this can be described as moderate or 'yellow'.

Ever-Increasing Focus on Defence

In November 2021, Croatia signed a contract to purchase 12 Rafale F3-R fighter jets from France. The value of this contract was around EUR 1 billion, including weapons, training, and logistics. Subsequently, in 2024 and 2025 the squadron of 12 planes was delivered to Pleso Air Base near Zagreb. In late 2024, Croatia announced the purchase of up to 50 Leopard 2A8 tanks from Germany, which will replace its Soviet-era tanks that will be sent to Ukraine in turn. The share of defence spending in Croatia from 2014 to 2020 varied somewhere between 1.5% and 1.8% of GDP and only in the last few years has Croatia been aiming for higher spending. To enable the purchase of the Rafales and Leopards, the country's defence budget has increased to 2% of GDP, with a plan to grow to 3% by 2030. Ever since the announcement of a further increase in spending for defence, some politicians from

H. Butković (✉)
Institute for Development and International Relations, Zagreb, Croatia
e-mail: hrvoje.butkovic@irmo.hr

M. Kaeding et al. (eds.), *Security, Defence, and the Future of Europe*,
https://doi.org/10.1007/978-3-032-18279-1_4

the opposition have expressed fears that this might come at the expense of the existing social spending. However, the government has repeatedly stated that this will not be the case since any increased spending is linked to expected economic growth, better fiscal capacities as well as greater utilisation of existing loans and grant opportunities.

Another significant development related to a deterioration in Europe's security situation was the 2025 reintroduction of mandatory military service, which had previously been abandoned in 2008. According to amended legislation, from late 2025 military service will be mandatory for men, while women will be able to join voluntarily. Basic training is planned to last 2 months, with a net monthly salary for the soldiers of circa EUR 1100, inclusive of contributions. The legislation makes provision for conscientious objection, in which case military service will be fulfilled by serving—without financial compensation—in the ranks of civil protection or by working in local public institutions.

Although increased focus and spending on defence is in line with the EU's proclaimed goals, Croatia is one of the strongest opponents of applying qualified majority voting (QMV) in the Common Foreign and Security Policy (CFSP). This came to the fore in relation to the 2023 German proposals to expand QMV in the CFSP without EU institutional reform. Together with Hungary and some other new Member States, Croatia wants to retain its veto right, seeing this as an important tool for influencing EU decisions, especially in relation to disputes with neighbouring states.

Different Views over Support for Ukraine

Prime Minister Andrej Plenković (leader of the centre-right HDZ party, which is a member of the EPP) and President Zoran Milanović (former leader of the centre-left SDP party, which is a member of the Progressive Alliance of Socialists and Democrats [S&D]) have expressed somewhat different views on the degree of support for Ukraine. The former advocates comprehensive backing, including diplomatic, economic, humanitarian and even military assistance, stressing that peace must not reward the aggressor or come at the expense of Ukraine's sovereignty and territorial integrity. By contrast, the latter has taken a more restrained stance. While he emphasises solidarity with the Ukrainian people, he distances himself from the Ukrainian government and firmly rules out any possibility of Croatian military involvement in the conflict. These different views hold significant political relevance because in Croatia's political system, the President oversees foreign policy in conjunction with the Prime Minister and acts as supreme commander of the armed forces.

However, the difference in how to support Ukraine extends beyond the positions of the Prime Minister and the President, reflecting a deeper political cleavage in the country. This became most visible in December 2022, when the Plenković government failed to pass through parliament legislation that would allow training for Ukraine's armed forces in Croatia as part of the EU Mission for Military Assistance to Support Ukraine. In 2024, a similar situation occurred following President Milanović's refusal to authorise a government proposal for participation of the country's military officers in the NATO Security Assistance and Training Ukraine mission. Subsequently, the government has sent this proposal to parliament, where backing is now needed to overcome Milanović's refusal with a two-thirds majority. However, faced with a low probability that the proposal will pass, the government has ultimately put voting on hold.

Perceptions of Security Threats

Public opinion in Croatia reflects a heightened awareness of security risks since Russia's invasion of Ukraine, though perceptions differ in intensity compared with countries on the EU's eastern flank. The Flash Eurobarometer surveys conducted since 2022 show that around two-thirds of Croatian respondents support the EU's Common Security and Defence Policy (CSDP), with firm approval for strengthening cooperation in military procurement and joint defence capabilities. Despite slight variances, this support has been consistent throughout the 2022–2025 period. Support for humanitarian aid to Ukraine is very high, while military assistance also enjoys majority backing, though less robust and with signs of gradual decline as the conflict continues. This suggests that solidarity with Ukraine remains strong, but concerns about the long-term economic and social costs of military engagement are growing.

When asked about perceived threats, Croatians identify Russia as the main external challenge to European and regional security. However, the sense of direct threat to Croatia is moderate rather than acute, or 'yellow' using the traffic-light assessment. Less than half of Croatian respondents believed the war could spill over directly into their country. Instead, instability in the Western Balkans, particularly in Bosnia and Herzegovina and Kosovo, is often cited in public debates as a parallel or even more immediate security concern. This perception explains why Croatian public opinion generally supports stronger European defence integration but still insists on close ties with NATO and the U.S. as indispensable security guarantees.

Recommendations

To strengthen its security, Croatia should prioritise enhanced political dialogue between the Prime Minister and the President. Establishing a clear and consensual stance on support for Ukraine would reduce domestic political ambiguity, reinforce the country's international credibility and provide citizens with a more realistic picture of current security risks.

At the same time, greater investment in transparent public communication on security and defence matters is essential. Explaining the rationale behind military spending, procurement decisions and reintroduction of mandatory service can help mitigate scepticism among citizens and foster a more resilient national consensus.

Moreover, while NATO remains the backbone of Croatia's security architecture, the country should actively support initiatives within the EU framework to ensure that national policies remain aligned with broader European trends.

At EU level, further efforts should be directed towards strengthening coordination with NATO. Avoiding duplication and reinforcing complementarity is vital, as NATO continues to serve as the indispensable foundation of European collective defence. Finally, EU institutions and Member States should pursue defence integration pragmatically, prioritising joint procurement, interoperability and capacity-building. Such an approach would deliver tangible results without being overshadowed by divisive debates such as that on establishing a fully-fledged European army.

Hrvoje Butković works as Research Advisor at the Institute for Development and International Relations (IRMO), Zagreb. His primary scientific interests are democracy at national and supranational levels, together with industrial relations in an internationally comparative perspective. The Institute for Development and International Relations, Zagreb, is a public, non-profit, scientific research organisation engaged in multidisciplinary research. It provides strategic decision support and analysis to decision-makers, ensuring the dissemination of research results and information through publishing activities.

European Security Challenges and the Case of Cyprus

Andreas Theophanous

Security perceptions within the EU remain highly fragmented, reflecting divergent historical experiences and national threat assessments. For Cyprus, Turkey remains the main threat, having occupied 37% of the island since 1974. Turkey's actions and overall revisionist objectives under the traffic lights analogy constitute a 'red' threat to the Republic of Cyprus. Ankara refuses to recognise the Republic of Cyprus and thus continues to employ hybrid forms of warfare against this island-state. These circumstances underline the existential nature of Cyprus's problem alongside the broader difficulty of developing a common European security and defence policy. The EU's limited and often inconsistent responses weaken its credibility and raise questions about its ability to act as a coherent international actor. The EU must articulate clear principles, address aggression against Member States without exception and adopt a comprehensive strategy that links all issues with the wider debate on Europe's security architecture and regional stability.

Introduction

Discussions about security, defence and the future of Europe have intensified following various developments in the last few years, stemming from Russia's invasion of Ukraine and the ongoing war. The implications are profound for the EU, particularly in terms of Europe's economy and its competitiveness. It is crucial to recognise different key perspectives between the EU and the U.S., particularly regarding the war, Russia and the future of NATO.

While there is continuing debate about Turkey's role in Europe's security architecture, one cannot ignore the fact that it still occupies 37% of the territory of the

A. Theophanous (✉)
Cyprus Center for European and International Affairs, University of Nicosia, Nicosia, Cyprus
e-mail: theophanous.a@unic.ac.cy

M. Kaeding et al. (eds.), *Security, Defence, and the Future of Europe*,
https://doi.org/10.1007/978-3-032-18279-1_5

Republic of Cyprus, an EU Member State. Furthermore, Turkey does not recognise the Republic and has not implemented the Ankara Protocol in relation to Cyprus, which was drafted in December 2004, with implementation expected in October 2005. Moreover, Greece also considers that its major security threat comes from the East, which means Turkey. Taken together, the experiences of Cyprus and Greece demonstrate that Turkey's stance is not a security concern limited to one Member State, but a broader challenge for the EU as a whole.

Perceptions in Cyprus on Security and Defence

The EU has not paid any attention to the security concerns of Cyprus and Greece. Turkey did not pay any price in relation to its ongoing occupation of the northern part of Cyprus and its hybrid warfare against the Republic. There have been no sanctions against Turkey, nor conditions for the financial support it has been receiving from the EU for years. Similarly, there were never any conditions for the EU's financial support to the Turkish Cypriot community (and settlers) in the occupied part of Cyprus. In addition, the EU failed to address democratic backsliding in Turkey promptly, with any reaction being rather symbolic than concrete and effective. It is one thing to support Turkish Cypriots; it is another to tolerate developments which violate the rights of an EU Member State, the Republic of Cyprus and the Union's value system.

The EU and most of its Member States have been noticeably quite silent regarding Turkish actions in Cyprus, the Eastern Mediterranean and the broader Middle East. Turkey is a revisionist power. One question raised is to what extent this can be reconciled with Turkey's participation in the European security architecture. Developments in the Middle East are a case in point and raise various concerns for the EU, including but not limited to immigration challenges and the humanitarian crisis in Gaza. The absence of clarity and consistency by the EU is crippling its foreign policy potential. It is essential for the EU to have a vision for addressing problems and challenges in the broader Middle East and implement that vision based on the principles it claims to espouse. The EU must work consistently and proactively to promote stability in the region. Implementing these objectives requires a clear vision, credibility and coherent policies. Unfortunately, the EU is absent from today's major negotiations and developments concerning the region's future.

These issues again raise some fundamental questions: Can the EU have a coherent and truly common foreign policy? Do EU Member States have the same perceptions about security threats? The answers to both questions are, unfortunately, negative.

These factors should be taken into consideration while trying to address relations with the U.S. and Russia. Sooner or later, relations between the EU and the U.S. will be redefined. Within this framework, the Euro-Atlantic partnership should be revitalised and European security issues addressed, especially regarding Russia. One must also remember that the EU is not expected to become a nuclear power (at least in the foreseeable future). Furthermore, we should be reminded of the agreements between the U.S. and the Soviet Union during the Cold War. It was a different period, but significantly there was no major war in Europe.

That brings us to the issue of EU-Russia relations. Geography cannot change and the EU's dilemma is whether it prefers a new Iron Curtain or a different set of arrangements. Furthermore, while in Europe today there is growing concern about Russia's actions, many analysts suggest that negotiations are preferable to confrontation. The meeting between Trump and Vladimir Putin in August 2025 provided grounds for cautious optimism regarding the possibility of a degree of normalisation of Russia-U.S. relations. At the same time, while we should not forget the Alaska and Washington summits aimed at producing a final resolution to the war in Ukraine, the outcome of those meetings is yet uncertain.

The Cypriot government has maintained a consistent position since the war broke out. It has condemned the Russian invasion and supported sanctions imposed by the EU and the U.S. It has also provided humanitarian aid to Ukraine. There are three general trends of thinking in Cyprus that may not necessarily be conflicting. Firstly, there is deep regret for the loss of life. Secondly, there is condemnation of the Russian invasion and its occupying parts of Ukraine. At the same time, Cypriots compare the Russian invasion of Ukraine to the Turkish invasion of Cyprus in 1974. In this regard, most Cypriots feel that the position of the West has not been consistent. Thirdly, the war in Ukraine is considered to be part of a larger clash between Russia and the West. Many believe it could have been prevented some years ago by meaningful dialogue among all parties involved.

Threats

The Cyprus problem is considered to be an existential threat. Turkey has occupied 37% of the island since 1974. Furthermore, in addition to ethnic cleansing, it has been colonising the occupied parts of Cyprus. Turkish Cypriots now constitute a minority in the occupied northern part of Cyprus and Greek Cypriot properties are being exploited. In this context, Turkey's presence on the island and sustained revisionist objectives constitute a 'red' high-level threat.

Since June 1964, military service has been compulsory for Cypriot males over the age of 18. The length of service was originally set at 26 months, but was reduced to 14 months in 2016. Since the early 2000s, the Republic of Cyprus has consistently allocated around 1.8% of GDP to defence. While Cyprus supports the idea of a new European security architecture, given its circumstances, its priority remains to enhance military service and defence spending to face the Turkish threat.

Cyprus is also concerned about volatility and instability in the Middle East, which constitute 'yellow', medium-level threats. Though not involved in any regional conflicts, the spillover effects, especially those pertaining to conflict, as well as economic challenges and climate-induced migration, are particularly concerning for the Republic. Cyprus receives the highest number of asylum seekers per capita in the EU, most of whom enter via Turkey or the occupied northern part of the island. This raises key concerns about demographic changes resulting from colonisation, migration and other factors. Furthermore, the purchase of land and fundamental assets by foreign interests raises additional concerns.

Cyprus maintains good bilateral relations with most neighbouring countries and has a strong reputation amongst these nations as a peaceful regional actor. Cyprus has repeatedly functioned as a humanitarian hub offering aid in regional conflicts. Furthermore, the Republic aspires to be a place of dialogue and cooperation.

Recommendations

The EU's vision for addressing challenges in neighbouring regions should clearly outline its red lines regarding security concerns, in addition to other priorities such as the protection of human rights and democracy. Guaranteeing the territorial integrity of all Member States should be a red line and respect for international law (non-selectively) a priority. Indeed, the EU needs to reassess its role and decide what it stands for. Finally, while Europe enhances its military capabilities, it is also important to consider that in the nuclear age, diplomacy and sophistication are also required to promote important objectives.

Professor Andreas Theophanous is the President of the Cyprus Center for European and International Affairs (associated with the University of Nicosia). The Cyprus Center for European and International Affairs, co-founded by Andreas Theophanous in 1993, is an independent, non-profit organisation whose mission is to advance multidisciplinary, scholarly and policy-oriented research, provide advisory services and promote open debate to address problems and challenges at national, regional, European and international levels.

Czech Security in the Face of the Russian-Ukrainian War: Growing Defence Capabilities and Their Sociopolitical Costs

Zdeněk Sychra and Petr Kratochvíl

The Czech position on national security and defence is characterised by a certain duality. On the one hand, there is a slowly increasing openness to deepening defence cooperation within the EU and on the other hand, the strong anchoring in NATO and relations with the U.S. continues to be seen as central to the country's needs, especially by the right wing of the political spectrum. Czech governments have long relied on NATO as the fundamental pillar of national security and all key strategic documents declare that European projects should complement and not replace the Alliance. The EU is seen more as a tool for streamlining procurement and strengthening the industry than as an independent security guarantor. The 2023 defence agreement with the U.S. and purchasing state-of-the-art F-35 fighter jets together with other military equipment show that successive Czech governments are consciously aiming to become part of the American ecosystem, not only by investing in U.S. weapons, but also through interoperability and access to the latest technologies. In the Czech political environment, there is a relatively broad, albeit recently narrowing, consensus based on historically strong transatlanticism and distrust towards the EU in security matters. Even though Europe must become more capable of action, the American presence remains a key security safeguard. That is why Czech diplomacy repeatedly emphasises the need to "keep the US at the table" while stressing that Europe must be prepared to cover any shortfall in the event of weakening by America's leadership, especially regarding the war in Ukraine. At the same time, though, increased focus on defence raises serious concerns about socio-economic impacts. As to threat perception according to the traffic light system,

Z. Sychra (✉)
University of West Bohemia, Pilsen, Czech Republic
e-mail: sychra@ff.zcu.cz

P. Kratochvíl
Institute of International Relations, Prague, Czech Republic
e-mail: kratochvil@iir.cz

M. Kaeding et al. (eds.), *Security, Defence, and the Future of Europe*,
https://doi.org/10.1007/978-3-032-18279-1_6

Czechia can be classified between the 'yellow' (direct attack) and 'red' (hybrid attacks) levels in the traffic light system, indicating a relatively high degree of risk.

NATO First, EU-Plus

From a Czech perspective, the EU's role is viewed in a highly pragmatic, even utilitarian light: if it can speed up joint procurement and help the European defence industry, then its strengthening is seen as welcome. The Czech government, therefore, supports initiatives such as 'Readiness 2030' and the new European Defence Industry Programme, but at the same time insists that the "buy European" rule must not jeopardise interoperability with NATO and U.S. systems. In practice, this means a combination of transatlantic platforms (supersonic fighters, air defence) with European supply chains (ammunition, ground equipment). In recent years, Czechia has also been trying to 'box above its weight', an example being the ammunition initiative for Ukraine, which demonstrated a quicker response time than the EU could achieve, signalling the country's ability to become a facilitator among Allies. Such an initiative strengthens Czechia's reputation, despite providing an easy target for populist parties at home, especially the Yes *(ANO)* (Patriots for Europe in the EP) and Freedom and Direct Democracy (Europe of Sovereign Nations Group in the EP) movements.

The U.S. has long viewed Czech governments as reliable security partners within NATO, which is reflected both in strategic documents and practical steps such as conclusion of a bilateral defence cooperation agreement together with the large-scale acquisition of American technology, led by F-35 aircraft. However, the context is changing radically: the U.S. is increasingly seen as problematic and at times a rival partner, whose President directly attacks the EU and its Member States, both politically and economically. The Czech discourse has, therefore, gradually been leaning towards strengthening European strategic autonomy, particularly regarding concerns about reducing U.S. engagement in Europe and its shift in attention to the Indo-Pacific. The U.S. thus remains a vital security guarantor, but at the same time there is growing awareness of building European defence capabilities as a safeguard against a possible weakening of the U.S. leadership.

In addition to its anchoring in NATO, Czechia also emphasises building its own resilience. The 2023 defence strategy draws attention not only to modernising the armed forces, but also to involving society as a whole through active reserves, strengthening cyber and hybrid defence, as well as mobilisation capacities. The army's priority projects include the establishment of a heavy brigade by 2030, centred on new CV90 infantry fighting vehicles and Leopard 2A8 tanks, layered air defence (SPYDER system, MADR 3D radars, participation in the EU's ESSI project) and rearming the air force with fifth-generation F-35 fighter jets. In addition, the helicopter fleet is being replaced and other key capabilities are being modernised. The Czech strategy is thus to be a reliable member of NATO and, at the same time, an active European player capable of delivering concrete results when needed, whether it be ammunition for Ukraine or the modernisation of its own army.

Between Strategic Ambitions and Fiscal Constraints

The financing of defence capabilities is a politically and economically sensitive issue. Czechia has been meeting its commitment to spend 2% of GDP on defence only since 2024, but the government has announced a towards 3% by 2030, at a rate of 0.2% per year. In this context, proposals contained in the 'White Paper for European Defence' are viewed pragmatically. Czechia sees them as an opportunity to accelerate implementation of modernisation projects and reduce fiscal pressure on the domestic budget. Interest in drawing on the European SAFE instrument to purchase Leopard tanks is a concrete example of this strategy. Another option is to use new EIB funds for coordinated European purchases of military equipment. From the Czech perspective, therefore, European initiatives do not represent a substitute for national funding, but rather a supplement that makes it possible to achieve the set goals faster and at a lower cost. There are currently no plans to reintroduce compulsory military service, which was abolished in 2005. However, the army has highlighted its need to strengthen reserves and increase the population's preparedness through voluntary or shortened training.

Defence funding will thus primarily come from the state budget. Fiscal space for growing defence spending is to be created from 2024 onwards by austerity measures: an increase in corporate income tax, a reduction in tax exemptions, adjustments to VAT rates and higher contributions for some self-employed persons. The reduction of certain non-investment subsidies is also significant. The defence budget is protected by law at 2% of GDP and is not among victims of the savings. As some opposition parties, and since 2025 the new ruling parties, have critically noted, increasing defence spending may come at the expense of social services, healthcare and education, harming the lower-income segments of Czech society. Despite stretching fiscal demands and significant socioeconomic costs, the previous center-right government appeared determined to sustain its investment in defence as a priority over the coming years. However, the long-term sustainability of these investments and their legitimacy in society are not a given, as demonstrated by the gradual shift in public opinion and the arrival of a new government coalition at the end of 2025.

Safety at the Lowest Possible Cost

The development of Czech public opinion on Russian aggression against Ukraine between 2022 and 2025 shows a shift from initial strong solidarity to more pragmatic attitudes. Support for military supplies has gradually declined and stabilised at around 40%, financial aid oscillates between 40–45%, while humanitarian support remains consistently high. Support for sanctions against Russia also persists, but with a rejection of deeper European integration of Ukraine. Overall, the Czech public combines basic solidarity with growing scepticism about long-term costs. These attitudes are significantly influenced by populist groups, which are highly critical of Ukraine and the West's approach, especially radical groups such as Freedom and Direct Democracy as well as *Stačilo!* (Enough!) (Independent in the

EP). However, even the strongest political entity, the ANO movement, is only moderately critical.

The issue of defence spending is a key point of contention. While roughly half of society considers the commitment to spend 2% of GDP on defence to be sufficient, support for further increases is limited: approximately one-fifth would accept an increase to 3% of GDP, and only a marginal portion would accept an increase to 5%. This attitude shows that although the public respects basic commitments arising from NATO membership, it is not willing to bear the significant additional costs associated with building modern defence capabilities. Maintaining adequate defence spending while ensuring socio-economic stability is, therefore, a key task for future governments.

In terms of defining the threat, the state's response and framing the adversary, attitudes differ among individual political formations. Moreover, attitudes within different segments of Czech society also differ. A significant shift in the government's attitudes is evident after the parliamentary elections in October 2025, as a result of which the opposition ANO movement won. It formed a government with the SPD and Motorists for Themselves (Patriots for Europe group), all of which have consistently criticised high defence spending.

At present, though, it can be said that the government ranges from 'yellow' to 'red' in all threat categories. This follows from a general understanding that Russia as the dominant adversary has significantly higher military capabilities than the Czech Republic, but lags behind both NATO and the EU in terms of collective power. However, direct military aggression against the Czech Republic is not expected in the near future, thus 'yellow' prevails here. By contrast, the state's response is closer to 'red', mindful of a significant increase in budgets and strengthening of civilian preparedness. Russia is also at the 'red' level in terms of framing the adversary, but here it is more in terms of a direct attack in relation to non-traditional, hybrid threats.

Recommendations

It is critically important for the Czech government not only to reflect publicly that increased spending will not socioeconomically affect already vulnerable parts of Czech society but also to pay sufficient attention to this policy's social aspects. Experience with the energy crisis and its social and political consequences is a serious warning about how not to proceed.

The government should also strengthen its information and education efforts regarding the security situation. In terms of communication, it should link defence investments to the specific protection of citizens in everyday life (air defence against missiles/drones, cyber protection of hospitals, ammunition for own reserves), because the public accepts humanitarian aspects more easily than general investments in defence.

Joint European procurement can reduce the cost and speed up military deliveries without putting pressure on national budgets. The EU should, therefore, make SAFE loans a long-term and permanent instrument with simple administration and clear prioritisation of capabilities. At the same time, the Union should allocate part of its defence investments outside the permitted deficit limits, as proposed in the 'White Paper for European Defence—'Readiness 2030''.

Zdeněk Sychra works at the Department of Political Science and International Relations at the University of West Bohemia and serves as an external associate at the Institute of International Relations in Prague. His research focuses on EU politics, with particular emphasis on the Economic and Monetary Union and EU governance. He is author or co-author of numerous articles and book chapters on European politics. The University of West Bohemia is one of the most visible in Czechia. The Department of Politics and International Relations of the Faculty of Arts is an academic institution offering a broad range of undergraduate, graduate and postgraduate study programmes, conducting research in political science, international relations and territorial studies.

Petr Kratochvíl is Full Professor and Senior Researcher of the Institute of International Relations Prague (IIR) and a member of the TEPSA Board. He has written dozens of monographs, book chapters and journal articles. His research interests cover theories of international relations, European studies and the religion-politics nexus. The Institute of International Relations Prague is an independent public research institution that has been conducting scholarly research in the area of international relations since 1957. As an institution originally founded by the Czech Republic's Ministry of Foreign Affairs, the IIR also provides policy analysis and recommendations. It aims to form a link between the academic world, the public and international political practice.

A Super-Atlanticist No More: Copenhagen Turns to Europe for Security and Defence

Mikkel Runge Olesen

For decades, Denmark has been among the most transatlantic-oriented countries in Europe. However, that position is currently changing. Russia remains the primary threat to Denmark, but Danish politicians and the general public are now increasingly also viewing the U.S.—Denmark's primary security provider—as a potential threat. For that reason, Russia is rated 'red' in this chapter, while the U.S. is rated 'yellow'. This drastic development can be attributed to the words and actions of the second Trump administration, especially with regard to Greenland. Consequently, Danish politicians are increasingly looking to Europe for their security needs.

Europe's New Role in Danish Security Thinking

Just a few years ago, EU defence cooperation was still merely a supplement for the Danish government and not a primary competence in Danish security policy. This held true even after a referendum to abolish the Danish EU defence opt-out in 2022. Danish Prime Minister Mette Frederiksen stated bluntly in July 2023 that there must never be so much as a "sheet of paper" between the U.S. and Europe, since it should be clear to all Europeans that "we cannot do anything without the Americans". The true change in Danish policy towards Europe happened, therefore, not with the abolition of the opt-out, but when Donald Trump won the U.S. election for a second time in November 2024.

The second Trump term is creating a rift between Denmark and the U.S. that is much more substantial than was the case during his first term. This is caused by Trump's antagonistic approach to Europe in terms of defence spending, his chaotic and wavering approach to supporting Ukraine against Russia and his

M. R. Olesen (✉)
Danish Institute for International Studies (DIIS), Copenhagen, Denmark
e-mail: mro@diis.dk

M. Kaeding et al. (eds.), *Security, Defence, and the Future of Europe*,
https://doi.org/10.1007/978-3-032-18279-1_7

confrontational trade policies. However, above all it has to do with the Trump administration's desire to acquire Greenland, an autonomous part of the Kingdom of Denmark. These factors led Prime Minister Frederiksen to state publicly in March 2025 that Denmark could no longer count on the U.S., thereby signalling a potential end to decades with the U.S. as the central pillar of Danish security policy. This has propelled Europe into the centre of Danish security thinking. However, it remains to be seen whether this will mean relying on the European pillar in NATO, relying on an ad hoc coalition of northern European powers or indeed relying on the EU to develop into a full-fledged security alliance. The Danish government's position on such options is as yet unclear, but likely to be positive to any development that increases European deterrence.

Defence Spending on the Rise

Traditionally on the low side, Danish defence expenditure has drastically increased in recent years, fuelled not only by a perceived rising threat from Russia or U.S. pressure, but also by a realisation that the present U.S. alliance may not last and that higher defence spending will thus be needed to prepare Denmark and Europe for that eventuality. Danish defence spending therefore increased from 1.29% of GDP in 2021 to an estimated 3.22% in 2025. Where will the money come from? The Danish economy is currently strong and much of the increased spending may be financed through extra revenue from current and future economic growth. Economic growth in Denmark was around 3.5% in 2024 compared to an EU average of around 1%. Furthermore, the country has a low national debt at only 7.4% of GDP compared to an average of more than 80% amongst EU Member States. Though Danish growth is expected to slow somewhat in 2025, the country's economy is likely to remain strong. For these reasons, the government has found it easier to make an argument for increased defence spending than other European countries, where the military build-up may require deep cuts for social security and welfare. Mindful of this dilemma, Prime Minister Frederiksen is very supportive of the EU's White Paper conclusions, designed to make it easier for European economies to shoulder the burden of military build-up.

A Worried Public

The Danish government has generally enjoyed broad public support for the recent budget increases as well as the general realignment of Danish security policy that is currently underway. The Danish support for Ukraine is very strong, with 86% of Danes polled in the Spring of 2025 being in favour of sending military supplies to the country. This is probably tied to a domestic consensus on this matter in the Danish parliament. While scepticism to Denmark's Ukraine policy can be found on the far left, this is motivated primarily by an anti-militarist sentiment rather than any kind of sympathy for Russia. 86% of Danes surveyed in January 2025 saw Russia as a threat to Denmark, while 75% of Danes polled in March 2025 viewed Russia as an enemy with whom Denmark is currently in conflict. This number may have risen even further as a consequence of presumed Russian drone incursions into Danish airspace in September 2025.

At the same time, though, 46% of Danes surveyed in January 2025 also see the U.S. as a threat to Denmark. By March 2025, 66% of Danes polled stated that they view the U.S. as an enemy of Europe, more than any European country in that poll. This high Danish number compared to the rest of Europe can probably be attributed to ongoing U.S. attempts to annex Greenland. Furthermore, there is a fairly broad consensus for these positions among Danish politicians. Though variations in policy of course exist, there are no clear pro-Russian parties in Denmark. When it comes to the U.S., many Danish parties, from centre-left to right, have, over time, been fairly pro-American, but mirroring popular opinion, sympathy for the U.S. has plummeted among Danish politicians of all colours following the Greenland debacle. The consensus is as much cause and effect regarding the high level of popular unity on threat perception. Public perceptions limit room for manoeuvre for the political parties, but political parties' unity also affects popular opinion, since without a party willing to take up a certain policy position, that position will seldom gain broad traction in Danish society.

Using a traffic light system, Denmark's view of *both* Russia and the U.S. currently falls between 'yellow' and 'red'. Danes do not, for the most part, fear an immediate invasion, but nevertheless the polls do paint a fairly pessimistic picture concerning security. As only the polls concerning Russia have a significant majority seeing Russia as both a threat and an enemy and since Russia is seen as a threat towards the Kingdom of Denmark in its entirety (Denmark, Greenland, and the Faroe Islands), Russia ultimately falls into the 'red' category. Since the poll numbers are lower for the U.S. and since the U.S. is mostly a threat towards Greenland and not the rest of the Kingdom of Denmark, this falls into the 'yellow' category.

The high level of perceived threat amongst Danes may also explain why there has been remarkably little debate concerning the expansion of mandatory military service in Denmark. While this has been limited in practice for many years, that may change now as the Danish defence services struggle with fulfilling political goals for a new heavy brigade. Instead, the limited debate that did take place focused on the introduction of mandatory service for women, which came into effect on 1 July 2025, tying together objectives of improving recruitment possibilities for the Danish armed forces with aspirations about gender equality.

Recommendations

European institutions should strive to create unity amongst its Member States in deterring Russia even without the U.S if need be. Both carrots and sticks will be needed.

On the one hand, unwillingness on the part of some EU countries to meet common defence goals should have consequences such as political isolation and sidelining from EU defence planning. On the other hand, the EU should continue to be as supportive as possible—as with the ReArm Europe Plan—with nations that want to shoulder their defence burden but face stiff financial difficulties in doing so. Having a solid financial base, Denmark could play a key role in promoting such a dual strategy.

Finally, the political parties of each European country need to find common ground, if not on policy, then at least on the security challenges that Europe currently faces. Should party unity be achieved, societal unity will be much easier to establish.

Mikkel Runge Olesen is Senior Researcher at the Danish Institute for International Studies researching Danish foreign and security policy, NATO and transatlantic relations as well as security in the Arctic and Nordic regions. The Danish Institute for International Studies is an independent public research institution for foreign, security and development studies based in Copenhagen.

Estonia: Small State, Big Resolve

Tony Lawrence

Among other indicators of a 'red' threat perception, the National Security Concept of Estonia identifies Russia as the greatest security threat facing the country and places a high priority on military defence. Strong political and societal consensus on these issues underpins Estonia's pursuit of an ambitious and expensive defence policy. Estonia believes that the EU, in its response to Russia's full-scale war in Ukraine, has proved its potential value as a defence capacity builder. However, it remains generally sceptical about the EU's defence role, for which NATO and U.S. engagement remain essential.

Threats

Estonian security and defence policy is driven above all by its perceptions of Russia, a country that both leaders and the general public regard as the source of the most serious threats, mainly military. Most Estonians believe that Russia's attempts to re-establish influence in its neighbourhood are a threat to global peace and security. This was measured at 82% according to Kantor Emor's government-commissioned survey 'Public Opinion on National Defence' during May 2025, from which other statistical information is drawn for this chapter. Other threats featuring prominently in public opinion polls are also related to Russia's foreign policy goals, such as: the war in Ukraine; disinformation; as well as military and cyber-attacks.

This threat perception, clearly in the 'red' category, has been present since Estonia re-established its independence, but has been amplified by Russia's later actions, especially its full-scale war in Ukraine and more recently through 'sub-threshold' activities such as its suspected attacks on underwater energy and

T. Lawrence (✉)
International Centre for Defence and Security, Tallinn, Estonia
e-mail: tony.lawrence@icds.ee

M. Kaeding et al. (eds.), *Security, Defence, and the Future of Europe*,
https://doi.org/10.1007/978-3-032-18279-1_8

communications infrastructure, along with extreme airspace incursions by its military aircraft. It is widely expected that Russia will reconstitute its armed forces rapidly once the war is over and will pose an existential military threat to its neighbours and beyond. Russia's strategic goal would be to weaken the West overall, but Estonia and its Baltic neighbours would be especially vulnerable due to their geographical location and small size.

Responses

Broad agreement about this threat is reflected in the country's strong consensus on security and defence policy. Estonia has consistently sought security through integration with international organisations and through the development of its own armed forces. It enjoys high levels of support for membership of both NATO (83%) and the EU (84%) as well as for allied military presence in the country (82%). Most Estonians (82%) believe that the state should be able to resist any attack by military means. Many routinely participate in defence through volunteer organisations, which have seen their numbers grow in recent years. Around 90% of the population believes that compulsory military service is "definitely" or "rather" necessary. Conscription has been mandatory for all young men since Estonia regained its independence, although in practice, health and fitness exemptions, deferrals and the training capacity of defence forces mean that little more than half the eligible population has served in recent years, hence a current push to increase this number significantly. Military service is paid and lasts for either 8 or 11 months. Alternative civilian service is also available for those who object for religious or moral reasons, though very few take up this option. Women have also been able to volunteer to serve as conscripts since 2013.

There is near-complete agreement among politicians from all parties about the need to increase defence spending, a position also supported by almost half the population despite recent high levels of inflation, as well as security-related tax increases and new taxes. After years of resisting borrowing, Estonia has also begun to issue bonds in part to fund defence development. It will spend a record EUR 1.4 billion (3.4% of GDP) on defence in 2025 (annual defence spending has hovered around 2% of GDP over the previous decade, rising to 3% in 2023 and 3.4% in 2024). Its mid-term defence development plan, approved in 2025, foresees expenditure well above 5% of GDP in the period 2026–29, with investment priorities that include intelligence gathering systems, air defence, long-range strike, larger armed forces and expanded ammunition stocks. Estonia has procured from a variety of sources, including the U.S. (rocket artillery), EU Member States (short- and medium-range air defence, infantry fighting vehicles), Israel-Singapore (coastal defence missiles), Turkey (military vehicles) and South Korea (howitzers).

Estonia also regards a satisfactory outcome to the war in Ukraine—including full territorial restoration, accountability for war crimes and reparations—as essential for its own and wider European security. In part due to its own historical experience, it is deeply apprehensive that a deal might be cut between the U.S. and Russia above

Ukraine's and other European countries' heads. Politicians have also been displeased about the exclusion of smaller states from 'coalition of the willing' negotiations.

On a percentage of GDP basis, Estonia has been the top bilateral provider of military, financial and humanitarian assistance to Ukraine throughout the war and support remains high amongst the population—67% of Estonians believe that the country should continue its military support to Ukraine. It is one of just a handful of countries to have announced its readiness to commit military forces to provide security guarantees to Ukraine in the event of a ceasefire and is a strong advocate of the country's accession to NATO and the EU.

Institutions and Allies

Estonian defence policy and public opinion clearly regard NATO as the primary guarantor of security. The U.S. is viewed as the partner most able by some measure to deter Russian military ambitions and its continued participation in European security affairs is seen as essential. Politicians, whatever their private views, are generally reluctant to criticise their U.S. counterparts or to acknowledge publicly that longstanding trends reshaping the transatlantic relationship, amplified during the second Trump presidency, may have negative impacts on Estonia's security. However, Estonia does not wish to be a passive consumer of U.S. benevolence. It certainly recognises the need for Europe to do more for its own security and places high priority on persuading fellow Europeans, including by its own example, to take defence more seriously and consequently to persuade the U.S. to remain involved.

Attitudes towards NATO have remained largely constant during the two decades of Estonia's membership. However, public support for membership has grown in the past few years, reaching a high of 83% in 2025. Feelings towards the EU as a defence actor have evolved substantially and positively since Russia's full-scale invasion of Ukraine, at least among the country's leadership. Estonia had long been sceptical of any defence role for the EU, seeing this as a distraction from NATO that would probably upset the U.S. However, it has enthusiastically supported the mobilisation of EU instruments to sustain Ukraine's war efforts and the development of new tools to encourage and support Member States' rearmament. Both, in Estonia's estimation, require levels of investment far above those that Member States are apparently ready to provide.

Estonia would welcome the EU becoming, in some form or other, a provider of military capability for Member States, NATO and the Union itself. It has, for example, applied for and received an initial allocation under the Commission's SAFE scheme of EUR 2.6 billion, almost twice its current defence budget. There are, though, limits to Estonia's eagerness for EU rearmament efforts. Because the threat immediacy demands a rapid response, Estonia will continue to resist policies that restrict acquisition options, such as "buy European" rules, or the exclusion of qualified third countries from EU initiatives. It is also investing in domestic production, with three Ministry of Defence-sponsored industrial parks planned for the manufacture of smaller items such as mines, explosives and missiles.

More broadly, Estonia remains sceptical of the EU taking any role in territorial defence. This, it believes, should remain a clear preserve of the Alliance. Similarly, it is suspicious of moves towards closer defence integration in the EU, such as a European army and notions of autonomy.

If NATO were to become untenable, perhaps because of U.S. disengagement, Estonia would probably be more confident in notional defence arrangements based on a coalition of neighbours in the wider Nordic-Baltic region than in EU-based arrangements. The region's countries think alike about Russia; elsewhere, there are differences regarding the seriousness of threat perceptions as well as the urgency and scale of the response required. Indeed, these differences may be factors behind a slightly worrying trend in Estonian public opinion that has seen small levels of growth in an equally small share of the population, which believes that NATO would not provide a full military response if Estonia were attacked.

Recommendations

European security is at a high-stakes turning point. Europeans need to be better prepared for a period in which they will face a hostile Russia to their east, with at best lukewarm backing from the U.S.

Firstly, to position themselves for these circumstances, they must take steps to ensure security for those states on the fringes of the continent on whom their own security depends. Immediately, this means providing maximum moral, financial and physical support to Ukraine in order that it can secure as just an outcome as possible from Russia's war. It also means locking Ukraine and other geographically peripheral states—in the Balkans and the Caucasus—into Western security structures to erase grey zones and build broad security; this, in turn, means rejuvenating the rather sluggish EU enlargement process.

Secondly, the EU must continue to build on its efforts to facilitate the development of the military capability needed to secure Europe's safety as well as the industrial and technical defence base that can support this.

Thirdly, the EU and its Member States must continue efforts to keep the U.S. engaged in European security matters. The U.S. may often choose to remain distant, especially under the current administration, but its ability to deter Russia, the primary threat to the continent, is unmatched.

Fourthly, the EU must recognise that NATO is, and must remain, the prime guarantor of security for most Member States and that NATO's regional defence plans will thus be the prime driver for those Member States' defence planning. The EU should focus on capability-building instruments that complement NATO and must, at the very least, ensure that its own capability planning initiatives (such as 'Eastern flank watch') are fully coordinated with the Alliance.

Tony Lawrence is head of the defence policy and strategy programme at the International Centre for Defence and Security, Tallinn, Estonia. His research focuses on various aspects of defence and deterrence in the Baltic region, including: defence policies of the Baltic states and other regional actors; defence cooperation; the role of NATO and the EU; military components of deterrence and defence; as well as the progress and impact of Russia's war in Ukraine. The International Centre for Defence and Security is the leading think tank in Estonia, specialising in foreign policy, security and defence issues. It aims to strengthen security and defence thinking in Estonia, the Nordic-Baltic region, NATO and the EU by offering timely and high-quality analysis and policy recommendations on issues of European and transatlantic security and defence.

Finland: Without Security, Everything Is Nothing

Tuomas Iso-Markku

As a small country bordering Russia, Finland takes security extremely seriously. It supports all efforts to strengthen Europe's military capabilities and the EU's defence dimension, but also wants to keep the U.S. involved. Finland's threat perception traffic light is set at 'red', albeit the country feels better prepared than most.

Security as a Priority

Finland's approach to security and defence has been shaped by the country's proximity to Russia and the memory of two wars fought against the Soviet Union between 1939 and 1944. These have translated into a heightened threat perception and conviction that security is the basis upon which everything rests. 79% of the population believes that if Finland were attacked, Finns should take up arms to fight the invasion.

Russia has always been viewed as Finland's primary (military) threat. To navigate the relationship with its eastern neighbour, Finland has relied on varying combinations of deterrence and reassurance. For decades, reassurance meant that Finland refrained from any military cooperation or alliance to which Moscow could have objected. At the same time, Finland did its best to maintain a credible national defence.

Finland's belief in non-alliance ended with Russia's full-scale invasion of Ukraine in February 2022. Following a radical shift in public opinion and a quick strategic reassessment by decision-makers, Finland applied for NATO membership in May 2022, joining the alliance in April 2023. Both Finnish decision-makers and the public perceive Russia as a serious long-term threat. Understandably, the Finns

T. Iso-Markku (✉)
Finnish Institute of Internatonal Affairs (FIIA), Helsinki, Finland
e-mail: tuomas.iso-markku@fiia.fi

M. Kaeding et al. (eds.), *Security, Defence, and the Future of Europe*,
https://doi.org/10.1007/978-3-032-18279-1_9

are very sympathetic towards Ukraine's battle against Russia's invasion, comparing it to Finland's own experiences and viewing its outcome as crucial for European security.

Throughout its history, Finland's defence has built on general conscription for men, which enjoys broad support. Around 75% of each age cohort is called up, with circa 20,000 men completing their military service annually. Women can serve on a voluntary basis and around 900–1000 do so every year. Military service lasts 165, 255 or 347 days depending on specialisation. Alternatively, a 347-day civilian service is chosen by some 2000 men annually.

Thanks to the large pool of trained reservists, Finland's envisaged wartime strength stands at an impressive 280,000. However, in the medium term, the Finnish model is challenged by the country's persistently low birth rates. Extending conscription to all genders or introducing a universal national service with both civilian and military tasks have been floated as options for the future, but not yet seriously discussed.

Another key pillar of Finland's security and defence policy is the concept of comprehensive security. It emphasises preparedness for all types of crises, with close cooperation between government authorities, the private sector, civil society and citizens seen as key to securing the vital functions of society under all conditions.

At present, Finland's defence spending stands at 2.5% of GDP and is set to reach 3% by 2029. This comes at a time when Finland's economic performance has been lacklustre and the government is executing large budget cuts. So far, defence spending hikes have proven uncontroversial, reflecting how seriously Finns take the current situation. Overall, Finnish society's readiness to invest in security demonstrates that for Finland the threat perception traffic light is set at 'red'. At the same time, Finland's starting point is better than that of many other EU Member States.

A Supportive but Pragmatic View of EU Defence

For Finland, which joined the EU in 1995, Union membership has always had a security dimension. In the 1990s, non-aligned Finland was still wary of extensive military cooperation. However, the EU offered the kind of shelter Finland was looking for, tying the country politically and economically to a group of Member States who henceforth had an interest in Finland's destiny.

With time, Finland overcame its hesitancy about expanding the EU's defence remit. Especially after Russia first invaded Ukraine in 2014, Finland adopted a highly positive view of anything that the EU could do to strengthen European defence. Illustratively, Finland became a vocal advocate of the EU's mutual assistance clause, Article 42.7 of the Treaty on European Union. However, Finnish interest in defence cooperation was not limited to the EU. The country also strengthened ties with NATO and worked in various bilateral and mini-lateral formats.

NATO accession has not changed Finland's view of the EU's relevance, with the country stressing that EU and NATO roles are mutually reinforcing. From Finland's perspective, the EU's main strengths lie in its ability to fund and foster the development of European defence capabilities and industry, as well as military mobility. Moreover, the EU's broad policy portfolio offers the Union tools to deal with hybrid threats.

To equip the EU for an era of radical uncertainty, Finland has also pushed the Union to learn from Finland's whole-of-society approach to security. Following a request from the President of the European Commission, Finland's former President Sauli Niinistö drafted a report on strengthening the EU's civilian and military preparedness, drawing heavily on the Finnish concept of comprehensive security.

While Finland thinks that Europe should take more responsibility for its own security, Finnish policymakers struggle to imagine European defence without U.S. involvement. NATO accession, a concomitant bilateral defence cooperation agreement with the U.S. and the procurement of 64 F-35 s demonstrate Finland's Atlanticism. However, the Finnish population is more sceptical about the current direction of U.S. foreign policy and hence around 65% of Finns support the idea of a common EU defence.

Recommendations

While Finland has achieved role model status in defence matters, it should not take this for granted. Since Finland's defence relies strongly on the contribution of Finnish society, the country should proactively address the challenges that loom on the horizon. Apart from the state of Finland's economy, these include the country's low birth rates and increased political polarisation.

Finland should also be more ambitious when it comes to European defence and the EU's role therein. Although cooperation with the U.S. remains essential in the short term, it should not give way to complacency. Finland should prepare for a scenario in which the U.S. is largely disengaged from European security.

Finally, Finland should continue its strong support for Ukraine's quest for sovereignty and security. As Finland has rightly acknowledged, the outcome of the war in Ukraine will decisively shape the European security order. Ukraine could be an important contributor to European security and defence after the war.

Tuomas Iso-Markku is a Leading Researcher at the Finnish Institute of International Affairs (FIIA). His research deals with the EU's role in security and defence matters, European defence cooperation, EU-NATO relations, German domestic politics, German foreign and EU policy, Finnish EU policy, Finnish foreign, security and defence policy as well as European party politics. FIIA is an independent research institute affiliated with the Parliament of Finland. FIIA studies Finnish foreign policy, international politics, global economic relations and the EU. Its mission is to produce high-quality research, support policymaking and participate in both academic and public debates in Finland as well as internationally.

"When Paris Sneezes, Europe Catches a Cold": Why the French Crisis Is Bad News for European Defence

Celia Burgdorff

France's deepening domestic crisis, marked by parliamentary deadlock, public discontent and Emmanuel Macron's waning authority, casts a long shadow over Europe's defence ambitions. Macron remains one of Europe's most vocal champions of strategic autonomy, yet his message increasingly falls on sceptical ears at home. The updated *Revue nationale stratégique* (RNS) (National strategic review) leaves no doubt: Russia is identified as the foremost threat to France, its allies and the European continent's stability. However, French public opinion paints a more nuanced picture, namely a medium to high ('yellow') threat perception, recognising Moscow's military and financial strength as well as its potential to act aggressively in the coming years, without succumbing to alarmism. This tension between official rhetoric and public sentiment highlights a deeper dilemma in France's strategic posture: how to reconcile European ambitions with domestic fragility and limited resources. If France is to remain a credible leader in European security, it must focus less on global pretensions and more on building the institutional backbone of a genuine EUSD.

At Home, Macron's Pro-Europeanism Meets Resistance

"*Notre Europe est mortelle*"—Europe as we know it could die, said Emmanuel Macron during his second Sorbonne Speech in April 2024. With this quote from French author Paul Valéry, he tried to send a message to his European counterparts as well as a warning to his own citizens. Only 2 months later, in June 2024, after disastrous results for his party, Renaissance, at the European elections, he decided to dissolve the National Assembly, provoking parliamentary elections. What followed was an ongoing political crisis: since then, the French parliament has been

C. Burgdorff (✉)
Le Fondation pour la recherche stratégique (FRS), Clichy, France

M. Kaeding et al. (eds.), *Security, Defence, and the Future of Europe*, https://doi.org/10.1007/978-3-032-18279-1_10

stuck between three blocs. In 2025 alone, four different Prime Ministers have come and gone, trying to build a majority that would enable them to reduce the country's alarming level of debt. This situation, though, did not prevent Emmanuel Macron from making use of his so-called 'reserved domain' foreign policy. During the last few months, the French President has been extremely active on the international stage, meeting European counterparts in Washington and Brussels and facilitating dialogue between members of the 'Coalition of the willing' in the Palais de l'Elysée.

This development could appear forced or opportunistic, but it is in fact part of Macron's political DNA. Emmanuel Macron is probably one of the most pro-European presidents France has ever known. For the first time in the Fifth Republic's history, he succeeded in making European questions part of a political identity. Moreover, pro-Europeanness might also be the last easily identifiable trait of Macron's once progressive, now centre-right-leaning party. This is bad news for Europe: as Macron is on his way to becoming one of the most unpopular French presidents ever, resentment towards him could easily evolve into a new form of Euroscepticism. Following Prime Minister François Bayrou's overthrow by parliament, a new protest movement emerged all over the country. Citizens of different social, political and geographical origins called for Macron's removal from office. Of particular concern for Europe, given that most claims are related to social justice, there are also some people who fear an imminent war and the deployment of French troops, whether in Poland or Gaza. There are also fears that the cost of defence to the public purse could be borne at the expense of social rights. These events could further destabilise an already fragile EU.

Among European leaders, though, Macron has been a key diplomatic actor on the path to an EUSD during the last few years. His 'Gaullist' conception of sovereignty, often labelled as 'strategic autonomy', has become ever more relevant since Russia's full-scale invasion of Ukraine. Furthermore, since the return of Donald Trump to the White House, the French President and his diplomats have also been actively lobbying for a European defence body, compatible with NATO, but independent.

Prioritise European Leadership over a Stronger Global Presence

The complex geopolitical context, coupled with France's domestic challenges, calls for a significant shift in the country's approach to European security and defence. The July 2025 update from the RNS testifies to the urgency of this situation. The document explicitly identifies Russia as a threat to "the interests of France, those of its partners and allies, and the very stability of the European continent and the Euro-Atlantic area," and calls for a "moral rearmament." This framing, together with recent French Institute of Public Opinion polls, points to a medium ('yellow') to high ('red') threat perception among French citizens. In line with this level, Russia, as a potential aggressor in the coming years, is viewed as having the financial and military capability to annex parts of Europe, with comparable or slightly superior capabilities to France. 72% of French citizens believe that Russia poses a threat to the sovereignty of EU Member States and 79% do not trust Vladimir Putin to respect a possible ceasefire. On a more practical level, the RNS foresees an increase in France's defence budget to EUR 64 billion (2.5% of GDP) by 2027 instead of 2030. While this is already ambitious given the country's financial constraints, France's European partners who are aiming for 5% of GDP might still deem this effort insufficient.

The RNS also highlights a deeper contradiction at the heart of French defence policy. On the one hand, France is committing to European procurement, strengthening an EUSD. On the other hand, the document requires that France develop its own industrial and technological defence base. This is symptomatic of France's split between its commitment to European integration and its enduring self-image as a global diplomatic actor. This second aspect is closely tied to the French Navy and overseas territories, which ensure a French military presence in strategic areas such as the Indo-Pacific. This is often overlooked by France's European partners. Both aspects are equally important in the newest RNS, thus not indicating a clear shift towards one or the other.

Considering the French financial and political realities—with public debt expected to reach 116% of GDP by the end of 2025—as well as European vulnerabilities, the French armed forces should prioritise European leadership over a stronger global presence in the coming years. This orientation will be supported by the EUR 16.2 billion France is set to receive from the SAFE fund, strengthening its defence industry base. Meanwhile, the government has announced plans for 'voluntary' military service, albeit without further details at this stage.

Recommendations

With just 1 year left before the presidential elections, France can no longer afford half-measures. In a world where the geopolitical ground is constantly shifting, Paris must finally deliver on its oft-repeated promise to "pivot to Europe." That means using its diplomatic clout not just to call for, but to secure deeper coordination of European security and defence.

The bold step would be to champion a treaty laying the foundations of a genuine EUSD, one that empowers EU institutions to act with authority in a domain that has become existential.

Beyond institutional reform, France should immediately align its defence investments and partnerships with European frameworks, prioritising joint capabilities and structured cooperation with key partners such as Germany. This would turn rhetoric about strategic autonomy into tangible progress, making defence financing more realistic through efficiency gains, while demonstrating France's credibility as Europe's security anchor.

Celia Burgdorff holds a PhD in History of International Relations (Université Paris 1 Panthéon-Sorbonne and Ludwig-Maximilians-University Munich). Her work focuses on the history of European integration, European diplomacy and the Franco-German relationship. She is an associate researcher at the Fondation pour la recherche stratégique (FRS). Founded in 1992, the Fondation pour la Recherche Stratégique (FRS) is an independent, non-profit think tank recognised as a public utility foundation in France. With a staff of 32, it specialises in strategic and international security issues, particularly defence and military affairs. FRS contributes to national strategic debates and promotes French perspectives abroad and is the only major independent French think tank dedicated exclusively to these fields.

Germany's *Zeitenwende*: All That Glitters Is Not Gold

Funda Tekin

Germany is operating on a 'yellow' threat perception level, which is reflected in its actions. Consequently, the *Zeitenwende* (turning point) has triggered fundamental reforms in Germany's security and defence policy, but the impacts on European security and defence policy are limited.

Zeitenwende in Times of an Epoch Break

Germany's approach to security and defence policy has been inextricably linked to its Second World War legacy. Ever since 1945, key pillars have been its strong commitment to multilateralism and a rules-based international order. Additionally, Germany's security and defence policy has been closely embedded in European integration—as a peace project—and the transatlantic partnership with NATO as the key pillar. Finally, Germany has focused on a comprehensive understanding of security with the constitution defining the Bundeswehr as a defence army, allowing it to take action collectively within the mandates of international organisations such as the United Nations (UN), NATO or the EU only. During the Cold War era, Willy Brandt defined the principle of "*Wandel durch Handel*" (change through trade) as a key feature of Germany's new Eastern policy. As with the European integration project, economic interdependencies with the Soviet Union and the Eastern bloc were meant to promote political modernisation and eventual democratisation. While this played out for most countries in the former Eastern bloc, which have now joined the EU, this strategy largely failed with Russia. The country's full-scale invasion of Ukraine on 24 February 2022 put a definite end to this approach and revealed Europe's and particularly Germany's high dependence on Russian gas and oil.

F. Tekin (✉)
Institut für Europäische Politik, Berlin, Germany
e-mail: Funda.Tekin@iep-berlin.de

M. Kaeding et al. (eds.), *Security, Defence, and the Future of Europe*,
https://doi.org/10.1007/978-3-032-18279-1_11

Additionally, multipolarity is taking over the global scene with the rules-based order in decline. Euroscepticism and far-right political forces are on the rise across Europe and the second Trump administration has rendered the transatlantic relationship unpredictable at best, with an enormous effect on Europe's security order.

So, it is no surprise that former centre-left Chancellor Olaf Scholz announced a "*Zeitenwende*" (turning point) in February 2022, and the current centre-right Chancellor Friedrich Merz spoke of an "*Epochenbruch*" (epoch change) when campaigning during general elections at the beginning of 2025. In his *Zeitenwende*-speech, Scholz committed Germany, amongst other things, to decreasing its dependencies on Russian gas and oil because energy security was part of national security and to complying with NATO's 2% goal for defence spending. Furthermore, he announced the establishment of a special fund worth EUR 100 billion for modernising the Bundeswehr. Defending freedom, democracy and the rule of law were to remain core elements of German foreign policy.

However, public and political debates ever since have lost Scholz's determination. There is general acknowledgement that the *Wandel durch Handel* strategy had been a mistake (this includes views from former Chancellor Merkel and parts of the Social Democratic Party of Germany [SPD]), whilst a commitment to increased military spending and delivery of military means persists. Some argue that Germany and the EU need to increase military capacities as a means of deterrence; others are convinced that militarisation will not pave the way to peace, but the contrary. Diplomacy would need to be the strategy, argues a manifesto issued by a group from within the SPD and co-signed by popular members of the party.

German Views at a Glance: Threat Perceptions and Military Readiness

The annual opinion poll and study on threat perceptions in Germany by the Bundeswehr Centre of Military History and Social Sciences disclosed in November 2024 that the population is rather undecided on whether weapon deliveries contribute to ending or prolonging the war in Ukraine and whether they represent protection or a threat to their own security. The same study, though, states that 65% of respondents perceive Russia's military actions as a threat to national security. Forty-one per cent recognise tensions between Russia and the West as a threat to personal security, which marks an increase of 7% compared with 2023.

This study also provides insights into the German population's military readiness, which is highly relevant for contextualising current debate on whether and, if so, how to structure reestablishment of compulsory military service, which was paused in 2011. In 2024, 49% of respondents supported the idea of compulsory military service, while 23% were undecided and 24% objected to it. Respective debates had different dimensions, including general support for military service, the effectiveness of compulsory military service, as well as an inter-generational dimension. Young people demanded a say in the debate that they had felt excluded from, even though such a policy change would affect their lives the most. Over the summer of 2025, the draft law had been blocked by the Minister of Defence Boris Pistorius from the SPD, who did not back the proposal by the Christian Democrats to draft soldiers via a lottery procedure. In the end, the government agreed on a voluntary military service that still requires all 18-year-old males to respond to a questionnaire and eventually undertake a medical examination.

In general terms, under the traffic lights analogy, Germany is operating on a 'yellow' threat perception level, with both the population and political elites being aware of the threat. During crisis times, political actions are marked by determination and strong rhetoric, but their respective debates and actions are marked by hesitation.

The Winding Path to European Defence and Security Policy

This recurrent hesitation in political debates on Germany's approach to European security in general and support to Ukraine in particular has left its mark. Even though, according to the Ukraine Support Trackers of the Kiel Institute for the World Economy, Germany is the third-largest supporter of Ukraine, ranking behind the U.S. and EU, the country is still being accused by other EU Member States of not delivering on its promises. The narrative of Germany delivering only 5000 helmets to Ukraine at the outset of Russia's war of aggression has stuck. Ongoing discussions on Taurus deliveries to Ukraine are also a case in point. In fact, since 2022 Germany's financial, humanitarian and military support has added up to EUR 76 billion (paid and/or provided). Regarding defence spending, Germany reached the 2% of GDP limit in 2024 for the first time and is also committed to attaining the 5% objective by 2035, as decided at the NATO summit in the Hague.

EU Member States might risk actual disappointment by putting their hopes on the special funds established by the *Zeitenwende* and the special fund on infrastructure and climate neutrality established in March 2025. The latter is part of a decision to loosen the debt brake for defence spending above 1% of GDP. The EUR 500 billion provided by this special fund is for improving the German population's everyday lives and undertaking infrastructure projects. EUR 300 billion and EUR 100 billion are located at federal and at the regional levels, respectively. An additional EUR 100 billion feed into a climate and transformation fund. These fundamental decisions represent important political signals that Germany is willing to take greater responsibility for security, strengthening the momentum for enhanced common projects at a European level such as within the framework of PESCO or the European Defence Fund, including SAFE. Nevertheless, some technological and industrial spill-over has resulted and the impact on European defence and security policy does have its limits. A great share of the special fund has been dedicated to national procurement and Germany is purchasing in the U.S. rather than from European industry directly. Additionally, implementation of the *Zeitenwende* special fund has been slower than expected. The special fund for additional investments in infrastructure and climate neutrality has built-in limitations regarding the purposes it can be spent on. Defence spending in 2025 has grown, but only to a limited extent from 2% of GDP in 2024 to an expected 2.4% of GDP in 2025. Still, the German brigade that has been stationed in Lithuania since 2024 represents the largest Bundeswehr contribution to the Eastern Flank of NATO.

How to End the War in Ukraine: No Straightforward Answer to the One Million Euro Question

One of the strongest proponents of ending military support to Ukraine and increasing diplomatic talks with Russia is Sarah Wagenknecht, a former member of the party *Die Linke* (The Left), and founder of the Alliance Sarah Wagenknecht. This opinion has not, though, translated into mainstream political strategy. Hence, Germany participates fully in sanctions against Russia and supports efforts to seize or redirect frozen Russian assets for Ukraine. Germany is part of the 'Coalition of the willing' for supporting Ukraine and hence is generally prepared to deploy troops in Ukraine as reassurance forces or to be present on the ground, at sea, or in the air to secure a peace settlement once it has been reached. It backs the concept of strengthening the European pillar within NATO. Germany is ready to work on the EU's own defence capabilities while remaining aware of the need for U.S. involvement in both achieving and preserving peace. Yet, Trump's attempts to negotiate peace without the involvement of the EU and/or even Ukraine are not supported.

Recommendations

Given the global context and the ongoing war in Europe, together with an unpredictable transatlantic partnership, the EU needs to increase its strategic autonomy. Germany is well aware of the fact that relations with the U.S. need to remain close—regardless of how difficult they are. In security terms, this requires three things. Firstly, more unity and solidarity among Member States is vital. Currently, Hungary and Slovakia are the outliers when it comes to decisions on Ukraine. However, the Czech Republic's 2025 presidential elections might have increased this to a club of three. Procedures for preserving the EU's capacity to act in spite of such veto positions are vital. Council summits producing multiple conclusions or lengthy coffee breaks for certain members of the European Council might serve as provisional solution only. A sustainable solution would result from extending QMV.

Secondly, defence spending within the EU should be boosted. To this end, programmes such as ReArm Europe, including the SAFE Programme, are essential. From a German perspective, more standardisation, simplification and scale to remedy Europe's fragmented defence industry, slow procurement processes and the need to increase military production rapidly is just as important.

Thirdly, flexibilisation and differentiation remain important tools within the CSDP. Formats such as E3 (Germany, France and the UK) or the 'Coalition of the willing', as well as PESCO projects, allow those Member States that are willing and able to cooperate on certain defence and security issues to do so. In order for this strategy to be effective, the EU's cohesion deserves careful consideration.

Funda Tekin is director of IEP and an honorary professor at the University of Tübingen. She earned her PhD in political science from the University of Cologne with a research focus on differentiated integration and enlargement. Prof. Dr. Funda Tekin was a member of the TEPSA Board. The Institute für Europäische Politik (IEP) is a non-profit, non-partisan organisation focused on European integration. It provides an accessible, European, interdisciplinary forum and a platform for expert debates on European policy. The institute is one of Germany's leading research institutions for foreign and European issues.

European Security in the Danger Zone: Greece's Strategic Role

Dimitris Tsaknis and Athina Fatsea

This chapter examines how Greece and the EU are experiencing a period of global strategic fragility. Greece has become a vocal proponent of European strategic autonomy, reaffirming its position on the side of a 'shaking' transatlantic alliance. With a 'yellow' level of threat perception, shaped by tensions with Turkey and instability across Europe's neighbourhood, Athens calls for decisive EU action to strengthen collective defence, thereby complementing NATO's presence.

In the 'Yellow' Zone: Greece's Security Challenges

Greece faces a number of intersecting security challenges on its borders. To its north, lie the unstable Western Balkan countries. In the east, an assertive Turkey is testing red lines in the Aegean and Eastern Mediterranean. Southeast, there is a deepening crisis in Middle East which continues to fuel humanitarian, security and radicalisation risks across the region, while fear of a new migration 'tsunami' threatens European governments. Finally, to the northeast, Russia's war in Ukraine drags on, with hybrid and actual threats already reaching into European territory. In September 2025, Russian drones and jets violated the airspace of numerous EU Member States and NATO Allies, such as Poland, Estonia and Denmark, triggering a NATO Quick Reaction Alert. Russia's aerial incursions into Europe were successfully intercepted by aircraft of the alliance and by missile systems, with drones in Poland being shot down. The escalation of Russian aggression against member countries of NATO can certainly be interpreted as a chess game that aims to test EU nerves. As a result, Russian provocation has given an additional boost to preparation of the EU's new defensive strategy, a necessary step to achieving so-called autonomy.

D. Tsaknis (✉) · A. Fatsea
European Public Law Organisation (EPLO); ELIAMEP, Athens, Greece
e-mail: dtsaknis@eplo.int; afatsea@eliamep.gr

M. Kaeding et al. (eds.), *Security, Defence, and the Future of Europe*,
https://doi.org/10.1007/978-3-032-18279-1_12

Public sentiment reflects regional instability, with 74% of Greeks concerned about the EU's defence and security in the next 5 years, according to the Spring 2025 Eurobarometer. Using the traffic light threat perception model, Greece falls into the 'yellow' category. While there is no imminent threat of war, it faces an explicitly stated threat from Turkey, including a long-standing *casus belli* declaration over territorial waters. Though regional instabilities further compound its security concerns, Greece's adversaries have broadly comparable capabilities, with its national posture focused on deterrence and preparedness rather than any expectation of imminent direct conflict.

Athens has responded decisively to these challenges. According to NATO's Defence Expenditure Report of June 2024, Greek defence spending had already reached 3.08% of GDP, one of the highest in the EU. This not only exceeds NATO's 2% threshold but aligns with the recent NATO commitment in The Hague to aim for 5% of GDP defence spending by 2035. More specifically, Allies will allocate at least 3.5% of GDP annually to core defence spending to procure military equipment and support personnel, plus an additional 1.5% to defence-related investments, such as the upgrade of infrastructure (transformation of rail, road, sea, and air corridors) with the aim of creating a 'military Schengen'. This includes dual-purpose investments that would enhance military mobility, cybersecurity, cooperation between military and civilian sectors and resilience on critical infrastructure. By 2025, the EIB estimated the astronomical cost for these expenses to be in the area of EUR 80 billion, an unaffordable cost in Greek terms as the state tries to rationalise the impact on public funds of spending on the armament race. The wounds that the economic crisis caused to the Greek state and the Greek citizens have still not fully healed 15 years later.

At the same time, Greece aligns itself with broader European efforts to develop a more autonomous defence capability, viewing this as essential for the EU's long-term strategic resilience. In this regard, Greece can capitalise on mandatory conscription with the continual mobilisation and presence of a significant deterrent manpower at the edge of Europe. Only a few know that the Greek army is experiencing a period of radical change in fields related to the military forces' organisation and administration, changes dictated by emerging security challenges.

Europe's Defence: Autonomy Within the Alliance

While Greece continues to value NATO, the shifting global order has raised questions about the Alliance's reliability. Repeated signals of unpredictability in U.S. foreign policy, especially under Trump's first presidency, and current political uncertainty have made EU Member States re-evaluate their dependencies. For Greece, the EU's strategic autonomy is not about replacing NATO, but about developing the capacity to act when NATO cannot. As described in the November 2016 Council conclusions, it means the "capacity to act autonomously when and where necessary and with partners wherever possible".

Greece has strongly supported 'Readiness 2030', the EU's flagship defence initiative. Athens was among the first to endorse the White Paper's pillars: bridging capability gaps, bolstering the defence industrial base and achieving joint procurement. It sees EU cooperation not just as symbolic, but operationally essential.

Above all, Greece's geography makes it an indispensable link between EU and NATO defence plans. It serves as a logistics hub for Ukraine-bound support, a gateway for energy security and a monitoring point for instability from North Africa to the Middle East. However, Greek officials have become vocal about the need for a European command structure and institutionalised burden sharing. Strategic autonomy for Greece means readiness without exclusion.

Strategic Investment Under Fiscal Pressure

Despite over a decade of fiscal strain, Greece remains committed to sustained defence investment. While Greece maintains consistently high defence spending, even under the Coalition of the Radical Left—Progressive Alliance (SYRIZA) (The Left in the EP) government, parliamentary debates often emerge around procurement priorities, strategic planning and fiscal limitations.

According to the Spring 2025 Eurobarometer, 72% of Greeks support financial and humanitarian support for Ukraine. However, the cost of this commitment is rising, particularly amid inflation and fiscal consolidation. In this context, Greece has supported European-level financing instruments such as the ReArm Europe Plan. With this Plan offering use of the Stability and Growth Pact's escape clause, countries such as Greece are given a way to balance strategic investments with budgetary discipline. Athens is also in favour of tools such as SAFE leveraging the EIB to finance dual-use infrastructure and cyber capabilities.

Recommendations

Greece should support efforts within the EU to institutionalise joint defence procurement and command, reducing fragmentation and enabling operational autonomy. It should advocate for permanent fiscal exemptions for defence within EU rules, ensuring financial flexibility at times of rising threats. Finally, Greece must invest in strategic communication, both domestically and across the EU, to clarify security risks and build public support for a united, capable European defence and security policy. Both Greece and the EU must design a pragmatic strategy that takes into consideration current geopolitics in a multipolar world, while the role and predictability of the U.S. as a longstanding transatlantic ally remain questionable. The nature of these challenges and the presence of an aggressive Russia in Europe's backyard awakens sentiments of insecurity among European societies, a factor that fuels the rise of Euroscepticism. Sanctions as a first step have to be followed by a larger military footprint, especially in the field of defence systems with short, medium, but also long-range capabilities.

Dimitris Tsaknis is responsible for the Academic Affairs of the ELGS Rome Office and Research Associate at EPLO. He holds a Master's Degree in International Relations from the National and Kapodistrian University of Athens.

EPLO is an international organisation, based in Athens, dedicated to the creation and dissemination of knowledge in the area of Public Law *lato sensu* and Governance. Fourteen countries have already ratified the International Treaty establishing EPLO.

Athina Fatsea is a Research Assistant and Project Manager at ELIAMEP, curating the Greek version of the Transatlantic Periscope, a project of the Bertelsmann Foundation. She is also a PhD Candidate at the Ionian University, Greece.

ELIAMEP is an independent, non-governmental, non-profit think tank established in Athens in 1988. Its mission is to conduct policy-oriented research and provide authoritative information, analysis and policy recommendations for the development of evidence-based responses to major European and foreign policy challenges.

Hungary: The Allied Outlier

Boglárka Koller

Despite its direct political confrontation with the EU and pro-Russian foreign policy stance, Hungary supports the EU's security and defence developments. Since 2017, it has modernised its military through European procurement and its own domestic industry. The EU and NATO remain central to its defence strategy, with Hungary participating in missions and joint capability projects. However, its foreign policy, which focuses on sovereignty, often complicates Allied cooperation. Threat perception in Hungary can be categorised as 'yellow'.

Strategic Change and New Developments

The 2014 Russian annexation of Crimea, the 2015 migration crisis and growing global rivalries prompted Hungary to re-evaluate its security and defence. Launched in 2017, the Zrínyi 2026 Programme was the most ambitious military modernisation initiative since 1989, combining capability upgrades, research and domestic arms production. The 2020 National Security Strategy expanded this security concept to include global challenges such as great power rivalry, migration, climate change, technology and economic dependence, while reaffirming NATO and the EU as core frameworks. The document emphasises national sovereignty and Hungary's pursuit of strategic autonomy to reduce its reliance on the EU and NATO. It emphasises the importance of digital and energy independence as well as responses to hybrid and cyber threats. It also takes a cautious yet partly aligned stance towards Russia and China. This focus on autonomy and sovereign deterrence was reinforced in the 2021 Military Strategy. These changes to the strategy resulted in significant

B. Koller (✉)
Institute of World Economics, Centre for Economics and Regional Studies at ELTE, Budapest, Hungary
e-mail: koller.boglarka@krtk.elte.hu

M. Kaeding et al. (eds.), *Security, Defence, and the Future of Europe*,
https://doi.org/10.1007/978-3-032-18279-1_13

organisational and fiscal changes. Transferring operational control from Parliament to the government signifies a greater degree of centralisation.

Implementing these new objectives has resulted in a substantial rise in Hungary's total defence expenditure. Hungary increased its defence spending from 1.79% of GDP in 2020 to 2.16% in 2024. At the 2025 NATO Summit, it pledged to raise this figure still further to 5% by 2035, with 3.5% allocated to core military capabilities and 1.5% to infrastructure, cyber security and other defence innovations. The country's commitment to defence is underscored by its participation in the EU's SAFE, which is expected to generate significant EU funding for defence procurement and investment. Hungary is allocated EUR 16.2 billion under SAFE. Paradoxically, Hungary was the only EU Member State that abstained from the vote to establish SAFE in 2025. Meanwhile, a significant portion of Hungary's defence industry has been consolidated under the control of a private company 4iG SDT. This Hungarian group acquired a majority stake (75+1%) in the state-owned N7 Holding, which holds shares in nine key companies, including Rheinmetall Hungary. The aim is to improve production coordination in Hungary and increase its export potential in the European market. However, privatisation and concentration also carry economic and political risks, as the state will have less control over the company.

The Connectivity Paradox

Hungary's evolving security and defence policy is framed within the foreign policy doctrine of 'connectivity', presenting the country as a mediator and bridge between the NATO/EU sphere and external powers. The strategy seeks to maximise national interests by engaging not only with traditional allies, but also Russia, China and Turkey, even when their positions conflict with those of the EU or NATO. While this approach could increase Hungary's international visibility and offer short-term benefits, it also poses significant long-term risks. For example, deepening economic ties with China could strain relations with the U.S. and maintaining reliance on Russian energy could isolate Hungary from other EU Member States. The connectivity concept favours bilateralism and personal ties over multilateralism and institutional linkages.

During Trump's second term as U.S. President, despite Hungary's evident economic losses due to his trade wars and new tariffs against the EU, Hungarian-U.S. relations have nevertheless become significantly more personal. By contrast, while most EU partners have distanced themselves from Russia as an aggressor state, Hungary's Foreign Minister has maintained a close and personal relationship with his Russian counterpart. It is important to note that any change in relationships between major powers can result in security risks and isolation for smaller states such as Hungary. Evidence of this can be seen in Hungary's exclusion from the British and French-led 'Coalition of the willing' for support of Ukraine. In the event of a serious security crisis or war, value-based choices and decisions are required of existing alliances such as the EU or NATO and the connectivity approach is not rewarded by the other members of these clubs. This will lead to the outlier being isolated, a situation that Hungary has only recently been experiencing.

Threat Perceptions of Hungarians

The prevailing Hungarian perceptions of security are influenced by a number of factors, including historical events such as the Treaty of Trianon and Soviet influence, the abandonment of the country by the West in 1956, its geographical location in the Carpathian Basin between the Western and Eastern parts of Central Europe and the fact that a significant number of Hungarian minorities live outside the country's borders. Mother-country nationalism is an everyday political and policy practice for the state. Consequently, Hungarians' attitudes are characterised by duality. On the one hand, they would like to maintain the security guarantees provided by NATO and the EU. However, they also consider it important to develop their defence autonomy, as the West has failed to provide sufficient security guarantees many times in the past. Furthermore, non-traditional threats are gaining prominence in contemporary Hungarian security discourse. These include economic uncertainties, migration, energy policy dependencies, cyber-attacks and hybrid warfare, all of which are becoming increasingly significant.

As a 2024 Policy Solutions survey indicates, in 2022, when the Russian-Ukrainian war broke out, Hungarians were more concerned about the possible outbreak of a global conflict, but a downward trend has been observed since then; today, only 32% of the population fear geopolitical threats. The official government rhetoric is that the war in Ukraine is not Hungary's war. It is a conflict between two Slavic nations, in which Hungary should not become embroiled. Since the war broke out, Hungarians have distanced themselves from Russia, but have not aligned themselves with Ukraine. Most Hungarians are opposed to Ukraine's EU membership, with 60% against the country's candidacy according to the Spring 2025 Eurobarometer survey.

Nevertheless, as the war is taking place in neighbouring Ukraine and there is a sizeable Hungarian minority there, citizens still perceive it as a direct security threat. Hungarians are also concerned about their dependency on Russian gas, particularly due to supply shortages and rising prices. The threat perception among Hungarians is therefore unique. While people are aware of the serious conflict nearby, many do not regard it as their own. They also view the question of ending the war as a matter for the major powers (the U.S. and Russia) to decide, with Europe playing only a minor role. This contradicts both the sovereigntist view and the idea that Hungarian citizens would prefer the EU to play a greater role in CSDP. According to the traffic light system, the threat could be categorised as 'yellow'.

While Hungarians list the Russian invasion of Ukraine as one of their main concerns at EU level (Eurobarometer), according to a 2025 Ipsos survey, only 6% of Hungarians choose military conflicts between nations among their top three worries (while 63% choose healthcare and 51% inflation). Global actors are perceived as having the financial and military capabilities to attack the country and cause significant damage. However, Hungarians do not believe that the major powers or neighbouring states are planning military action against Hungary in the immediate future. Nevertheless, they would like to be prepared for the negative consequences of any new security crises, particularly another large-scale influx of migrants. The 'yellow' category threat perception is also reflected in public opinion about the army and the possible reintroduction of conscription. The 2025 Policy Solutions survey indicates that Hungarians are generally satisfied with the work of their armed forces, with more than 40% expressing satisfaction with the quality of national defence and the military. According to a 2024 survey by the John Lukacs Institute for Strategy and Politics at Ludovika University, only 36% of Hungarians would support the reintroduction of conscription in Hungary.

Recommendations

Hungary's fundamental national interest lies in securing the safety guarantees that come with EU and NATO membership. To ensure this, Hungary must pursue a more trustworthy and cooperative foreign policy with its allies. In times of crisis, this requires decisions that are grounded in shared values and financial solidarity. Accordingly, it would be worthwhile reconsidering what kind of EU and foreign policy could most effectively contribute to enforcing Hungarian national interests in the fields of security and defence in the long term.

Cooperation among the Visegrád Group (V4) countries has weakened in recent years, particularly since 2022, largely due to Hungary's pro-Russian foreign policy and anti-Ukrainian rhetoric, which have created tensions and reduced trust among the other V4 states. It is of high importance to strengthen regional partnerships within the framework of the V4 or other Central European cooperation initiatives, as these coalitions provide Hungary with an opportunity to influence EU decision-making processes more effectively, participate in joint projects with other Member States and balance the interests of major powers.

Hungary should continue to invest in developing its own defence industry and technology, particularly critical capabilities, to enhance national security. Similarly, the country should continue to participate in EU defence initiatives such as PESCO and programmes funded by the European Defence Fund. Hungary should also continue with its active participation in the ESSI. Projects should be chosen that contribute to modernising and developing the Hungarian armed forces, while also boosting civilian economic development as well as the competitiveness of Hungary and the EU. Lastly, policy steps should address the threat perceptions of Hungarian citizens, particularly the demand for stronger border protection.

Boglárka Koller, Senior Research Fellow at the Institute of World Economics, Centre for Economics and Regional Studies at Eötvös Loránd University (ELTE), as well as a Full Professor, Jean Monnet Chair and Head of the CORE Jean Monnet Centre of Excellence at the Ludovika University of Public Service. She is President of the Central European Political Science Association (CEPSA).

The Institute of World Economics is the oldest and most experienced Hungarian research Institute specialising in international and development economics, with a distinct research group focusing on European Studies.

Militarily Neutral, But Not Politically Neutral—A View from Ireland

Barry Colfer

Ireland has a longstanding policy of military neutrality and one of the lowest rates of military expenditure in the world, standing at around 0.2% of GDP. However, for a range of factors, military expenditure is expected to grow significantly over the next 5 years.

It is difficult to categorise the threat perception in Ireland based on the traffic light system, but the country probably falls somewhere between 'yellow' (medium) and 'green' (low). Tending towards medium, it is widely understood that the country's defence capabilities are below what any potential adversary could muster and hence, over recent years the government has taken steps to upgrade the country's military capabilities. This is driven by a general acceptance, which predates the current conflict in Europe, that the country should invest more in its military rather than being purely motivated by any increased threat perception. Tending towards 'green', while the country is taking steps to increase its military expenditure, it is also assumed that there will be no military action against the country in the near future. This is explained in large part by a view that the country's neutrality and geography provide protection and make invasion by any adversary unlikely.

Ireland Remains Neutral

The discourse around security and defence in Ireland is fairly peculiar by European standards. Ireland is a small country of some five million people. It has a longstanding policy of military neutrality and is not a NATO ally, albeit engaging with the Alliance through the Partnership for Peace programme. Ireland has one of the lowest rates of military investment in the world at 0.2% of GDP, although this is

B. Colfer (✉)
Institute of International and European Affairs (IIEA), Dublin, Ireland
e-mail: barry.colfer@iiea.com

M. Kaeding et al. (eds.), *Security, Defence, and the Future of Europe*,
https://doi.org/10.1007/978-3-032-18279-1_14

expected to at least double over the next 5 years. Indeed, a 2023 Irish Times poll shows strong support (55%) for "significantly increasing Ireland's military capacity", particularly among older voters, with the figure rising to 66% of respondents in a 2025 Irish Independent poll supporting "a significant increase in public spending on Ireland's defence".

Irish neutrality is not enshrined in the country's constitutional architecture—unlike Austria, for example, where it is part of federal constitutional law—but rather became government policy over time. The origins of Ireland's military neutrality policy date to the country's independence from the UK in 1921. Thereafter, neutrality became a feature of Irish government policy partly in a bid to assert the fledgling nation's sovereignty, but also to distance itself politically and militarily from the erstwhile colonial power. There remains a strong attachment to the principle of neutrality among the public, particularly but not exclusively on the left, with over 63% expressing support for the current model of neutrality in a 2025 opinion poll, also in the Irish Times.

Today, through a 'Triple Lock' mechanism, any overseas deployment of more than 12 military personnel from Ireland requires consent from the government of the day, *Dáil Éireann* (the Irish lower house of Parliament) and the UN Security Council or General Assembly. Recent deployments include the EU Training Mission in Mali (2013–) together with UN missions in the likes of Kosovo (1999–) and Liberia (2003–2007). Given the present paralysis of the UN Security Council in particular, it is increasingly accepted that the Triple Lock mechanism is untenable and likely to be replaced over the current government's lifetime.

Military Activity

Ireland has an unbroken track record of service with UN peacekeeping operations since its first deployment in 1958 with the UN Observer Group in Lebanon, the forerunner to the UN Interim Force in Lebanon, which is set to be wound down in 2026–2027. The Irish Defence Forces have also participated in various EU CSDP missions and operations, including those in Bosnia and Herzegovina, Kosovo, Mali and Somalia, as well as the Mediterranean naval mission.

When it comes to Russia's war in Ukraine, from summer 2025 the government has provided EUR 250 million of non-lethal military support to Ukraine and contributes expertise, including mine clearance, to the EU's Military Assistance Mission. The provision of non-lethal equipment sees the government testing the limits of Irish neutrality, declaring the country to be "militarily neutral, but not politically neutral" when it comes to support for Ukraine. Around 120,000 Ukrainians have obtained temporary protection status in Ireland since the full-scale invasion in February 2022, one of the highest rates as a percentage of population for any country that does not share a border with Ukraine. Moreover, Ireland is among the most vocal proponents of Ukraine's future accession to the EU.

Changing Context: Security Policy Meets Industrial Policy

Ireland's geography, as an island behind an island, and the period of ethno-nationalist conflict which took place on the island from the 1960s to the 1990s, commonly referred to as 'the Troubles', shaped the country's unique take on security and defence for most of the last century. The Irish military comprises approximately 7500 personnel, with an additional 1700 personnel in the Reserve Defence Forces, which is small by international standards. Active personnel are divided between the Army, Air Corps and Naval Service. In 2022, a government-issued report recommended increasing the total size of the military to around 11,500. Notably, even before Russia's full-scale invasion of Ukraine, this report had recommended a sustained increase in military expenditure, but recruitment and retention are ongoing challenges for the Defence Forces.

A major risk to Ireland's security, and a strategic vulnerability for Europe, relates to the presence of subsea cable infrastructure within Irish waters. These cables support a strategically significant proportion of Europe's internet, banking and communications traffic. Of the more than 550 reported international subsea cables, nearly 75% pass through or close to Irish waters. Russian vessels attempted to undertake manoeuvres in Ireland's Exclusive Economic Zone just weeks before the full-scale invasion of Ukraine in 2022 and Russia's shadow fleet could seek to sabotage or damage subsea infrastructure. In 2025, the Chair of the U.S. Senate Foreign Relations Committee Jim Risch argued that Ireland's "strategic position" comes with "significant responsibility", given the potentially devastating impact that damage to any subsea cable infrastructure could have across Europe. The country's health service was also subject to a crippling cyber-attack in 2021, which further highlights Ireland's potential vulnerability, given the changing character of warfare.

Meanwhile, Ireland imports around 80% of its energy. There is a single pipeline carrying gas to Ireland from the UK, as well as three operational electricity interconnectors connecting Ireland to Great Britain and one to France that is under construction. Ireland's industrial model relies heavily on foreign direct investment, with almost 1000 U.S. firms alone active across financial services, technology, pharmaceuticals and medical technology in particular. Foreign direct investment accounts for more than 10% of employment in Ireland, with the country positioning itself as a leading global hub for data centres. Clearly, Ireland will need to be able to display its ability to protect its subsea cable infrastructure, deter threats and maintain energy security in order to maintain its industrial model.

Furthermore, the transatlantic relationship's changing nature means that the U.S., with whom Ireland has historically close ties, can no longer be regarded as a reliable security partner given President Trump's 'American First' agenda. Meanwhile, the reset in Irish-UK relations following the tumultuous Brexit years may allow for closer engagement with the UK military, although this will probably be mediated at EU level.

Recommendations

In Ireland, there is an understanding that the country's military capacity has traditionally been limited by international standards and any potential adversary would be viewed as superior by comparison. Still, there is a low (tending towards 'green') risk perception *vis-à-vis* potential military action against Ireland, although this may change given the range of security vulnerabilities that Ireland and Europe now face. The narrative around security and defence is also changing amid a clearer understanding that investing in military and defence capacity does not necessarily defy the country's policy of neutrality. There will be sustained investment into Ireland's security, capacity, including the acquisition of primary radar, by upgrading the country's naval capacity and hiring personnel, albeit expenditure is likely to remain far below the EU average.

In order to maintain the country's industrial model, the Irish authorities must invest significantly in the state's security and defence capability, particularly with respect to the protection of subsea cable infrastructure. The authorities will also need to identify areas for potential military cooperation, with a renewed emphasis on engagements at EU level, in keeping with findings from the 'EU White Paper for European Defence—Readiness 2030', potentially through joint procurement of military systems and building up the defence industry's readiness as well as dual-use industries. Various companies based in Ireland would certainly plan to explore opportunities afforded by dual-use technologies, including the likes of cybersecurity and telecommunications. Finally, the EU should play a central role in peace negotiations and a final settlement in Ukraine. With its own particular experience, Ireland could have something to offer to this enterprise, given the success of the Northern Ireland peace process.

Barry Colfer is the Director of Research at the Institute of International and European Affairs (IIEA) in Dublin. He holds a Ph.D. from the University of Cambridge and has undertaken fellowships at the University of Oxford, Harvard University and the European University Institute (EUI) in Florence, Italy. Previous to this, he worked at both the Irish and European Parliaments as well as with leading European and American think tanks.

The Institute of International and European Affairs is the main public policy and international affairs think tank in Ireland. The IIEA is independent and neutral, seeking to promote informed discourse around public policy and international affairs.

Italy in Security and Defence: A Reluctant Actor

Federico Castiglioni and Luca Cinciripini

In Italy, defence is not considered a priority, with this view being broadly shared by both the public and a significant portion of political actors. Although Italians acknowledge a global shift in the security environment, any threats appear to be geographically distant, creating a sense of reassurance that allows domestic concerns to remain at the forefront. Nonetheless, there is widespread awareness that Italy cannot disengage from its allies and must align, albeit reluctantly, with the new defence agenda. Public opinion reveals a traffic light threat perception as follows: 'green' for Russia's direct threat, 'yellow' for European defence and 'red' for Italy being dragged into conflict.

Between ReArm Europe and U.S. Disengagement

The ReArm Europe Plan aims to boost European defence spending by expanding the fiscal capacity of Member States. The main instruments to achieve this goal are temporary suspension of the EU Stability Pact and a dedicated mechanism, SAFE, designed to provide loans to Member States. Italy, given its high public debt, has greeted the ReArm Europe Plan with a high degree of scepticism, calling for a renaming (Readiness). While left-wing parties have criticised the decision to leave national rearmament largely uncoordinated at the European level, even conservative parties have shown caution, expressing particular concern about further increases in national debt. For now, Italy has indicated interest in borrowing around EUR 15 billion through the SAFE mechanism to finance already planned acquisitions, likely to be in the land systems sector. The challenge for Italy is to raise defence spending to meet NATO's new requirements while using EU instruments to ease pressure on

F. Castiglioni · L. Cinciripini (✉)
Istituto Affari Internazionali (IAI), Rome, Italy
e-mail: f.castiglioni@iai.it; l.cinciripini@iai.it

M. Kaeding et al. (eds.), *Security, Defence, and the Future of Europe*,
https://doi.org/10.1007/978-3-032-18279-1_15

the national budget, being fully aware that even lower-interest loans ultimately create fiscal obligations that future governments will have to meet.

The question of America's commitment to Europe's security looms in the background. Italy is seeking to preserve its role as a bridge across the Atlantic, a priority Prime Minister Giorgia Meloni has cultivated since President Trump's return to the White House. While a complete U.S. withdrawal from Europe or NATO is unlikely, Washington is fundamentally redefining the transatlantic relationship and rethinking its commitment to European security as we have known it since the end of the Second World War. This trend leaves Europeans under pressure to take the lead on their own security. The Ukraine war makes this clearer than ever: the EU can no longer assume unwavering American backing in the face of Russian escalation. For Italy, this creates a delicate balancing act.

On the one hand, it is recognised that the Union must mature strategically and develop greater autonomy; on the other hand, there is a reluctance to loosen ties with Washington, an ideologically close ally, materially indispensable in defence and still central to Italy's geopolitical outlook. However, domestically, Italy's scope for action is currently sharply curtailed by financial pressures. The Italian welfare system is under close scrutiny and represents a central concern for both politicians and citizens. Meloni's government has so far been criticised by the opposition primarily for the long waiting times to access public healthcare and the resulting drift towards privatisation, which disproportionately disadvantages lower-income groups. Another pressing issue is pensions: the system is under severe strain and pension allowances are expected to decline significantly in the coming years. Against this backdrop, defence spending is not perceived to be a national priority.

The current government's key political challenge—and probably that of successors—will be to preserve the welfare system while keeping public debt under control in an evolving geopolitical context. Traditionally, Italian governments have pursued a strategy of reclassifying expenditure as defence spending even when primarily serving other sectors. These include infrastructure (both physical and cyber), logistics hubs, as well as research and development. Such practices allow Rome to make its defence budget more sustainable and the 5% of GDP commitment undertaken at the latest NATO summit credible. Despite this disguise, a substantial increase in direct armaments acquisition is unavoidable in order to move from the former pledge of 2% to the required 5% and many purchases have already been planned (such as air defence and medium battle tanks).

Public Opinion and Peace Talks: A Cautious Approach

Public opinion in Italy remains cautious about the war in Ukraine and Europe's push to boost defence spending. According to a poll conducted in March 2025, conflict is widely seen as distant from national interests: support for Ukraine has fallen from 57% to 32% since 2022. Only 13% favour sending Italian troops, while roughly 33% oppose any Italian contribution to Kyiv's security guarantees. This caution carries over to European rearmament. Following a June 2025 survey, 57% of the adult population opposes higher military spending. Italians appear less alarmed by Russia's threat to Europe (low: 'green') than by the threat that escalation could drag Italy into conflict and worsen economic fallout from the war (high: 'red'). When it comes to European defence spending, Italians remain hesitant, seeing stronger military capabilities to defend Europe from external threats as a distant, rather than urgent, priority (medium: 'yellow'). This attitude reflects not only a preference for diplomacy over force; it also stems from a fragmented and polarised political landscape that inevitably shapes voters' views and limits Rome's room for manoeuvre.

As far as peace talks are concerned, according to a May 2025 survey the relative majority consider Vladimir Putin the main obstacle to peace (28%), while a minority (24%) attributes responsibility to both Putin and Volodymyr Zelensky. Only 10% believe that Zelensky alone is responsible for the stalemate in negotiations. This perception, though, does not translate into support for a direct Italian or EU role in enforcing a ceasefire. In recent years, populist political forces such as the Five Star Movement (The Left) and the League (Patriots for Europe) have grown increasingly critical of continued arms deliveries to Ukraine, even though the Italian government has maintained military support. In parliamentary debates, only a few actors (such as the liberal Azione—Renew Europe party) consider negotiations with Russia unacceptable today and virtually no one supports Italy acting alone. On the contrary, there is a broad consensus that any negotiation should take place within a European framework, though opinions differ on the format: whether led by major EU countries (the League), coordinated through EU foreign policy structures (Partito Democratico [S&D] and Forza Italia [EPP]), or pursued via a hybrid approach (Brothers of Italy [European Conservative and Reformist Group]). Tellingly, security and defence are among the few policy areas in which there is consistent consensus for EU action. July 2025 polls illustrate this ambivalence. Only 16% of Italians say they would be willing to fight for their country, an attitude shaped by the perceived absence of direct enemies, but 58% favour a stronger EU defence and greater coordination among Member States, if not the creation of a European army.

This generally positive attitude among Italians toward strengthening the European framework for military readiness does not, though, translate into equally broad support for the reintroduction of mandatory military service, which was suspended in 2005. According to a September 2024 survey, public opinion is almost evenly divided on the issue, with 47% in favour and 46% opposed, indicating a significant deadlock. Party positions mirror this ambivalence. Aside from the right-wing populist League, which has long advocated a return to conscription and has formally submitted a proposal to Parliament, most political actors—including the current Minister of Defence Guido Crosetto—remain sceptical. This scepticism is closely linked to how military service is framed in Italian public debate: supporters justify it primarily as a tool to discipline youth rather than as a response to security needs, while critics oppose it because they deem such a rationale inappropriate. In the event of any reintroduction, there is a cross-party agreement that conscription would need to be accompanied by an alternative form of civilian service open to both young men and women.

Recommendations

Italy's public institutions cannot ignore the tension between fiscal constraints and security demands, but they can adopt an honest and transparent approach in dealing with them. Many Italians still believe that while phenomena such as migration may put pressure on the welfare system conflict will not. This assumes that Italy can always navigate crises successfully because it lacks a 'real enemy'. Psychological reliance on external actors, the under-communication of security threats and the consequent reluctance to make unnecessary sacrifices are all assumptions that must be disavowed in a world defined by war and political violence. Public institutions should explain why investments in security and defence matter and how they could also deliver tangible benefits in the civilian sphere.

Against this background, the Italian government should accompany a campaign to change the prevailing narrative with a serious exploration of European solutions in security and defence. Italians need to see that efforts are underway to leverage the full political weight of the EU for conflict prevention and resolution, which includes stronger military coordination. Keeping public opinion on board is key if the EU and national governments want to succeed. In this sense, initiatives taken at EU level to help Member States upgrade their defence systems and improve their general readiness while avoiding duplications should be accelerated, prioritised and more actively publicised in Italy, making clear that the government is lobbying for these ends.

Ultimately, Italy's relevance will depend on its ability to strike a delicate balance, strengthening Europe's capacity to act while maintaining the transatlantic bridge, indispensable to both Washington and its European partners.

Federico Castiglioni is a researcher in the programme EU, politics and institutions at the Istituto Affari Internazionali (IAI). Previously, he worked at the EP as policy advisor for a Member, and then as a political analyst for the consultancy company Zanasi & Partners. In 2020, he earned a PhD in European Studies from the Roma Tre University, becoming adjunct professor of European Governance at the University of Naples 'L'Orientale' shortly afterwards. Currently, he teaches at the Link Campus University in Rome.

Luca Cinciripini is a researcher in the programme EU, politics and institutions at IAI. He holds a PhD from the Catholic University of Milan and was a visiting researcher at University College London and the University of Edinburgh. He graduated in Law from LUISS Guido Carli and obtained a first-level Master's degree in International Relations from the Catholic University. His research interests include EU foreign and security policy, EU-UK relations, international terrorism and climate security.

The Istituto Affari Internazionali (IAI) is a private, independent non-profit think tank, founded in 1965 on the initiative of Altiero Spinelli. It seeks to promote awareness of international politics and contribute to the advancement of European integration and multilateral cooperation. IAI is part of a vast international network, interacting and cooperating with the government and its ministries, European and international institutions, universities, major national economic actors, the media and the most authoritative international think tanks.

Former Weakest Link of European Defence: The Case of Latvia

Karlis Bukovskis and Janis Sarts

For close to three decades, Latvia, along with the other Baltic countries, has relied on Euro-Atlantic security structures. NATO, the U.S. and to a lesser degree the EU have been instrumental in Latvia's security and defence, but its own capabilities, especially after 2022, have rapidly become the focal point for the country and its society. Substantial mobilisation of diplomatic, financial and political resources towards geopolitical security over recent years has offset the old perception of Latvia as the weakest link in European defence. The Latvian case clearly demonstrates a 'red' traffic light in terms of threat perception, given that the Russian Federation is seen as capable of invading and annexing parts of Latvia. Russia is both seen and named as the main threat to Latvia in the State Defence Concept and hence accelerated preparations to defend the country have been underway for some time.

(Re)building and Contributing

Latvia's security architecture today rests on three pillars: NATO, the U.S. and its own capabilities. The country has been rapidly rebuilding its military infrastructure and industry since 2014, a process that has intensified since 2022. Eradicating all remains of the Soviet military complex during the 1990s was of paramount importance along with entry into NATO. Underinvestment in the military until 2014 was both a deliberate domestic choice and dictated by a geopolitically stable international situation, with political relations between Latvia and Russia demonstrating signs of pragmatism. The 2008 war in Georgia and especially the 2014 start of

K. Bukovskis (✉) · J. Sarts
Latvian Institute of International Affairs, NATO Strategic Communications Centre of Excellence, Riga, Latvia
e-mail: karlis.bukovskis@rsu.lv; janis.sarts@stratcomcoe.org

M. Kaeding et al. (eds.), *Security, Defence, and the Future of Europe*,
https://doi.org/10.1007/978-3-032-18279-1_16

Russia's incursions into Ukraine, paved Latvia's path towards consistently improving its own military capabilities and securing the much-needed multinational Enhanced Forward Presence group on its territory from 2016. It was in February 2022 when Latvia started on the irreversible path of advancing its own defence capabilities to meaningful levels.

Prior to 2014, Russia was not widely seen as an immediate threat. Thus, as with many European nations, Latvia underinvested in defence and, despite fearing an increasingly aggressive Kremlin, was unable to find the necessary political resolve to invest in defence unless there was a dire turn in the international situation. NATO membership and participation in global missions sometimes masked the urgency of addressing any vulnerabilities. In 2026, Latvia is due to spend more than 4.9% of GDP on its own defence, amounting to EUR 2.2 million. The country already has a positive track record in this regard, having spent above 2% since 2018. To achieve its intended defence expenditure for 2026, Latvia has increased its budget deficit in accordance with the exemption of defence spending from EU fiscal rules and issued government bonds. These partially cover increased military expenditure, while the rest results from reducing public sector expenditure, reallocating certain EU funds for defence purposes and utilising profits from state-owned companies.

In addition, Latvia has been among the most significant supporters of Ukraine, with military assistance currently set to be 0.25% of Latvia's GDP. Ukraine's resistance is perceived as the main factor limiting Russia's potential for further military aggression. In their 'red' traffic-light threat perception of Russia, Latvians tend to reckon that greater risks for Europe might arise after Russia stops attacking Ukraine. Hence, an understanding has emerged in recent months that Ukraine is no longer the main concern, but rather Latvia's own capabilities are, both among decision-makers and the general population. Discussions about the necessity for defence, coupled with debates on Latvia's preparedness for potential Russian aggression, have become regular both at public and private levels. Grasping that war is not an impossibility has certainly struck Latvian society. According to Latvian State Chancellery-commissioned research in July 2025, almost 45% of Latvians supported increasing the defence budget to 5% of GDP, with about the same number objecting. Support for strengthening Latvia's defence at the expense of reducing bureaucracy reached above 80%.

Revered Partners

NATO and the U.S. by far dominate the European alternatives in Latvian security calculations. NATO's Enhanced Forward Presence of 14 nations led by a Canadian brigade is an integral part of Latvia's defence. Latvia's position on an EU army has been critical, with government ministers publicly expressing scepticism about the idea, as any rash moves could hinder the "keep the Americans in" strategy. Immediacy of protection is Latvia's central concern and the EU's future plans cannot currently provide sufficient response against potential aggression from Russia. At present, only the U.S. through NATO possesses the full spectrum of practical military capabilities that can respond immediately to threats. The EU's defence investments and infrastructure together with military planning, including military applications of artificial intelligence (AI) are still lagging behind.

Meanwhile, there are military aspects in which Europe can act independently without the U.S., such as airlifts, strategic precision, intelligence and space. Latvia sees that Europe's progress is possible, but full-spectrum military readiness remains only an idea. A capable army is not about creating an institution or office, but about immediate, tangible capabilities that can be deployed effectively. Germany's increasing military role is indispensable, but it may be expanded only collectively in parallel with France, the UK and all EU countries. Cold War levels of commitment to defence from all countries are what is needed for Europe. Political volatility in the main European partner countries is still a challenge. Commitment to defence and protection against Russia too often depends on election results rather than being an undisputed national interest in every EU country.

With a multipolar world emerging, which sees China and Russia contesting the West's global role, this is a 'make or break' moment for Europe. Europe must be part of the Ukraine peace negotiations and continue playing a geopolitically decisive role in Moldova. The U.S. shift towards Asia-Pacific from a Latvian perspective is unavoidable and Europe must therefore increase its independent capacities accordingly. However, the U.S. exit should be gradual and managed. A Europe that is militarily capable and technologically advanced is a more valuable partner for the U.S. The EU's ability to act as a solution rather than a problem in international security depends on decisive investments. Technological and military advancements are the only things that will provide Europe with a global standing in the coming decades.

The Baltics are often perceived as NATO's weakest point, but today this is misleading. Latvia is in a challenging situation, but over the past years it has significantly improved both its own capabilities as well as international support. Moreover, war is not only kinetic, but also non-kinetic, including hybrid warfare operations that Latvia has been dealing with for close to a decade now. Russian and Belarusian actions have increased the resilience levels of Latvia against vulnerabilities. From a practical policy perspective, Latvia focuses its policies heavily on security and addressing vulnerabilities. Building a capable, technologically advanced and strategically coherent defence is considered essential not only for Latvia's own security but also for maintaining its role as a credible partner in the international system. Over recent years, Latvia has increased military spending and enhanced its military capabilities, purchasing equipment and engaging in practical collaboration with Estonia and Lithuania, which includes building the Baltic Defence Line. Latvia has also been preparing its civil society for the possibility of war. Adversaries are named and framed as 'enemies'.

Recommendations

The Latvian-UK-led Drone Coalition should gain full political and financial support *inter alia* from EU institutions. This is a project based on the coordination of efforts to secure drone manufacturing and supply chains among Western countries to provide stable supplies to Ukraine. Becoming an EU-wide project rather than a case-by-case only 'coalition of the willing' would allow the project to transform into a fully EU defence effort.

For the purpose of simplification and coherence, all EU defence-related formations such as the European Defence Agency, PESCO and the European Defence Fund should be integrated, unified and renamed. EU defence headquarters might then be chaired by the EU's Commissioner for Defence, which would send a clear message both domestically and externally that the EU cares and therefore invests in common defence.

Dr. Karlis Bukovskis is Director at the Latvian Institute of International Affairs (LIIA), an Associate Professor at Riga Stradiņš University and Chairman of the Foreign Policy Experts Council under the Ministry of Foreign Affairs of Latvia.

Janis Sarts is Director of the NATO Strategic Communications Centre of Excellence (NATO StratCom COE) in Riga and a former State Secretary of the Ministry of Defence of Latvia.

The Latvian Institute of International Affairs is Latvia's oldest and internationally most recognised think tank specialising in international affairs. LIIA conducts research, issues publications and works on international policy issues, collaborating with Latvian and foreign partners on its projects.

NATO StratCom COE is a multi-national, NATO-accredited international military organisation, which is not part of the NATO Command Structure. It contributes to improved strategic communications capabilities within the Alliance and Allied nations.

Lithuania's Security and Defence Policy: From Overreliance on Collective Defence to Leading by Example

Ramūnas Vilpišauskas

Since the early 1990s, Lithuania's security and defence policy has been aimed at reducing its dependencies on Russia and, in particular, joining NATO and the EU. Although EU membership always included a security element, collective defence within NATO and a strategic partnership with the U.S. were seen as key for deterring an increasingly aggressive and authoritarian Russia. However, concerns about Russia as a long-term threat and U.S. unpredictability under Donald Trump led to domestic political consensus on rapidly increasing defence spending, supporting Ukraine and advocating the EU's role in coordinating defence policies. This third component is viewed as strengthening Europe's capacities within NATO, thereby maintaining rather than replacing a U.S. presence. Lithuania's threat perception, according to the traffic light system, can be classed as 'red'.

Energy Security and Relying on Collective Defence

Since EU accession in 2004, Lithuania's security priorities have focused on advocating reforms for its Eastern neighbours and supporting their integration into the EU (and NATO) in the hope of extending an area of stability, prosperity and peace further east. At the same time, the country's relatively early experience of Russia's weaponising energy supplies resulted in efforts to move away from Russia by integrating into the EU's energy and transport networks.

Integration into the EU was seen as a necessary way to reduce dependence on Russia by diversifying infrastructure connections and reorienting them towards neighbouring EU Member States. The Baltic Energy Market Interconnection Plan,

R. Vilpišauskas (✉)
Institute of International Relations and Political Science (IIRPS) of Vilnius University, Vilnius, Lithuania
e-mail: ramunas.vilpisauskas@tspmi.vu.lt

M. Kaeding et al. (eds.), *Security, Defence, and the Future of Europe*,
https://doi.org/10.1007/978-3-032-18279-1_17

established to facilitate regional energy market integration, is a case in point. It originated from Lithuanian political elites' efforts to deal with the consequences of closing the Ignalina nuclear power plant by the end of 2009—an obligation written into Lithuania's EU accession treaty. Coordinated by the European Commission, which also helped to reach agreements with Lithuania and other Baltic Sea neighbours, it was aligned with the EU's energy policy objectives and co-funded by the EU. The focus on energy security was also visible in the country's initiatives within NATO, as it successfully established NATO's Energy Security Centre of Excellence in Vilnius in 2012.

Efforts to diversify away from Russia were marred by delays and disputes both domestically and with regional neighbours, but later accelerated by a growing sense of urgency and EU membership. This eventually allowed the Lithuanian government to declare in spring 2022, soon after Russia's full-scale invasion of Ukraine, that it would become the first EU Member State to stop all purchases of energy resources from Russia. This was seen by political elites as an example to be followed by other EU Member States and used by diplomats as an argument for the feasibility of broader sanctions on Russia's energy sector and a complete ban on its imports into the EU by 2027.

During the first decade of EU and NATO membership, Lithuania's defence spending was close to 1% of GDP, signalling reliance—some called it free-riding—on collective alliance in deterring potential aggressors. The main efforts in terms of NATO contributions were directed towards participation of Lithuanian special forces in NATO anti-terrorist missions, such as in Afghanistan after the 11 September 2001 terrorist attacks and political support for the U.S. operation in Iraq. NATO (led by the U.S.) was seen as the main security and defence organisation, while initiatives to strengthen the EU's role in security and defence were regarded cautiously as an unnecessary duplication or weakening of the U.S. role in European security.

Early Wake-Up Calls

Lithuania, often in coordination with Poland, has been increasingly sounding the alarm about Russia's aggressive intentions since the 2000s, for example, after the Russian war with Georgia in 2008. However, it was Russia's annexation of Crimea and occupation of eastern Ukraine in 2014 that became a wake-up call in terms of increasing defence spending and strengthening defence against hybrid attacks, especially in the field of cybersecurity.

The country started increasing its defence spending from 0.88% of GDP in 2014 to 1.95% in 2018 and slightly exceeded 2% in 2020. It also changed its defence policy from being based on professional service to introducing compulsory conscription in 2015 (currently, young men are recruited, while women can volunteer, although the overall numbers are still limited by infrastructural constraints). Meanwhile, the unpredictability of Donald Trump's first U.S. presidency triggered a rethinking of the country's cautious position with respect to defence cooperation within the EU, which started to be seen as complementary to NATO rather than a duplication. The leading role of Germany within NATO's Enhanced Forward Presence and especially the agreement to station a German brigade of around 5,000 troops in Lithuania by 2027, showcased the intention to strengthen cooperation with European NATO members.

In the field of cybersecurity, institutional reforms led to responsibilities being centralised in the newly established National Cyber Security Centre under the Ministry of Defence. This was soon reflected in Lithuania's rapid rise in the World Cybersecurity Ranking from 57th in 2017 to 4th place in 2019. Lithuanian officials became active in advocating for a rapid response cyber team within the EU. The EU Rapid Reaction Cyber Team (PESCO initiative) led by Lithuania was established in 2020. It currently includes participation by Austria, Belgium, Denmark, Estonia, Croatia, Latvia, the Netherlands, Poland, Romania, Slovenia and Italy (with Greece, Spain, France and Finland as observers). Lithuanian officials also contributed to EU negotiations on securing network and information systems—the so-called NIS2 directive. This followed from the country's already having accumulated experience in strengthening the protection and resilience of critical information infrastructure.

Authoritarian Russia: An Existential Long-Term Threat to Europe

After Russia's full-scale invasion of Ukraine in 2022, Lithuania emerged as one of the most active supporters of Ukraine and advocates of stricter and wider sanctions against Russia and its geopolitical ally Belarus. In 2022–2025, it figured among the leading EU countries in terms of support for Ukraine as a share of GDP. It also gradually reformed its institutions responsible for sanctions policy to strengthen their capacities, thereby contributing more effectively with proposals for EU-wide sanctions targeting Russia. Before that, in response to rigged presidential elections in Belarus accompanied by massive repressions in the summer of 2020, Lithuania introduced national sanctions against the regime in Minsk, called for an EU-wide response and hosted opposition activists from Belarus.

In summer 2021, after being the first EU Member State to experience a massive surge in irregular migration orchestrated from Minsk, Lithuanian authorities actively cooperated with the European Commission and Frontex in aligning the crisis response. It soon led to the construction of a physical barrier along the border with Belarus and successful efforts by Lithuania to convince EU institutions to adopt the concept of weaponised migration in their official terminology. Some years later, Lithuania, in cooperation with other Baltic states and Poland, also succeeded in convincing the European Commission to dedicate resources to strengthening the EU's borders with Russia and Belarus, as symbolised by the visits of Ursula von der Leyen to seven Eastern frontline states in August-September 2025.

However, further shift in Lithuania's defence policy and its view of the EU's role in this area was triggered by the re-election of Donald Trump in 2024. His deliberations about the transactional nature of America's commitment to the security of its allies in Europe and the unfair burden sharing within NATO led the Lithuanian authorities early in 2025 to announce their intention to increase defence spending in the coming years to 5%–6% of the country's GDP, from slightly above 3% in 2024. In October 2025, the Government adopted a budget for 2026 with 5.38% of GDP to be allocated for defence-related needs.

Allocating more resources for defence spending and supporting Ukraine reflects a relatively wide consensus among political parties and the country's population, seeing Ukraine's defence as that of the whole democratic and free Europe, reflecting a high threat perception, in traffic light terms, from 'yellow' after 2014 to 'red' since 2022. In line with this, Lithuanian authorities have been vocal about the dangers of appeasing Russia and any sort of peace deal reflecting its demands. Vilnius has been stressing the need for a just and sustainable settlement that respects Ukraine's sovereignty and territorial integrity. Lithuanians are also among the most enthusiastic supporters of a stronger EU role in defence policy. In the Spring Eurobarometer survey 2025, 54% of respondents from Lithuania indicated defence and security as an area where the EU should focus, compared to the EU27 average of 37%.

It also became more supportive of cooperation with EU countries in security and defence matters. A stronger EU role in this field, especially a policy of more defence spending by European NATO members, started to be seen as an argument to convince the U.S. that European countries were shouldering their fair share of the collective burden and it serves U.S. interests to remain part of the alliance. In June 2025, this was supported as the key message from the NATO summit in The Hague. EU-NATO cooperation is now seen as essential for the security of Europe.

Recommendations

An aggressive Russia and unpredictable Trump 2.0 have been the main triggers for a significant shift in the country's defence policy, becoming increasingly supportive of strengthening the EU's role in the defence area.

Currently, Lithuania's official position is to support joint EU borrowing for investing in defence and coordinate the defence policies of its Member States more actively, including more flexible rules on borrowing for defence. It was among the 19 EU Member States to ask for funding from the EUR 150 billion SAFE facility, which is likely to amount to EUR 6.3 billion for Lithuania.

The country's authorities also welcomed proposals from the European Commission to allocate more funding for defence, military mobility, protection and resilience of critical infrastructure in the next MFF 2028–2034. After incidents involving the incursion of undetected drones into Lithuanian territory during the summer of 2025, debate focused on enhancing air defence and transforming NATO air police in the Baltic States into NATO air defence.

Lithuania should continue to invest in its military capabilities and societal resilience as a way of strengthening its security and that of its allies. The transparency of allocating increasing investments into defence is crucial in maintaining public trust and support for these deterrence measures, as well as the practical implementation of a comprehensive security concept and societal resilience. Maintaining support for Ukraine is also vital, learning from its experience in strengthening the protection and resilience of critical infrastructure against hybrid attacks.

Taking into account that the U.S. remains indispensable for European security, it is important to maintain its interest and presence in Europe and its Eastern frontline states, particularly until European NATO members develop sufficient capabilities to deter aggressors. At the same time, Lithuania should continue cooperating closely with like-minded Baltic and Nordic countries, together with Poland, Germany, France and others, including formats such as the 'coalitions of the willing' (for instance, the Joint Expeditionary Forces [JEF], which include the UK).

To conclude this chapter, Lithuania's turn towards European NATO partners is best symbolised by the intention to inscribe the statement of German Chancellor Friedrich Merz on the walls of Vilnius's town hall, as made there in 2025 on the inauguration of the first German military brigade, that "the security of Lithuania is also our security". There is already a precedent for such a symbolic move—since 2002, the words of U.S. President George W. Bush, "anyone who would choose Lithuania as an enemy has also made an enemy of the United States of America", pronounced back then in Vilnius, have been inscribed on it.

Ramūnas Vilpišauskas is Professor at the Institute of International Relations and Political Science (IIRPS) of Vilnius University. In Autumn 2025, he was a visiting professor at Turin University (Italy), teaching European integration. In Autumn 2024, he was a Konrad Adenauer visiting scholar at Carleton University (Ottawa), teaching a course on transatlantic relations. In 2020–2023, he was Jean Monnet Chair professor at Vilnius University. From 2009 to 2019, he was Director of the IIRPS. In 2004–2009, he worked as Chief Economic Policy Advisor to the President of Lithuania, Valdas Adamkus.

The Institute of International Relations and Political Science of Vilnius University is one of the most prominent social sciences institutions in Eastern Europe and the Baltic region. IIRPS is also a member of TEPSA.

Luxembourg: Security on the Cheap

Josip Glaurdić

Luxembourg has adapted to Europe's security challenges by emphasising cyber, space and joint niche projects. Yet in monetary terms, the country is still paying little for its security. In terms of threat perception based on the traffic light system, Luxembourg registers overall as 'yellow'. For Europe's defence union to be credible, countries such as Luxembourg must turn their wealth into measurable commitments, not just rhetoric.

Luxembourg is Europe's wealthiest country, but also one of its most reluctant spenders on defence. Russia's invasion of Ukraine shattered many illusions across the continent, yet in Luxembourg, the shock has been cushioned by geography and prosperity. The Grand Duchy has moved quickly into symbolic niches—cyber, space and joint projects with Belgium—but in truth, it still buys its security cheaply. The uncomfortable reality is that Luxembourg prefers the safety of alliances and the image of solidarity, while outsourcing the real costs of deterrence to others.

The country's contributions have always been niche-driven. Secure satellite communications, cyber capacities and the much-publicised IT Coalition for Ukraine are welcome innovations. Luxembourgish instructors in EU training missions and the announcement of a joint reconnaissance battalion with Belgium do demonstrate a willingness to move beyond the purely symbolic. Yet in financial terms, these gestures remain modest. The widely touted EUR 2.6 billion procurement package for the Belgian-Luxembourg battalion, stretched over a decade, is hardly transformational for the richest state in Europe. Luxembourg presents itself as a champion of "smart small-state defence", but 'smart' in practice has often meant minimal. This gap between capacity and commitment poses a wider problem: can an EUSD be credible if its richest members continue to spend proportionally less than those exposed to Russia's frontline threats?

J. Glaurdić (✉)
Institute of Political Science, University of Luxembourg, Esch-sur-Alzette, Luxembourg
e-mail: josip.glaurdic@uni.lu

M. Kaeding et al. (eds.), *Security, Defence, and the Future of Europe*,
https://doi.org/10.1007/978-3-032-18279-1_18

Dependence as Doctrine

The question becomes sharper when set against the U.S.; Luxembourg's reliance on NATO and Washington is not only a matter of policy but also of habit. The political class has never truly contemplated a scenario in which Europe must defend itself with limited American help. Even now, with the volatility of U.S. politics and reliability of transatlantic guarantees in doubt, Luxembourg's reflex remains unchanged: trust NATO, hope for the best and allow others to shoulder the burden. Any rhetoric about building a European pillar is sincere; however, the practice remains minimalist. In this sense, Luxembourg epitomises the paradox of strategic autonomy. It argues for more Europe in defence while quietly assuming that the ultimate backstop will still be American.

The financial picture exposes this gap most clearly. In its most recent national security strategy, Luxembourg has promised to raise defence outlays gradually, reaching 1% of national income by 2028. Although this figure was surpassed 3 years early in 2025, this arguably remains unambitious given NATO's already outdated 2% benchmark. Luxembourg will rely heavily on EU pooling instruments such as SAFE and 'Readiness 2030' to soften the fiscal impact. Officials insist that Luxembourg's added value lies in high-tech niches and dual-use research rather than in traditional mass. That argument carries some weight, but it cannot disguise the imbalance. Allies who face direct threats judge solidarity in money and material, not in branding exercises. Measured as a share of national capacity, Luxembourg still secures its defence at a discount—and in wartime Europe, that is a hard reality to explain away.

Complacency and Public Detachment

The persistence of this posture is explained by politics and public opinion. Luxembourgers are not indifferent to security. Recent Eurobarometer surveys show that large majorities of more than 80% view the world as increasingly dangerous, regard Russia's war in Ukraine as a threat to Europe's stability and want more European CSDP. Support for Ukraine also remains strong, with more than 70% of respondents in the spring 2025 Luxembourg Times survey favouring continued assistance. Yet this awareness coexists with a sense of isolation. Luxembourg is surrounded by allies, distant from Russia's borders and sheltered by prosperity. Defence rarely features as a campaign issue.

When military and government officials called for public debate on the issue of reintroducing conscription in late 2024, public reaction was at best tepid. A petition opposing conscription gathered hundreds of signatures. Although it failed to reach the legal threshold needed for parliamentary debate, the government was quick to state that the reintroduction of conscription was "off the table". The result is a pattern of empathy without urgency. In terms of threat perception, Luxembourg occupies a middle ground or 'yellow', using the traffic light system. Moscow is now labelled a direct threat in official strategies and budgets are rising, but the sense of immediate vulnerability remains muted. The mindset is cautious rather than complacent: Luxembourgers recognise the danger, but still hope that diplomacy and collective deterrence will suffice to contain it. The conflict may feel existential in Poland or the Baltics, but in Luxembourg, it still feels distant.

Diplomacy is where Luxembourg is most at home and it is right to insist that the EU must be central when peace talks eventually open. Yet credibility at the negotiating table requires leverage away from it. 'Diplomacy first' cannot once again mean 'diplomacy only', let alone 'diplomacy on the cheap'. Security guarantees for Ukraine, sustained reconstruction aid and a clear EU accession path are not optional add-ons. They are the very price of a stable peace. Luxembourg's record on Minsk shows the risks of betting on formulas that reward aggression. Without hard security commitments, a return to premature deals would simply defer the next crisis.

Recommendations

The conclusion that follows is stark. Luxembourg can remain small and still be serious, but only if it shifts from symbolic gestures to measurable effort. That means codifying a multi-year financial glide-path with a transparent floor for core defence and a separate envelope for broader security. It means pledging a multi-year Ukraine package, benchmarked to national income and reported with precision, so that allies see promises turned into capacity. It means building a volunteer reserve that provides real personnel for the reconnaissance battalion as well as operationalising cyber and space projects as genuine alliance capabilities rather than prestige showcases. It means increasing rotational deployments and hosting exercises to make Luxembourg visible in collective defence. It means producing annual reports with hard metrics, convening citizens' panels and explaining that deterrence, though costly, is cheaper than defeat. It also means tying any Luxembourgish push for EU mediation to enforceable security guarantees, sanctions that bite and reconstruction finance that lasts.

Luxembourg's lesson for Europe can either be double-edged or exemplary. It can continue to brand itself as a pioneer of 'smart small-state defence' while free-riding on the sacrifices of others. Or it can demonstrate that even the smallest state can pay its fair share, convert niche expertise into real capacity and speak with diplomatic authority because it has 'put some skin in the game'. In an age of war, credibility is not earned through rhetoric. It is measured in budgets, deployments and delivery. For Luxembourg, as for Europe as a whole, that is now a choice—and one that cannot be postponed.

Josip Glaurdić is full professor of Political Science at the Institute of Political Science of the University of Luxembourg.

The Institute of Political Science pursues research on governance, democracy, conflict, EU integration and political economy, combining multilingual, comparative and policy-relevant approaches at the intersection of European and global challenges.

Maltese Neutrality and the Challenge of EU Defence and Security Cooperation

Mark Harwood

Malta's strategic position at the centre of the Mediterranean has often made the island an attractive base for various powers dominating the area. From the Phoenicians to the Romans to the French, regional powers have sought to dominate Malta and lay claim to its natural harbours. The last foreign power to hold sway over Malta, the UK, stayed from 1800 to 1964, during which time the island's status as a military base was clearly seen during the Second World War. Indeed, it became one of the most bombed places in the world, with more bombs falling on the island in 2 months than would fall on London throughout the entire Blitz. However, following independence, the history of military occupation has been replaced with a commitment towards neutrality from a country that sees itself as a bridge across the Mediterranean, not as a frontline state, very much within the 'green' zone of threat perception. With greater security and defence cooperation, the EU is entering waters that the Maltese will find difficult to navigate.

Unwilling to Commit to Defence Cooperation

Malta's first post-independence government, the centre-right Christian Democrats, sought closer economic ties with the European Community, discussed the prospects of joining NATO and focused on building a diplomatic service. However, the Socialists elected in 1971 closed NATO's headquarters in Malta, joined the non-aligned movement and incorporated neutrality into the constitution in 1987. This now states that Malta is "a neutral state actively pursuing peace, security and social progress among all nations by adhering to a policy of non-alignment and refusing to participate in any military alliance". Since 1987, there has been general consensus

M. Harwood (✉)
Institute for European Studies, University of Malta, Tal-Qroqq, Malta
e-mail: mark.harwood@um.edu.mt

M. Kaeding et al. (eds.), *Security, Defence, and the Future of Europe*,
https://doi.org/10.1007/978-3-032-18279-1_19

between the two main parties and the population about the importance of Maltese neutrality, including Malta's status as linking the northern and southern shores of the Mediterranean. There is also agreement that defence is not guaranteed by its armed forces, but by a network of cooperative relations with its neighbours. Malta spends 0.5% of its GDP on defence. Mindful of this, there are no discussions around increasing military capacity or of introducing any form of military service, which has neither been mandatory at any point in Maltese history nor part of its political discourse.

When Malta applied to join the EU in 1990, the issue of its neutrality and ability to participate in the EU's CFSP was highlighted by the Commission as a potential obstacle. While Malta always maintained that its neutrality was compatible with membership, it took the additional step of annexing a declaration to its accession treaty stating that participation in the EU's CFSP would not compromise its neutrality.

Post-membership, some have argued that Malta is aligned with and integrated into European defence and security cooperation, but is nevertheless not prepared to commit actively. In this way, Malta has participated in various EU missions, notably the EU Border Assistance Mission Libya as well as the Central Mediterranean Naval Operation Sophia. In 2024, Malta also voted in favour of strengthening European defence and reducing Europe's dependency on other countries, even though it was one of four Member States that expressed their initial reservation about this measure. The conundrum of a neutral state participating in European defence and security cooperation is exemplified by the domestic furore that erupted in March 2025 regarding Malta's involvement in the EU Military Assistance Mission supporting Ukraine. The Prime Minister initially indicated that Malta was participating before the armed forces issued a statement countering his declaration by stating that only one Maltese national, based in the UK rather than the field, was involved. More importantly, Malta decided not to join the PESCO and remains the only EU country not to participate, having adopted a wait-and-see policy. Furthermore, while Malta has voted in favour of increasing EU defence spending, the country has made no commitments to increase its own military spending (0.5% of GDP), beyond the normal fluctuations it sees in its annual budget allocations. Moreover, with Malta still under an EU excessive deficit procedure, it seems unlikely that the government would be able to increase defence spending substantially.

On the flip side, successive Maltese governments have expressed how they see the EU's 'mutual assistance clause' and the 'solidarity clause' as providing additional guarantees for the country's security, an uncomfortable position considering that Maltese people do not wish to pay for the Union's defences. It seems that, in not obstructing greater European defence and security cooperation, Malta backs a Union eager to bolster its capabilities, but it does not see neutral states as obliged to finance that initiative. This further echoes the government's view of the country as enjoying 'green' light status in terms of security threats with few, if any, threats to Malta's security on the horizon. Even in terms of U.S. involvement in European defence, as a country outside NATO which maintains close bilateral relations with the U.S., Malta rarely engages in debates around EU-NATO relations, its focus remaining squarely on its bilateral relations with the U.S., the UK and the EU.

Ambivalent Public Support

In terms of public support for military and security cooperation, 72% of Maltese respondents in April 2025 supported a common defence and security policy, up from 57% in autumn 2024. However, only 26% mentioned security and defence as two main areas they would like to see the EU budget go towards. Furthermore, while Malta saw the biggest increase in support for the CSDP, it was still the fourth-lowest in the EU, on a par with Ireland. Malta and Ireland were the second least likely Member States to reference defence as a budget priority. While respondents in Malta stated that the most important issue facing the EU was Russia's invasion of Ukraine (35%), at a national level, the main concern was inflation (35%). In this way, the Maltese seem to understand the significance of international developments, such as the war in Ukraine and the need to counter aggression with force, but do not see this as necessitating Union money.

Recommendations

Going forward, it seems clear that the issue of further European defence and security cooperation will prove a difficult issue for this neutral state to address. In countries such as Malta, while standing squarely behind support for Ukraine, many leading politicians and academics have gone public in expressing their frustration over a lack of EU action regarding Gaza. Much of this frustration has been directed at Roberta Metsola, the Maltese Member of the EP who also sits as its President. The Union needs to ensure greater consistency in its external relations or accept that support for European defence and security cooperation will falter when the EU fails to meet the next security challenge. The Union must also harness the benefits of AI to improve its communication skills. There is no excuse for the Union to stick to a 'one message fits all' approach. Eurobarometer metrics allow mapping to show what issues raise greater concern in which EU countries, especially when promoting its actions overseas. It provides little comfort for a Mediterranean state to be faced with EU information campaigns that focus exclusively on the Union's eastern borders. What is being achieved in the Mediterranean? Why think that the Maltese will respond to the same information campaigns as the Estonians when addressing EU security and defence?

Finally, it is an awkward truth, but countries such as Malta cannot deliver one message in Brussels and a different message back home; that game leads to Brexit. If a country is expecting the mutual assistance clause to underwrite security tomorrow, then make clear that this comes at a cost, not in terms of greater military spending, but rather of speaking honestly to a domestic audience.

Mark Harwood is a professor at the University of Malta. Having previously worked for the European Commission as well as the Maltese Government, his area of research is the impact of EU membership on Malta.

The Institute for European Studies was founded in 1991 as a teaching and research institute within the University of Malta. Offering a full range of degree programmes up to PhD level, the Institute has over 1000 alumni. The Institute is also a member of TEPSA.

Poland: All (Not So) Quiet on the Eastern Front

Marcin Zubek

The Russo-Ukrainian war continues to have a significant impact on Poland and its policies. Taking into account recent changes in the global political landscape (such as Trump's second U.S. presidency term) and internal political competition (government change in 2023 and presidential elections in 2025), Poland struggles to conduct a security policy that is in line with the European project, not against the new U.S. administration and acceptable to its own citizens. All this is being contemplated against the looming threat of war, which Poles sense as being somewhere between 'yellow' and 'red'.

Over 3 years have now passed since Russia invaded Ukraine, an event which has had deeply negative consequences in terms of Polish security. It is easy to view 24 February 2022 as the newest critical juncture in the Polish (geo)political calendar, replacing most probably 10 April 2010, when the Polish presidential plane crashed in Russia, killing all souls on board. Whilst both events have a significant Russian component and include tragic loss of life, there is also a key difference. The 2010 disaster left the Polish nation heavily divided regarding who to blame, whereas the outbreak of war in 2022 seems to have united all levels of society against a common enemy. It was finally clear where the real threat was and this was realised not only in Poland, but also by others in Europe. Poland was finally able to say to some of our Western European partners, albeit with little satisfaction, "We told you so".

M. Zubek (✉)
Jagellonian University, Krakow, Poland
e-mail: marcin.zubek@uj.edu.pl

M. Kaeding et al. (eds.), *Security, Defence, and the Future of Europe*,
https://doi.org/10.1007/978-3-032-18279-1_20

Between Brussels and Washington

In late 2025, at the time of writing this chapter, such clarity seems to be waning and trends in threat perception are changing. However, unaltered since 2022 is the position regarding security, which remains on top of the political agenda. In the first half of 2025, Poland presided over the Council of the EU with a programme entitled "Security, Europe!", very much centred around various aspects of security, including defence and disinformation, but also food, health and economic security. It is, though, not surprising to find that 'hard security' has been the most important dimension. Poland has been pushing for the possibility of using EU funds for defence purposes and was ultimately successful. Around a third of all allocations in the SAFE fund, roughly EUR 44 billion (out of EUR 150 billion) for 2026-2030, are earmarked to be spent in Poland. Warsaw has also been spending significant amounts of money on defence from its own budget, which in 2026 will amount to circa 4.5%–4.8% of its GDP, a significant achievement. Not only was Poland able to attract European money to fund its own security, but it also helped amplify this idea at EU level. This seems to have realised a long-standing fantasy in Polish public opinion, which on the one hand has always supported a stronger common European defence and security policy, yet on the other hand tended to be sceptical when it came to the possibility of a federal Europe.

Persuading Brussels to move in this direction at last did need some external provocation, though. The election of President Donald Trump in the U.S. certainly helped Europeans realise that Washington can no longer be considered a reliable partner. However, what happened in America was neither properly interpreted nor fully appreciated by certain Polish political elites, especially those further to the right. There seems to be a conviction that Trump has a genuine soft spot for Poland and that some sort of special U.S.-Polish relationship can be forged (or even already exists). Polish President Karol Nawrocki, while still in the presidential race, even went so far as to blame the EU for planned U.S. tariffs, perhaps hoping for some appreciation from the White House. From an international relations perspective, it is clear that a special relationship between Warsaw and Washington will be considered special only for the former and will end up in a classical 'bandwagoning' situation no matter who is the U.S. President.

Poland is indeed in a difficult position regarding its transatlantic relations. On the one hand it is significant that U.S. troops are based on Polish territory, as they deter Putin from being too reckless. On the other hand, this American presence could be withdrawn overnight, leaving the Europeans to fend for themselves. Hence, keeping a balance between making sure that the unpredictable, arguably anti-European Trump remains friendly and not antagonising EU allies by currying too much favour with Washington is a difficult task. The Kremlin has also been testing NATO's reactions more boldly, of late. At the time of writing in September 2025, NATO air defences have just been called upon to shoot down the very first mass incursion of Russian drones into Polish airspace since the outbreak of war. Despite the fact that nobody died or was injured, this was nevertheless an escalatory and provocative move by Russia. Historically, wars have broken out following much more trivial events. However, reaction from the White House was almost non-existent, while Ursula von der Leyen made last-minute changes to her State of the Union speech because of the incident.

The Struggle Within

Looking at more endogenous considerations of Polish security, including threat perceptions in society, immediately after the drone incident on 10 September 2025, a massive wave of disinformation was launched. It was claimed that the drones marked Ukraine's attempt to pull NATO into the war, rather than Russia's testing Polish defences.

As already mentioned, this *was* of course Russia trying to exploit Polish societal and political divisions in an effort to convince citizens that the enemy is to the west, not the east. According to an Institute for Market and Social Research poll from February 2025, it is military security and the possibility that Poland could be pulled into the war that are the biggest fears shared by over 50% of the population. That being so, according to the Eurobarometer over 40% of Poles claim that the EU should play a greater role in protecting its citizens and that it should also boost its actions in defence and security. Other polls show that over 60% of Poles believe that Europe cannot efficiently support Ukraine without U.S. involvement (yet, over 50% negatively perceive Trump's involvement in the conflict). Almost 70% also oppose any Polish military personnel being deployed to Ukraine as a part of a potential peacekeeping effort. In a nutshell, Poles are afraid and tired of war. Perhaps for that reason, government have decided not to tamper too much with the regulations concerning conscription. Poland aims to build a professional army and no *levée en masse* is in the pipeline.

Those fears are exploited especially by the far right to deepen political divisions and alter the threat perception. Moreover, these exploits have been effective to a certain degree. In the 2025 presidential election, both far-right candidates took third and fourth places, together accumulating over 21% of the votes. The third-placed candidate was clearly anti-EU and the fourth-placed openly pro-Russian and anti-Ukrainian. Later in the summer, a big campaign was launched by the radical right aimed at shifting the threat perception, instigating fear of immigration. A so-called 'Border Protection Movement' was launched, a grassroots initiative where volunteers would survey border crossings significantly between Poland and Germany, rather than Poland and Belarus. They unlawfully stopped people and vehicles trying to identify illegal migrants allegedly pushed back to Poland by the 'evil' Germans. The media effect was very strong, coupled with the political consequences of temporarily reinstating border controls by state authorities. This was certainly another blow to Schengen and freedom of movement. The far-right activists were rapturous and so was the Kremlin.

Needless to say, the basis on which this immigration threat from Germany was conceived was fake news and disinformation, hence the last two statistics in this chapter. According to the Financial Times, in 2024 the number of fake news items in Poland rose by 100%. It is obviously becoming one of the biggest security threats worldwide. Meanwhile, according to the Institute for Market and Social Research poll cited earlier, this has yet to be fully appreciated by the Poles, especially those voting for the right and far-right parties. Only 13% of those voters realise that disinformation can be dangerous. Awareness of 32.4% among those voting for centre and left-oriented parties is somewhat better, albeit still relatively low. It is easy to conclude, therefore, that Polish society is generally filled with existential fear, not only unable to distinguish facts from fake news, but also largely unaware that disinformation is dangerous. One could say that the greatest source of insecurity is coming from within, which invites exploitation from outside.

Mindful of these opinion polls, in traffic light terms, the present threat perception could be translated into a darker shade of 'yellow'. The adversary (Russia) is not yet entirely capable, but most likely willing to engage in violent exchanges. It certainly does not have the capability to annex territories, but is able to attack identified targets with some degree of success. Poland has been taking precautions against such a situation through defence investments as well as building and sustaining political alliances.

Recommendations

Polish authorities would be well advised not to stray from the European track. This implies constantly advocating, consulting and persuading European allies that Polish security is central to the whole EU and that it is strictly connected with military and diplomatic support for Ukraine. Regarding the U.S., perhaps it would make sense to be pragmatic and focus on what is behind the scenes and behind the main actor. Donald Trump is unpredictable, with a delicate ego. It might make more sense to engage more with lower American administration levels and civil society, where grounds for sowing Polish ideas might be more fertile, and let those implanted ideas travel towards the top. Lastly, when it comes to internal politics, transparency, less divisive language and in the long term proper civic education might be able to create a psychologically less vulnerable and more resilient society.

Marcin Zubek obtained his PhD in political science in 2018. His research interests revolve around issues connected to the domestic sources of foreign and security policy and their democratic control, as well as international security, conflict and peace studies. He has been involved in numerous research and educational projects, including the Jean Monnet Networks, Jean Monnet Modules, as well as the Horizon Europe and Erasmus Mundus projects.

The Institute of European Studies at the Jagiellonian University in Kraków was established in 2004 and presents an interdisciplinary approach in researching Europe, dynamically joining the processes of Europeanisation and internationalisation of science. The Institute team comprises both experienced and young researchers, all experts in the fields they represent.

Atlantic Anchor, European Pulse: Portugal's Take on Security and Defence

Sandra Fernandes and Alice Cunha

Portugal seeks to leverage its geographic marginality through a multidimensional foreign policy anchored in Atlanticism, Europeanism and Lusophony. Rather than resisting peripherality, Portugal reframes itself as an asset, being positioned as a connector and contributor to a broader, more inclusive European security framework. Within the traffic light system, Portugal's threat perception is best captured as 'yellow' (a medium threat level), although Russia's superior military capacity could justify either 'green' (low likelihood of direct conflict) or 'red' (capacity to occupy significant Portuguese territory), with an attack remaining unlikely in the near future.

Peripheral But Not Passive

Portugal might sit on Europe's Southwestern edge but nevertheless sees itself as a bridge between continents—between the Atlantic and European mainland, between diplomatic activism and strategic commitment. Portugal's long-standing Atlantic vocation and its participation in multilateral organisations, such as NATO, the EU and the Community of Portuguese Speaking Countries (CPLP), illustrate a diplomacy rooted in various axes of belonging. Far from being a handicap, its geographic peripherality has been re-signified as strategic marginality, enabling Portugal to operate as both a committed European actor and a node of broader Atlantic and Lusophone linkages. Its multilateral posture—described by officials as a "360-degree

S. Fernandes (✉)
University of Minho, Braga, Portugal
e-mail: sfernandes@eeg.uminho.pt

A. Cunha
Universidade Nova de Lisboa, Lisboa, Portugal
e-mail: alice.cunha@fcsh.unl.pt

M. Kaeding et al. (eds.), *Security, Defence, and the Future of Europe*,
https://doi.org/10.1007/978-3-032-18279-1_21

diplomacy"—positions Lisbon as a policy-taker and increasingly as a policy-shaper within European security debates.

This self-perception certainly shapes Lisbon's approach to EU enlargement, defence and transatlantic relations. Although not perceiving Russia as an imminent threat before 2022, thereafter the country has acted firmly: deploying troops to NATO's Eastern flank, training Ukrainian forces and contributing over EUR 122 million in military aid. The geopolitical shock caused by the Russian invasion of Ukraine has heightened the country's awareness of a shifting international order and the need for Europe to assume greater responsibility for its own security. Portugal argues that NATO and the EU should not be considered as mutually exclusive, but rather as complementary pillars of European defence.

Not Just About Russia

Portugal's strategic priorities are not merely a reaction to Russia's aggression. Instead, they are embedded in a long-standing foreign policy based on three main pillars: Atlanticism, Europeanism and Lusophony. Lisbon advocates for NATO's renewed attention to the Southern flank, underlining that instability in North Africa and hybrid threats in the Atlantic are as significant as developments on the Eastern front.

Furthermore, an economy of defence is in the making. Portugal's growing, albeit modest, defence industry reflects its increasing contribution to European defence as a security consumer and an industrial partner. The 2019 Military Programming Law and its 2023 revision signal Lisbon's intention to strengthen its capabilities through EU cooperation frameworks such as PESCO and the European Defence Fund. Portugal participates in dozens of projects and coordinated three in 2025, namely: the EU Cyber Academia and Innovation Hub; Automated Modelling, Identification and Damage Assessment of Urban Terrain; and Maritime Unmanned Anti-Submarine Systems.

However, the country still falls short of NATO's new 5% of GDP spending target. Still, in less than a year, Portugal has already advanced beyond the previous 2% set for 2025–2029. To achieve the revised NATO goal, Portugal has asked for a loan from the European Commission through the SAFE mechanism, with a tentative allocation amounting to around EUR 5.8 billion. This evolution appears to be part of an effort by the new government, which took office in February 2025, to stress its international commitment. Yet, the success of this shift will depend not only on the amount of investment, but also on its quality. Following the outbreak of war in Ukraine, the idea of reinstating military conscription, suspended since 2004, became the subject of renewed debate. In 2024, the former Chief of Staff in the Portuguese Navy proposed a new recruitment model to ensure a sufficient number of military personnel. Political parties, civil society and various military associations strongly opposed what was interpreted as support for conscription. Most parties preferred to advocate for strategies aimed at attracting more individuals to military careers voluntarily.

Public Support, Political Consensus—Yet Fragile Commitment

Regarding Ukraine, as a reflection of its society Portugal remains one of the EU's most supportive members, consistently surpassing the European average, as highlighted in successive Standard Eurobarometers. Furthermore, in 2025 Portuguese respondents demonstrated a high level of satisfaction with the EU's response to the invasion of Ukraine. However, around 23% of people state that they are "not very concerned" about the EU's defence and security in the coming five years. This attitude contrasts with their generally positive views regarding any specific actions the EU has taken to support Kyiv. Backing for military, financial and humanitarian aid to Ukraine remains strong, rooted in a broader sense that European values—not just borders—are under threat. Defence spending enjoys a broad cross-party consensus, although debate intensifies when sovereignty is at stake, particularly regarding suspicious attitudes towards creating a European army. Nonetheless, as in many EU countries, intentions often collide with institutional inertia.

Portugal's approach to European security is underpinned by a flexible understanding of centrality that embraces its Atlantic past, Lusophone outreach and continental commitments. Lisbon's foreign policy is less about choosing between centres of power and more about leveraging marginality into influence, promoting inclusion, connectivity and solidarity across different geographic and normative spheres.

Portugal's placement in the traffic light system is not clear-cut. Overall, the threat level is medium, which fits best with 'yellow'. However, in some cases, 'green' would be more appropriate, since Russia's superior military strength makes direct conflict with Portugal unlikely. At the same time, 'red' could also apply, as this strength would allow Russia to seize large parts of Portugal if it chose to do so. Still, a Russian attack on Portugal is considered unlikely in the near future.

Recommendations

Europe must speak with one voice within a broader understanding of security. Portugal's approach offers an important reminder: European security cannot be built solely around threats perceived by its Eastern members. A stronger EU requires a comprehensive strategy that integrates the varied geographical, historical and political orientations of its Member States. Portugal's insistence on the Southern flank, its investment in Atlantic partnerships and its political support for Ukrainian accession are not contradictory, but complementary.

Political will is not enough and there are public choices to be made. Enhancing Portugal's defence capacities is both clear and desirable. This means modernising the armed forces, investing in cybersecurity and deepening EU defence cooperation. However, ambition alone is not enough. These goals require sustained increases in defence spending, which will either compete with other public policy priorities or demand alternative funding sources. Mechanisms such as SAFE offer potential solutions, but the government has to be transparent about trade-offs. The public must be told why higher defence spending is necessary, how it will be financed, along with what Portugal can gain in terms of security and influence within Europe.

Portugal's Atlantic vocation and extensive Exclusive Economic Zone—an area of the ocean that typically extends up to 200 nautical miles beyond a state's territorial waters, over which the state has jurisdiction—are not just historical legacies, but also assets. By investing in naval modernisation, maritime surveillance and the protection of submarine infrastructures as well as greater alignment of defence priorities with the blue economy, Portugal could further consolidate its role as a provider of security across the Atlantic. Its participation in PESCO projects related to maritime security provides concrete opportunities to advance these efforts.

Sandra Fernandes is professor at the University of Minho (Portugal), holding a PhD in Political Science with a specialisation in International Relations from Sciences Po Paris. She holds the position of Pro-Rector for International Cooperation at the University of Minho. She also served as the director of the Research Center in Political Science (CICP). Her research interests include the external action of the EU, its relations with Russia, the post-Soviet space, geopolitics, multilateralism, foreign policy analysis and international security.

The Research Center in Political Science (CICP) has positioned itself as a distinguished research hub since its establishment in 2015 and has consistently received an "Excellent" rating from the Portuguese Foundation for Science and Technology (FCT). CICP is actively committed to fulfilling the three core missions of academic institutions: conducting high-quality research, transferring valuable knowledge and providing training.

Alice Cunha, Ph.D., is Professor with Habilitation in International Relations at the NOVA University of Lisbon and Researcher at the Portuguese Institute of International Relations (IPRI-NOVA), where she works on European Union Studies, an area in which she has published extensively. Her main research interests are related to enlargement studies, Europeanisation, European funds and Portuguese foreign policy.

The Portuguese Institute of International Relations (IPRI-NOVA) is a research institute founded in 2003 and dedicated to advanced studies in Political Science and International Relations. IPRI-NOVA promotes scientific research, specialised training at doctoral and post-doctoral levels, knowledge transfer and social value creation. It has been recognised as a Public Utility Institution for services rendered to the community. IPRI-NOVA is a member of TEPSA.

Romania's Security Is Inextricably Linked with the Transatlantic Relationship

Mihai Sebe and Eliza Vaş

Starting from reshaping transatlantic relations and considering the current debate on creating an EUSD, Romania is analysing ways of enhancing its European posture while dealing with economic issues and hybrid warfare challenges. In this context, the Russian Federation can be considered at least a medium ('yellow') threat to the country's security and sovereignty. Hence, there is a need to open new paths of cooperation with the U.S. administration to retain its military commitments in Europe.

From a Civilian Mindset to Readiness in Romania

Romania is seeking to become a more relevant actor in the field of European security and defence, as the EU's peace project is shifting to a more dynamic mode, given the harsh international reality and the spread of hybrid warfare. Switching from a civilian-centric to a readiness-based project, due to the perception of Europe being under threat, Romania is intent on underpinning the Eastern flank as an impregnable cornerstone of European security. To this end, over recent years our country has been an active contributor to PESCO missions and projects, such as those focused on cybersecurity (Cyber Rapid Response Teams and Mutual Assistance in Cyber Security) and maritime mine countermeasures (Maritime Autonomous Systems for Mine Counter Measures).

With its direct access to the Black Sea, Romania has built its strategic documents on a triad of objectives: increasing Romania's role and efforts in the EU; strengthening its strategic profile in NATO; as well as deepening and expanding the Strategic Partnership with the U.S. Accordingly, Romania tries to use all existing and

M. Sebe (✉) · E. Vaş
European Institute of Romania, Bucharest, Romania
e-mail: mihai.sebe@ier.gov.ro; eliza.vas@ier.gov.ro

M. Kaeding et al. (eds.), *Security, Defence, and the Future of Europe*,
https://doi.org/10.1007/978-3-032-18279-1_22

upcoming instruments, for instance 'Readiness 2030' and SAFE, to modernise the military, strengthen defence capabilities and revitalise the national defence industry. Additionally, in an opinion published by the Foreign Affairs Committee of the Chamber of Deputies concerning 'Readiness 2030', it is stated that the EU must adopt a holistic and horizontal approach by integrating defence and security dimensions within most of its policies. Although defence remains a national responsibility, this view underlines the point that Romania needs better coordination in areas such as military mobility, collaborative public procurement and investment in its own defence capabilities.

Moreover, Romania's defence plans have been drafted in cooperation with the Allies, under NATO's umbrella, as part of a unified response to potential threats. However, based on current public discourse, it is unlikely that a European army will soon replace NATO, given that this Alliance remains the foundation of any real and credible defence for many EU Member States. Hence, Romania has committed to increasing its defence expenditure and building defence capabilities, signalling a continuing commitment to implement and act in accordance with its obligations.

Since 2007, military service has been voluntary in accordance with peacetime conditions. This has led to a decrease in the number of military reservists and thus there are discussions about legislative proposals to update this situation by building a modern framework for the armed forces. Against this background, an opinion poll published in October 2025 shows that around 48% of respondents do not believe that reintroducing compulsory military service is a good idea, while 43% believe the opposite. Moreover, the 2025 GLOBSEC Trends Report indicates that 83% of Romanian respondents back defence capacity-building through voluntary military service.

Strengthening NATO's Umbrella and Keeping the Americans in

Following the U.S. administration's appeals for increased defence spending within NATO, Romania committed to reaching 3% of GDP by 2027. This is in line with Romania's perception of the U.S. not just as a security guarantor for Europe and the Euro-Atlantic area, but also a key strategic partner in the bilateral relationship.

Building on the defence agenda, there is a belief that we should remain on the same path with the U.S., taking into account its efforts aimed at ensuring the stability and security of Europe. Essential elements for maintaining the U.S. as a security partner/provider are seen as: continued support for democracy and freedoms; investments as well as reciprocal, fair and balanced trade relations; developing common advanced technologies, including AI, data centres, specialised naval construction; energy (liquefied natural gas and nuclear projects); as well as interconnectivity projects (such as the Three Seas Initiative).

Regarding the U.S. and EU's joint goal of a free and resilient Ukraine, it is expected that this can be achieved through consolidated European involvement. In this context, Romania is aiming to become a key player in reconstructing Ukraine, with some officials mentioning that those countries that have supported Ukrainians from the beginning should also be central to the reconstruction process. This should open up participation for all relevant stakeholders, such as Romania, who are already actively involved in construction, IT, architecture, energy, defence and other related services.

Money for Defence in Times of Austerity

Negotiations on the MFF 2028–2034 are expected to generate a national debate on budgetary requirements for an EUSD. Although Romania has long advocated keeping high levels of cohesion and agriculture funds, some political actors are nowadays in favour of directing more resources to defence, while others call for the development of public/private partnerships as alternative financing sources.

Regarding defence expenditure, in 2017, Romania committed itself to spending at least 2.0% of GDP annually by 2027. For 2025, the estimate has already risen to 2.28%. This gradual increase is endorsed by political decisions to use EU money for defence, as Romania will benefit from EUR 16.68 billion in funding through the SAFE programme. This is the second largest allocation established at EU level and represents a strategic opportunity to enhance Romania's defence capacity, while supporting the national defence industry.

Mindful of Romania's twin deficits (budget and current account) alongside the 2025 austerity measures, a question looms regarding the level of domestic resources needed to reach defence objectives. Additional military spending would entail extraordinary pressure on the budgets for education and social policies, thereby increasing public discontent. Romania provides financial support for a series of EU incentives, such as: exclusion of defence spending from deficit calculations; exemption from VAT for European common projects; optimisation of procurement directives. Romania's Parliament has also considered the following measures: extending the EIB's financing framework for dual-use projects and other types of equipment; deepening the dialogue between Member States on defence sector bonds; simplifying defence legislation through a future Omnibus proposal adopted at European level; and more flexibility regarding categories related to activating the national escape clause within the Stability and Growth Pact.

Major Concerns and Threat Perception Among Citizens

The Standard Eurobarometer 103—Spring 2025 shows that in comparison with general perceptions at EU level, Romanians view Russia's invasion of Ukraine as the most important issue the EU is facing at the moment, enhanced by resultant general international uncertainty. Domestically, key issues concerning Romanian citizens are rising prices/inflation/cost of living (40%), the economic situation (26%) and health (14%). Regarding actions at EU level that would have the highest positive impact on lives in the short term, Romanians favour increased job opportunities (35%) and measures aimed at ensuring peace and stability (32%). Actions to strengthen European defence are supported by just 18% of respondents. This can be explained by Romanians' tendency to associate the EU with economic prosperity, achieved through cohesion and agriculture funds, which they would like to maintain through the next MFF.

In terms of threat perception, a comparative annual survey published by GLOBSEC in 2024 shows that Russia is seen as the main security threat to Romania, dramatically increasing from 30% in 2020 to 73% in 2024. A follow-up question revealed that 33% of Romanian respondents perceive "Western societies and their way of living" as a threat to Romanians' identity and values. This distribution of results indicates a range of threats from internal (especially how we view ourselves in relation to others) to external (directly observing the effects of Russia's aggression against Ukraine and growing instability in the Black Sea Region).

The 'GLOBSEC Trends 2025: Ready for a New Era?' survey indicates that 64% of people consider the Russian Federation to be a threat to Romania. The same report simultaneously shows a record-high backing for the EU with 91% of respondents in Romania supporting EU membership—the highest level recorded in the country over the past 6 years.

Regarding public support for increased defence spending, a national poll from 2025 indicated that 76.2% of Romanians would be in favour of such a decision, which is completely understandable considering heightened awareness of a Russian threat. Furthermore, a similar regional analysis from 2025 shows that 86% of Romanian respondents agree that the country should increase its defence spending, making it the second country after Poland in Central and Eastern Europe (among EU Member States) with such a high support.

In conclusion, based on the traffic light system of threat perception, Russia can be considered as at least a medium ('yellow') threat to the country's security and sovereignty. This is backed by evidence of the hybrid war conducted in Romania at the time of the 2024 elections.

Recommendations

Romania should advocate at the EU level for opening new paths of communication and cooperation with the U.S. administration in order to maintain American military commitments to Europe.

In the context of increased financial stress and a number of key priorities, it should also further enhance its public-private partnerships and attract other sources of financing that do not put extra pressure on the national budget.

Furthermore, Romania should support EU enlargement to the Republic of Moldova, Ukraine and the Western Balkans as a means of increasing the region's stability, expanding the internal market as well as reinforcing the area of freedom, security and justice.

Finally, the country should build awareness and situational capacities to counter hybrid war-related threats and fully transition to a whole-of-society approach with regard to resilience and readiness.

Mihai Sebe is Interinstitutional Relations Coordinator, European Institute of Romania (EIR) and lecturer at the University of Bucharest. He gained his PhD in Political Sciences. His current research interests include: European affairs, the impact of new technologies, regional cooperation formats.

Eliza Vaş is Coordinator of the Studies Unit at the EIR and Editor-in-Chief of the *Romanian Journal of European Affairs*. Additionally, she is Vice President of the Young Initiative Association and actively engaged in the European non-profit sector.

The European Institute of Romania (EIR) is the only national public institution dedicated to European Affairs, with more than 25 years of uninterrupted activity. Coordinated by the Romanian Ministry of Foreign Affairs, its mission is to provide expertise in the field of European Affairs to the public administration, the business community, the social partners and civil society. Studies, training, translations and communication are EIR's key areas of activity.

Estranged in Mind, Entwined in Reality: Security and Threat Perception in Slovakia

Matej Navrátil

Slovakia lives in two security realities at once. In part of the public imagination, threats feel distant or inflated; mistrust of NATO and the U.S. endures and a considerable part of society is receptive to pro-Kremlin narratives. Yet the country is simultaneously a frontline neighbour of Ukraine, bound to collective defence through NATO and deeply embedded in the EU. Slovakia also embodies the EU's wider dilemma. On paper, it is firmly integrated in NATO and EU structures, entwined in reality. However, in the minds of its citizens, it remains estranged, hesitant to act decisively and vulnerable to the Kremlin's disinformation. Unless Europe bridges this gap, it risks having strong armies, but weak societies. Slovakia's lesson is clear: deterrence requires not only tanks and treaties, but also trust. Winning the battle for hearts and minds is as urgent as any arms race. Slovakia's case is a bellwether of how fragile European unity can become when public opinion drifts so far from security realities that it turns into a strategic vulnerability. Slovakia's case illustrates the strategic ambivalence of a state caught between frontline geography and divided public sentiment, in line with a 'yellow' traffic light or medium threat perception: it is taking steps to defend itself, yet a considerable part of the public remains unsure whether the danger is real or imagined.

Security and Threat Perception in Slovakia: The State of Affairs

Many Slovaks still treat Russian aggression as something far away, even though the frontline lies just across the eastern border. This contradiction is measurable. A poll conducted in 2025 shows one of the region's highest support rates for NATO membership, around 70%, yet the 2025 Eurobarometer shows that Slovakia remains

M. Navrátil (✉)
Comenius University in Bratislava, Bratislava, Slovakia
e-mail: matej.navratil@uniba.sk

M. Kaeding et al. (eds.), *Security, Defence, and the Future of Europe*,
https://doi.org/10.1007/978-3-032-18279-1_23

markedly less willing than most EU citizens to back lethal aid to Ukraine. From polling at the start of 2025, a non-trivial 16% of people would even prefer a Russian victory. The strategic consequence is a chronic gap between what keeps Slovakia safe and what parts of the Slovakian population wish were the case. Officially, Slovakia sees NATO as the cornerstone of its security. In practice, this means heavy security dependence on the U.S.

Yet 2025 polls show a paradox: while Slovak security rests on U.S. guarantees, 35% of Slovaks see the U.S. as a top security threat, compared to 50% who view Russia in the same way. Yet, 32% also see Moscow as a key strategic partner. This estrangement leaves the Slovak government caught between external commitments and internal delusion. The country is entwined with Washington's security umbrella, but its citizens often prefer the illusion of neutrality, an idea that has also been recently uttered by the Prime Minister and gained considerable traction in the media (almost 31% of respondents favouring Slovakia becoming neutral). Neutrality may sound appealing, but in reality it would mean dependence on the goodwill of stronger neighbours—a lesson learned from Slovak history in 1938.

Public opinion matches a 'yellow' threat perception. The country acknowledges Russia as a threat and has taken steps to strengthen its defence, but public opinion remains divided, with significant pro-Russian sentiment and reluctance to bear the costs of security. Yet, the Ministry of Defence launched the National Defence Forces training programme—voluntary defence training—for which Slovakia lowered the minimum age from 19 to 18, effectively putting formal conscription on the back burner.

How to Walk to an EUSD

Since Russia's invasion of Ukraine, Slovakia has increased its defence budget and purchased modern U.S. F-16 fighter jets, inching closer to NATO's expenditure benchmark. In 2022, Bratislava was among the first to deliver heavy weapons to Ukraine, including the S-300 air defence system, unused and uneconomic MiG-29 fighter jets, together with some of its KUB air defence systems. Yet, even though these pieces of military equipment were partly refunded by the EU or exchanged for more effective and modern systems used by NATO allies, these steps were often contrary to domestic opinion.

For a state of 5.5 million people, Slovakia punches above its weight where it matters most today, namely in the realm of artillery. Arms exports surged to about EUR 1.15 billion last year, powered by 155-millimetre shells and the Zuzana-2 howitzers. New lines in Snina and the revival of Chemko Strážske are together building a full chain of military ammunition on Slovak soil, with European demand guaranteeing the market. Zuzana-2 s are already firing in Ukraine via a Denmark–Germany–Norway arrangement. These are not abstract contributions: they are tonnes of steel and powder that translate into deterrence and survival.

Credibility is also capability. When senior politicians openly toy with 'neutrality' or dismiss EU security summits as 'war summits', partners hesitate, even if Slovakia ultimately signs the same *communiqués* and taps the same funds. Cost is opportunity: in a Europe accelerating common procurement, mixed signals can mean slower access to joint projects and the financing that follows. A small state cannot afford to waste the compound interest of trust. Simply put, although Prime Minister Robert Fico often criticises EU policies, Slovakia ultimately supports key initiatives, but this very questioning of allies seriously undermines Slovakia's credibility amongst its partners.

The direction of travel is no longer vague. The EU's 'Readiness 2030' White Paper names seven practical priorities (air and missile defence; artillery; ammunition and missiles; drones and counter-drones; military mobility; AI, quantum, cyber and electronic warfare; as well as protection of critical infrastructure and strategic enablers). These match Slovakia's own capability gaps almost line-for-line. The financing architecture is also in place: national fiscal flexibility through the Stability and Growth Pact's escape clause and, crucially, the new SAFE instrument—up to EUR 150 billion in long-maturity EU-backed loans—to catalyse joint procurement and production. Brussels has also started to cut red tape: the Defence Readiness Omnibus fast-tracks permits streamlines procurement and eases intra-EU transfers that not so long ago used to trap spare parts behind a wall of bureaucratic paper.

The U.S., NATO and 'European Army' Mirage

However, none of this replaces NATO. In June 2025, allies set a historic benchmark to invest 5% of GDP on defence: 3.5% for troops and weapons, with 1.5% security investment for resilience, industry and critical infrastructure. That decision is a map for Europe's large-scale capabilities and readiness inside, not outside of NATO. For Slovakia, the arithmetic is tight: a planned average of just over 2% of GDP for defence between 2025 and 2028 and a budget deficit still near 5% means that every euro must work twice. The government now faces stark budgetary trade-offs. Economic stagnation and populist pressures mean that higher military spending often comes at the cost of welfare policies. This is politically explosive in an already divided society where the incumbent government runs its political messages primarily on the social agenda by increasing the minimum wage and pensions. While Bratislava aligns with EU initiatives on joint procurement and capability upgrades, it lacks both the fiscal room and public backing to be an enthusiastic driver of an EUSD. The smart play is to file multi-year, bankable plans aligned with EU priorities, so that European flexibility and SAFE money pay for air defence batteries, ammunition, drones and military mobility while EU recovery funds and grants are used for dual-use projects such as bridges and railways.

In broad terms, the U.S. remains a partner, but a tougher one. Washington's message is simple: Europe must carry more of Europe. That does not argue for a standalone 'European army'; it argues for European large-scale capabilities, industry and readiness that are fully interoperable under NATO planning and command. The Alliance is the roof; a stronger EU is the scaffolding and pillars that keep the roof secure.

Peace, But From Strength

Calls for a ceasefire and 'balanced' diplomacy with Russia are common in Slovak politics. This mirrors public mood, but risks undermining European unity. Such calls for talks will keep growing. Europe should play a larger diplomatic role, but anchored in Ukraine's 10-point peace formula and the European Council's demand for a comprehensive, just and lasting peace. Any concessions while Russian missiles still fall would merely validate aggression and invite the next war. The sequence matters: air defence, ammunition, drones and sanctions enforcement now; reconstruction money and sanctions relief only when the guns fall silent. Deterrence first, diplomacy second: that is how peace settlements become durable.

Recommendations

Slovakia should move from ambivalence to intent.

Firstly, adopt a partly classified National Strategy for Defence Industry Development aligned to 'Readiness 2030', that would be discussed and approved across the political spectrum and clear away the domestic bottlenecks in procurement, certification and intra-EU transfers while contracting strategic reserves at home.

Secondly, use the escape-clause space and SAFE loans to co-finance air defence, artillery, drones and strategic enablers, while shifting dual-use mobility into cohesion and recovery funds.

Thirdly, lock in scale with multi-year orders for 155-millimetre ammunition and artillery, accelerate factory lines and enable domestic maintenance for new fleets from Patria and CV90 to F-16 and ground-based air defence.

Fourthly, rebuild credibility at home and abroad: reaffirm NATO anchoring, professionalise strategic communication and treat the information space like the operational domain that it is.

Finally, pooling of resources pays dividends—regional joint planning and mobility corridors, common air-defence nodes—and enables a stronger European pillar to sit firmly inside and not beside NATO.

Matej Navrátil, PhD. works as an Associate Researcher at the European Council on Foreign Relations and as a researcher at the Faculty of Social and Economic Sciences, Comenius University. His research focus includes the EU, organisation theory, study of institutions/institutional theory, as well as EU foreign and security policy. Matej was a visiting scholar at the Norwegian Institute of International Affairs. His work has appeared in the Hague Journal of Diplomacy and he has co-authored book chapters in international scholarly volumes.

The Faculty of Social and Economic Sciences is an integral part of Comenius University in Bratislava. Academics and researchers provide expertise in different fields of social science for national decision-makers, running research and popularisation projects in Slovakia and abroad. The faculty's foreign professors, students from abroad and European research projects give it a truly international feel. In the last decade, it has earned a reputation as one of the best social science faculties in Slovakia. The Institute is also a member of TEPSA.

A Free-for-All: Slovenia and EU Defence Commitments

Jelena Juvan and Boštjan Udovič

This chapter presents Slovenia's engagement in EU security and defence, highlighting a large gap between its declarative approach and reality, usually evidenced by the lack of consistent leadership and hence constrained capabilities. It explores defence spending trends, societal perceptions and strategic ambivalence, situating Slovenia's role within broader EU security dynamics. There are both challenges and opportunities for Slovenia to enhance its credibility through political will, niche contributions and proactive coalition-building. Using the traffic light analogy, Slovenia can be categorised within the 'green'/'yellow' range, reflecting an overall low to moderate threat perception among the Slovenian public, depending on the type of threat.

Slovenia and EU Security and Defence

Slovenia consistently affirms its support for the EU's ambition to develop into a stronger, more coherent and credible security and defence actor. However, this support has largely been expressed at a declarative level, with limited translation into concrete national initiatives or leadership within EU frameworks. Slovenia's engagement in the CSDP, PESCO and other EU security mechanisms reflects more the determination to remain a part of collective processes than an ability to shape their outcomes decisively. This tendency is linked to Slovenia's relatively small size, limited defence capabilities as well as constrained financial and human resources, which restrict its capacity to exercise influence beyond symbolic or supportive contributions. As a result, Slovenia has predominantly followed prevailing EU positions rather than articulating distinct or pioneering national stances on

J. Juvan (✉) · B. Udovič
Faculty of Social Sciences, University of Ljubljana, Ljubljana, Slovenia
e-mail: Jelena.Juvan@fdv.uni-lj.si; Bostjan.Udovic@fdv.uni-lj.si

M. Kaeding et al. (eds.), *Security, Defence, and the Future of Europe*,
https://doi.org/10.1007/978-3-032-18279-1_24

pressing security challenges. Western Balkans and EU enlargement have been defined as priorities. However, Slovenia has missed the opportunity to take advantage of the benefits stemming from its historical and cultural ties with Western Balkan countries.

The two notable exceptions that demonstrated Slovenia's potential for greater activism were its Presidencies of the Council of the EU in 2008 and 2021, when it was temporarily thrust into a leading role in facilitating consensus and steering EU security debates. These episodes underscored that Slovenia is capable of playing a more visible and constructive role in shaping EU security and defence policy when called for by institutional conditions, but such activism has remained episodic rather than systemic. Today, the EU's security discourse is profoundly shaped by Russia's aggression against Ukraine, a conflict that will have long-lasting consequences for Europe's security order and for the EU's credibility as a security and defence actor. For Slovenia, the war highlights both the necessity for deeper engagement in EU security initiatives and the risks of remaining a predominantly declarative participant.

Slovenia and the Financing of Defence and Security Investments

Slovenia's defence spending trajectory illustrates both a strategic adjustment to evolving security dynamics and a persistent ambivalence toward long-term capability development. For decades, expenditure hovered at 1.2–1.3% of GDP, far below the NATO benchmark of 2%, reflecting limited political will and the perception that Slovenia's security was primarily guaranteed through its Alliance membership rather than national investment. The recent pledge to increase spending to 2% of GDP in 2025, increasing to 2.2% in 2026, represents a rhetorical alignment with NATO expectations, yet the question remains whether the officially declared commitments are going to be translated into practice.

The establishment of the state-owned defence investment company DOVOS (Society of defence, security and resilience) has been presented as evidence of strategic modernisation, with ambitions to foster technological innovation and strengthen industrial capacities. However, the company's initial capitalisation is modest, raising doubts about its capacity to effect meaningful change in the short to medium term. Moreover, Slovenia's politically contentious withdrawal from the Boxer armoured vehicle programme in 2025 reflects a recurring pattern of reversals and fragmented procurement strategies that undermine credibility both domestically and among allies. While the formal increase in spending signals a shift from declarative support toward more concrete action, Slovenia still faces structural constraints—most notably limited fiscal space, underdeveloped defence-industrial infrastructure and low societal support for prioritising defence—that cast doubt on whether these investments will translate into durable capability enhancement.

Slovenia's Public Opinion and Awareness

Public opinion and awareness about security issues in Slovenia reflect a persistent mismatch between strategic realities and societal perceptions. While survey data suggests that the majority of Slovenians view NATO membership as having improved national security, this acknowledgement has not been translated into sustained public support for defence spending or capability development. Instead, citizens consistently rank non-military issues such as corruption, crime, economic insecurity and social welfare as more pressing than external or military threats, underscoring a narrow and civilian-centric understanding of security. Such perceptions risk marginalising debates on collective defence, as security is predominantly interpreted through the prism of governance and social stability rather than strategic vulnerabilities.

Moreover, in domains where awareness is crucial, such as cybersecurity, evidence points to limited institutional and societal preparedness, with decision-makers often underestimating the scope of emerging hybrid threats. This gap between declarative support for security frameworks and the absence of deep societal engagement is compounded by low levels of trust in state institutions, with fewer than half of the population confident that the government would effectively safeguard lives in an emergency. Consequently, Slovenian security policy is challenged not only by resource constraints, but also by public discourse that remains detached from strategic imperatives, raising doubts about the long-term societal legitimacy of national defence commitments together with Slovenia's credibility as a reliable partner within NATO and the EU.

In applying the traffic light framework, the country can be categorised within the 'green'/'yellow' range, reflecting an overall low to moderate threat perception. Slovenia does not identify any state as an adversary or perceive a direct military threat to its territorial integrity. According to Slovenia's defence strategy, its security environment is largely shaped by stable relations with all neighbouring countries as well as its membership of NATO and the EU. Nonetheless, Slovenia acknowledges indirect and non-traditional security challenges, such as hybrid threats, cyber incidents, disinformation as well as regional instability in the Western Balkans and Eastern Europe. According to a poll conducted by the University of Ljubljana, Natural disasters are the number one threat perceived by the Slovenian public.

Consequently, Slovenia's national discourse and strategic documents emphasise cooperative security, resilience and crisis management, rather than deterrence or territorial defence, situating it firmly in the low ('green') to medium ('yellow') range of threat perception.

Recommendations

There are three recommendations that should be followed to align Slovenia's defence and security approach towards the CSDP. Firstly, the EU must actively empower smaller Member States by creating structured pathways for them to provide niche capabilities that directly strengthen Europe's collective defence posture. Within the European Defence Fund, the EU should establish instruments specifically dedicated to supporting projects led by smaller nations. Such an instrument would incentivise these states to develop and contribute niche capabilities, such as cyber defence, counter-drone technologies, or advanced logistics, where they possess comparative advantages.

Secondly, the EU should urgently enhance coordination and accountability in defence investment programmes, ensuring that reversals and fragmented procurement do not undermine credibility.

Thirdly, Slovenia should adopt a more assertive and vocal approach in articulating its positions within the international arena. Equally important, though, is the need for the country to engage first in a coherent and strategic process of formulating its stances domestically. This entails fostering informed debate, building cross-sectoral consensus and clearly defining national priorities on issues that are crucial for Slovenia's long-term interests and future development, independently and within EU.

Jelena Juvan is Associate Professor and senior research fellow at the Chair of Defence Studies and Defence Research Centre at the Faculty of Social Sciences, University of Ljubljana. She teaches courses on: EU Security and Defence Policy; Security in the Information Society; Defence and Security System; and Cyber Security. She is head of the Chair of Defence Studies and a vice-president of the Euro Atlantic Council of Slovenia.

Boštjan Udovič is Professor in diplomacy and a researcher at the Centre of Diplomatic, Economic and Legal Studies, at the Faculty of Social Sciences, University of Ljubljana. He has been guest professor at the University of Salzburg and the University of Regensburg as well as a member of different national and international strategic bodies in the field of diplomacy and foreign policy.

The Faculty of Social Sciences (FDV), University of Ljubljana, is the biggest interdisciplinary faculty in Slovenia, covering fields from political science, sociology, communication, European studies, defence studies, diplomatic studies to cultural studies. Its members have been collaborating in different international and national research projects and as scientific advisors to enterprises and public entities.

A Reluctant Spender with a Focus on the South: Spain and European Defence

Pablo del Amo, Raquel García Llorente, and Ignacio Molina

Spain's strategic vision on defence combines NATO alignment with a push for European autonomy. Its army possesses non-negligible capabilities, although constrained by budgetary limitations and a cautious public attitude toward more spending due to a low-threat perception or 'green' under the traffic light analogy. Yet, Spain does acknowledge that the continent as a whole is at risk and, shaped by its geographical context, pursues a comprehensive '360-degree' security approach. This entails a broader definition beyond the military sphere, while ensuring that strong support for Ukraine and Eastern allies against Russia does not neglect the need also to uphold Southern stability. Spain promotes much stronger EU military-industrial integration compatible with transatlantic cooperation, even if relations with the Trump administration are chilly.

Spain's View on Security and Defence

Spain shares a strategic identity with its Euro-Atlantic allies, but it displays a somewhat distinct security agenda, shaped by recent history—no war against a foreign enemy for over a century—and its unique geographical position. Madrid is the second furthest European capital from Moscow, while Spain is the only European country with a land border in Africa. This is where interconnected sources of insecurity converge: radicalisation, organised crime, human trafficking, regional rivalries and environmental degradation.

The country is also unique within Europe, having suffered large-scale terrorism from three different sources: nearly 1000 killings by the separatist group ETA; more than 200 victims in jihadist attacks; and over 100 people murdered as a result of

P. del Amo · R. G. Llorente · I. Molina (✉)
Real Instituto Elcano, Madrid, Spain
e-mail: pdelamo@rielcano.org; rgarcia@rielcano.org; imolina@rielcano.org

M. Kaeding et al. (eds.), *Security, Defence, and the Future of Europe*,
https://doi.org/10.1007/978-3-032-18279-1_25

far-left and far-right extremism. This has fostered a culture of prevention and resilience; hence, vulnerability is much lower today. Non-conventional threats, in some cases at a level of risk well above the European average, have meanwhile gained relevance: climate-related disasters (floods, megafires, extreme weather), irregular migration flows, cyber intrusions, disinformation, health disruptions and energy weaknesses (a major power blackout in April 2025 left most of Spain and Portugal without electricity for many hours). This broader definition of threats is reflected in the 2021 National Security Strategy.

Spain has thus played a key role in promoting a more balanced concept of security within NATO, embodied in the 360-degree notion. This is a comprehensive doctrine for a number of reasons: it goes beyond the traditional military domain; it spans the entire risk lifecycle, from prevention to recovery; and it seeks to ensure that the geographical focus is not solely in the East, but that challenges from the Mediterranean-Sahel are also addressed by the Alliance. In theory, this integrated approach has been adopted by NATO at the 2022 Madrid Summit and in the 2024 report on the Southern Neighbourhood.

Spanish Strengths and Weaknesses

This sensitivity has been compatible with a defence policy guided by Spain's multilateral Western vocation and its consistent participation in most missions promoted by NATO and the EU (in addition to UN peacekeeping operations). In the last two decades, Spain has been present in locations most crucial to Euro-Atlantic security: Afghanistan, the Allied border with Russia, the Indian Ocean, the Mediterranean Sea, the Middle East and the Sahel. It has acted as a reliable and experienced partner, with an average of 3000 military personnel permanently deployed and possessing the necessary air and naval capabilities, though it is true that these efforts have been oriented more toward stabilisation and counterinsurgency than toward high-intensity military operations.

Indeed, in terms of capabilities, the Spanish armed forces are competent and well-structured. According to comparative indexes that measure the capacity of force projection abroad, Spain ranks as NATO's sixth power (despite being only ninth in total military spending in 2024). With 117,600 military personnel, Spain maintains a medium-sized force by European standards. It has an Army with more battle tanks than France or Italy and a navy well equipped with frigates as well as a light aircraft carrier. However, it also faces notable shortfalls, partly because it has neither increased its military spending nor taken steps to prepare for a potential conflict over recent years. For example, Spain needs more submarines and tanker aircraft and suffers from a lack of long-range missiles, which limits its medium-term operational and deterrent capacity. The gap between available means and strategic ambition (given the wide variety of threats it faces) means that Spain lacks autonomy in regard to security and is, therefore, ultimately dependent on the U.S. This problem also affects other European allies regarding intelligence, logistics and high-end military capabilities, as the war in Ukraine has clearly demonstrated.

From a more positive perspective, Spain's defence has another strategic pillar. This is a domestic industry which enjoys a relatively solid position in regard to: the naval sector (Navantia is one of the largest shipbuilders in Europe); aerospace (participation in Airbus Defence and Space); and a number of private companies with high technological potential (Indra, Escribano, Oesía).

The two U.S. bases in Andalusia (Naval Station Rota and Morón Air Base) are also important assets for the security of NATO Allies. Both function as key logistical platforms for operations in Europe, the Middle East and the Sahel. Any major reduction in this American military presence would compel Spain to strengthen its own logistical and projection capabilities.

Domestically, the professionalisation of military service, concluded in 2001 with the abolition of conscription, thereafter completely transforming the armed forces' structure and organisational culture. The current all-volunteer system ensures higher quality commitment and specialisation, although it creates size constraints and makes long-duration operations more difficult to sustain. Anyhow, unlike the situation in other EU countries, there is no debate about reinstating compulsory military service, which was characterised by operational discontinuity and very low popularity among the urban youth. There is also no discussion in today's political agenda about alternatives to conscription. Recruitment promotion instead relies on salary increases and career benefits, as the low basic pay has so far tended to result in professional soldiers remaining in the armed forces for only a few years before moving to better-paid positions in the police (local or national) and the Civil Guard.

The Politics of Security and Defence Policy

With regard to public opinion, recent polls show that the armed forces are Spain's most valued institution. Moreover, 85% of Spaniards support NATO membership and 57% believe Europe should spend more on armaments, although support decreases if such expenditure requires cuts in welfare programmes. Notably, in the EP's Eurobarometer published in September 2025, Spain was the only country in which "defence and security" was not cited as the primary area on which the EU should focus to strengthen its role in the world; Spaniards instead prioritised "education and research".

This finding, together with evidence from other studies, such as the 2025 Elcano Royal Institute Barometer, leads to the conclusion that Spain still falls predominantly within the 'green' category under the traffic light system, indicating a low perception of threat and a stable, peaceful view of international security. In fact, 60% of Spaniards believe the country faces no threat from any other state. Among those who do perceive risks, Morocco ranks first (this neighbouring country claims the cities of Ceuta and Melilla, home to around 200,000 fellow nationals), followed by distant Russia. Scepticism prevails about a Ukrainian victory after the Russian invasion, although there is strong support for European military aid and, to a lesser degree, for sending Spanish troops. However, the conflict occupies a secondary place in Spain's political and media debate, particularly compared to the war in Gaza.

The Spanish government, a left-wing coalition reluctant to expand its military budget at the expense of social priorities, has officially declined to endorse NATO's 5% of GDP spending target agreed at the 2025 Hague Summit. It argued on the basis of: fiscal sustainability problems; European industry's inability to absorb such a huge investment; as well as Allied efforts, which need to be measured in operational capabilities and actual contributions to missions. In April 2025, Spain announced a budget increase that would bring defence expenditure to around 2.1% of GDP, a level of spending that would be held indefinitely, claiming that this would suffice to meet NATO capability goals. Nonetheless, this modest stance caused friction with some European allies (who have accepted expenditure of at least 3.5%) and led to verbal clashes with U.S. President Trump, who even suggested Spain's expulsion from the Alliance.

Rethinking European Defence Beyond Spending Targets

Nevertheless, the current context offers an opportunity to strengthen the country's position within the European defence industry. Spain has the fourth-largest GDP in the EU and its starting point of spending is very low. Hence, even theoretically small figures announced by the government will help considerably to expand current production and diversify it with possible new programmes of high technological content (integrated air defence, medium-range missiles, drones and naval systems) that will also help address capability shortfalls.

Beyond the national budget, Spain advocates European-level spending solutions, funded by borrowing and subsequent grants—similar to the NextGenerationEU precedent—in line with proposals for defence by the Draghi Report. To date, the European Commission's financial proposals have focused on funds that need to be repaid. The SAFE programme offers up to EUR 150 billion in loans, but since Spain does not wish to take on additional public debt, it has requested only EUR 1 billion, as compared with EUR 16 billion requested by France and EUR 15 billion by Italy. Madrid also argues that progress toward a European security and defence policy cannot rely merely on purchasing U.S. equipment, but preferably on a common industrial framework to enable joint investment, generate economies of scale and advance genuine strategic autonomy.

Moreover, Spain thinks that the increase in EU defence expenditure cannot be reduced to a strictly military dimension. This led to sending a request to the Commission, together with Italy, to rename its ReArm Europe Plan programme 'Readiness 2030'. In this spirit of promoting a broader concept of security, Spain also considers that spending on climate change mitigation should be counted as part of the effort.

In the long run, both Spanish elites and public opinion would probably support the idea of a European army; however, in practical terms, Spain—as with most Member States—remains reluctant to cede sovereignty over defence matters. In the meantime, Madrid supports a stronger European pillar within NATO and a gradually more integrated EU with greater defence capabilities that may advance, if necessary, through enhanced cooperation among the most committed states.

Regarding the most urgent concern for the continent's security, Spain's military assistance to Ukraine has evolved significantly over time, from initially non-lethal material to the delivery of heavy weaponry and the training of more than 8000 Ukrainian soldiers on Spanish soil. There has also been firm political support and humanitarian aid, with around 240,000 refugees received. In comparative terms, Spain's total assistance to Ukraine amounts to approximately EUR 1.47 billion, hence 15th place among global donors.

Spain believes peace efforts with Russia must reflect the views of Ukrainians and ensure that the process does not turn into a bilateral negotiation between Moscow and Washington. Europe, in Spain's view, should give continuing military and economic assistance to Ukraine, as well as promote the country's future reconstruction, a clear EU accession horizon and security guarantees against the Russian threat. Nevertheless, Madrid has adopted a more cautious stance than some 'coalition of the willing' members regarding a tentative deployment of troops on the ground.

Recommendations

Spain should continue developing key defence capabilities through sustained national investment in close coordination with European initiatives. Given the country's size and resources, simply meeting the target of spending 2.1% of GDP on defence would unlock very high potential in different domains, thus enhancing its role as a regional security provider and strengthening European autonomy. Doing so would also help dispel the debate—artificially fuelled by the inflated figures demanded by Trump—about Spain's real commitment to the continent's security.

At the same time, the government needs to explain better to its citizens the importance of solidarity with partners on the Eastern flank. That effort should focus on Member States that share a border with Russia and above all Ukraine, maintaining the strong political support it has already provided (by backing Kyiv's EU membership bid and hosting large numbers of refugees) and increasing military aid, which remains comparatively limited.

Finally, Spanish diplomacy should articulate more clearly in European capitals and in Washington its distinctive stance on '360-degree security', understood as an integrated approach both thematically (since traditional military threats are not the only ones that matter) and geographically (since the Southern dimension cannot be ignored as a central component of the continent's collective security strategy).

Pablo del Amo is a Fellow at the Elcano Royal Institute.

Raquel García Llorente is a Fellow at the Elcano Royal Institute.

Ignacio Molina is a Senior Fellow at the Elcano Royal Institute and Professor of Political Science at the Autonomous University of Madrid.

The Elcano Royal Institute is Spain's leading think tank for international and strategic studies. It was established in 2001 as an independent private foundation, that engages with public institutions, the business community, academia and civil society.

Sweden: Supporting Europe by Supporting Ukraine

Gunilla Herolf

For Sweden, the overriding security tasks at present are supporting Ukraine as well as strengthening itself and Europe generally against ongoing Russian aggression. To quote the Statement of Foreign Policy on 12 February 2025, "We—Sweden, the EU and NATO—are in the midst of a long-term confrontation with Russia. Our task is inescapable: we will constrain Russia's capability to do us harm, particularly through our support to Ukraine." In traffic light terms, Swedes perceive a 'red' threat level as highly appropriate.

Defending a Europe of Many Shapes

Since for Sweden the defence of Europe is primarily related to the Russian threat, rather than institutions, support for its defence takes many forms. Since 2022, Swedish aid to Ukraine has amounted to SEK 105 billion (EUR 9.6 billion), of which SEK 92 billion (EUR 8.4 billion) is in the form of military aid. For 2026 and 2027, the government proposes SEK 40 billion (EUR 3.7 billion) each year in the form of military aid, whilst civil aid will amount to SEK 10 billion (EUR 913 million).

Nordic cooperation in military and civil defence is constantly growing, with Swedish-Finnish cooperation being particularly close. After Finland and Sweden joined NATO in 2023 and 2024 respectively, the Nordic and Baltic countries' relations have similarly grown closer.

For Sweden, due to its geographical proximity to Russia, only NATO is seen as capable of serving as a basis for collective defence. After joining NATO in 2024, Swedish contributions to European security grew substantially. Its territory is

G. Herolf (✉)
Swedish Institute of International Affairs, Stockholm, Sweden
e-mail: gunilla@herolf.se

M. Kaeding et al. (eds.), *Security, Defence, and the Future of Europe*,
https://doi.org/10.1007/978-3-032-18279-1_26

crucial for reinforcements of units, defence material and civilian goods to reach Finland and the Baltic states. Military contributions include ground units to NATO's Enhanced Forward Presence in Latvia, naval vessels to NATO's Standing Naval Forces and combat aircraft to air policing and response preparedness. Sweden will also become the framework nation for an army base in northern Finland. Other contributions are in the form of a military industry (such as combat aircraft and submarines), troops trained for combat in harsh weather conditions and naval units well acquainted with difficult conditions in the Baltic Sea.

Sweden's traditional system of conscription was suspended in 2010, but in 2017 a new, now gender-neutral, system was instated. People between 16 and 70 have a legal duty to contribute in some form to Sweden's total defence. The 18-year-olds are required to undergo mustering and, if selected for military training, they are obliged to participate. Civilian service is still suspended (since 2010), but a commission has recommended its reintroduction. Public opinion is largely in favour of the conscription system.

Sweden has traditionally labelled the EU as its most important foreign policy actor. The EU's role in security matters has grown due to its essential role in civil defence and, more recently, the urgency in building up European defence. Sweden is a driving force in EU efforts to develop a specific strategy to address Russia's hybrid activities. It is also a strong supporter of Ukraine, Georgia and Moldova becoming EU members.

The times are changing and, as stated in the February Statement of Foreign Policy, Sweden cannot take the transatlantic link for granted: "European NATO countries need to take joint responsibility for the defence and security of Europe, including Ukraine." This statement reflects well the Swedish preference (seen also in the EU's PESCO) to include non-EU countries in forming a stronger Europe. It also points to the deep insecurity which exists when it comes to the U.S. role regarding the defence of both Europe and Ukraine.

Agreement with Reservations

Sweden shares the view expressed in the Commission 'White Paper for European Defence—Readiness 2030' that European preparedness and defence capacity must be strengthened. Sweden has also expressed its interest in taking a leading role in various projects. Furthermore, the government supports the goal of facilitating loans for procurement (SAFE), under the condition that it enables a broad, open and competitive market.

However, Sweden's intergovernmentalist inclination also comes out in its view that Sweden retains its previous position of being very critical towards collective EU debts, believing that Member States should control development. Moreover, in these and similar contexts, the term EUSD is not used, and rather than seeing EU development as replacing NATO, the complementarity of the two is underlined.

Exceptional Unanimity of Views

Swedish military appropriations, which have doubled during the last few years, will continue to increase. Between 2024 and 2025, the enhancement was 10%, meaning an additional funding of SEK 13 billion (EUR 1.2 billion) and a total of 2.4% of GDP. For Sweden, the increase is financed by the exceptional means of a SEK 300 billion (EUR 274 billion) loan. Swedish finances are robust (government debt at 33.5% of GDP) and there will be no cuts to cover the costs. Sweden has not applied for means from SAFE.

All political parties agree on the need for Swedish rearmament and for military, financial, as well as political aid to Ukraine. There is also total political support for the fiscal policy framework mentioned above and this unanimity is furthermore reflected among the public. Swedes see the Russian war as a threat against European values as well as a military threat to Sweden and other countries if the aggression continues. This situation is perceived as serious and hence a threat perception of 'red'.

The Swedish view is that Russia has no wish for a fair peace and hence a strengthened Ukrainian position must precede negotiations, which requires more support from Europe and the U.S. In negotiations, apart from Ukraine, Russia and the U.S., the EU must also participate.

As described in Eurobarometer 103 of spring 2025, Swedes stand out as being either the most or second most positive among the citizens of EU countries when answering questions related to support for Ukraine: Asked about the view on EU's actions of welcoming people fleeing the war, Sweden was second (77% of respondents agreed and 20% tended to agree) which was also the case when asked whether countries agreed with EU's activities in granting candidate status as a potential member of the EU to Ukraine (55% agreed and 28% tended to agree). When asked about the EU imposing economic sanctions on the Russian government, companies and individuals, Sweden was the most positive country (74% agreed and 20% tended to agree), which was also the case when asked about the EU's activities to provide financial and humanitarian support to Ukraine, (78% agreed and 19% tended to agree) and the view on the EU's action to finance the purchase and supply of military equipment to Ukraine (72% agreed and 22% tended to agree).

Recommendations

European states should stop importing Russian oil and gas, rather than indirectly financing Russia's war against Ukraine. There are alternative exporters.

Russian funds in European banks should be used to help Ukraine. As the aggressor against Ukraine, it has forfeited these funds. The risks for this should not be carried only by Belgium.

Russia is now testing the continent, gradually escalating its activities against European countries. They should be met firmly—for the Russians, anything else is a sign of weakness.

Gunilla Herolf (PhD, Stockholm University) is a Senior Associated Research Fellow at UI. Her areas of research are European security cooperation, Nordic security and transatlantic cooperation.

The Swedish Institute of International Affairs (UI) is an independent institute and a platform for research and information on international relations and foreign policy. UI was founded in 1938.

The Netherlands and EU Security and Defence: A Reluctant Partnership

Auke Venema

This chapter focuses on the ability and willingness of the Netherlands to contribute to the EU's future security and defence. Russia's invasion of Ukraine provided the final incentive for a Dutch decision to invest heavily in the country's armed forces, culminating in acceptance of the 5% NATO GDP pledge at the NATO summit in the Hague. Simultaneously, the Netherlands confirmed its support for the policies and initiatives needed to strengthen EU security and Defence, including 'Readiness 2030' and the European Defence Industry Programme. However, despite the war in Ukraine and wavering American support for NATO, Dutch enthusiasm for EU security and defence remains lukewarm. The Dutch position *vis-à-vis* recent EU defence initiatives remains dominated by traditional financial concerns. Most mainstream political parties stick to 'NATO first', with the EU in a complementary role. The Netherlands' 2025 top five threat perceptions are included later in this chapter. Dutch public opinion reflects a medium to high ('yellow') threat level perception, showing that concern has grown about the possibility of involvement in war and the lack of European military capacity to defend itself.

Introduction

Since the Second World War, Dutch security and defence have been firmly rooted in NATO, resulting in close ties to the U.S. and the UK in particular. For decades, this Atlanticist orientation went hand in hand with the Netherlands' strong interest in European economic integration. Co-founding the European Economic Community, the Netherlands secured a continually growing export market; in 2023, 70% of Dutch services and goods exports went to the EU. Following the Cold War, this

A. Venema (✉)
The Clingendael Institute, Wassenaar, The Netherlands
e-mail: avenema@clingendael.org

M. Kaeding et al. (eds.), *Security, Defence, and the Future of Europe*,
https://doi.org/10.1007/978-3-032-18279-1_27

underlying principle has remained unchanged, with the Netherlands positioning itself as a bridge builder between NATO and the EU. The Dutch armed forces were modernised successfully, ending conscription and focusing on crisis management operations. This transformation came at a heavy price, though. Repeated and substantial budget cuts eroded readiness and sustainability. Nevertheless, the Netherlands remained relevant by contributing to many crisis management operations (NATO, EU and coalitions of the willing). Simultaneously, the Netherlands continued its advocacy of international law and has remained an active supporter of the UN.

While Under Pressure, Traditional Guidelines Persevere

However, the traditional guiding principles of Dutch foreign and defence policy are under pressure. What will the Europeanisation of NATO result in, even if the U.S. under Trump does not withdraw from NATO altogether? What will the end of the war in Ukraine bring? Whatever happens, to defend and deter against new threats, the Netherlands, as part of the EU and Western Europe, will have to take unprecedented steps in the area of security and defence. This may go well beyond the current EU scope on enhancing defence (industry) collaboration and investment mechanisms. The future of Europe's security architecture may prove that the traditional guidelines of Dutch foreign, defence and security policy are untenable.

However, since the Russian invasion of Ukraine, no major changes have been made in the orientation of security and defence policy. The 2024 government coalition agreement kept NATO in first place, with the EU in a supporting role. The invasion of Ukraine did have a significant impact on defence spending, finally raising the NATO GDP percentage from 1.1% in 2014 to 2% in 2025. The 2025 defence budget (EUR 24 billion) enables the Netherlands to strengthen its armed forces, refocusing on deterrence and Article 5 operations, which are to do with collective defence. At the NATO Summit in the Hague on 25 and 26 June 2025, the Netherlands agreed to raise NATO defence spending to 5% of GDP by 2035, implying a budget rise to EUR 35 billion by then. The total Netherlands' support of Ukraine since 2022 has amounted to EUR 8.7 billion (by September 2025). The military assistance included 24 F-16 fighter jets, Leopard tanks, air defence systems, ammunition and medical support.

Immediately before the June 2025 NATO summit in the Hague, an Ipsos opinion poll also demonstrated substantial support (42%) for the rise of defence spending to 5% of GDP. 20% of respondents were against and 25% neither agreed nor disagreed. However, were this increase to be implemented at the expense of spending in, say, health care and education, support would drop to 31%, 28% would neither agree nor disagree and 38% would be against. 72% agreed that Europe is too dependent on the U.S. Only 23% considered the U.S. an ally. Nevertheless, trust in NATO was at 50%, while trust in the EU was at 42%. In July, after the Summit, an Ipsos poll showed a majority of respondents supporting continuation of military support to Ukraine (64%). 15% of the respondents were against continuation.

In March 2025, the Clingendael Institute published the results of its yearly threat perception poll, ranking threats on a 1–10 impact on security and prosperity scale. Cyber-attacks and physical attacks against critical infrastructure were rated first and second respectively in the hierarchy of threats. They were followed by three war-related threats: involvement in a war because of an attack on NATO against a NATO/EU ally; involvement in a nuclear war; and concern about EU Member States' military shortfalls. The Clingendael 2025 top five threats reflect growing public awareness about the threat of war and Europe's lack of military capacity to defend itself. These specific threats were outside the top five in 2023. Dutch public opinion now reflects a medium to high ('yellow') threat level perception. Russia may consider military actions in the coming years.

Against this backdrop, regarding threats to the Netherlands, public opinion does show major concerns as well as growing consensus. The further increase in defence spending, for now at least, is not fundamentally challenged. There is a clear understanding that European military capacity has to be strengthened. A majority supports the continuation of military assistance to Ukraine. While being uncomfortable with European dependence, yet lack of trust in the U.S. public opinion does not reflect any demand for major changes.

Nevertheless, there are calls for change in the Netherlands' defence and security. The two main government advisors for foreign, security and defence policy point to the profound geopolitical changes and their impact on the Netherlands. The Scientific Council for Government Policy stresses that the Netherlands will have to make "far-reaching and sometimes painful" choices in "a wide range of policy domains and domestic social relations". The Advisory Council on International Affairs advises the government to strengthen the European pillar within NATO. This requires a more significant European share in the NATO command structure and targeted investments in strategic capabilities (air defence, strategic transport, electronic warfare, long-distance weapons), as well as the need to think about a credible European nuclear deterrent. The Council considers defence to be an essential European public good. Accordingly, the Council urges the government to support current European plans (ReArm, SAFE) and help implement them quickly.

EU Security and Defence: The Dutch Perspective

Since launching PESCO in December 2017, the EU has provided a framework for deeper defence cooperation, allowing Member States to extend their operational readiness, invest in shared projects and develop defence capabilities jointly. Over 60 PESCO projects have so far been launched, with the Netherlands participating in many, including: military mobility; cyber response soldier systems; and countering maritime mines. The Netherlands considers the EU Strategic Compass as an important contribution to a safer Europe. However, the position *vis-à-vis* the Compass clearly identifies the Dutch European security and defence parameters: (1) NATO first, with the EU in a complementary role; (2) fiscal frugality and efficient procurement; (3) parliamentary control over troop deployments. Within those, the Compass can deliver an important contribution to a safer Europe.

Since Russia's invasion of Ukraine, the European Commission has launched various initiatives to speed up military production and promote joint procurement, thereby rationalising production and bringing down costs. At the time of writing, the European Defence Industry Programme still has to be finalised. During the development of ASAP, the European Defence Industry Reinforcement Plan and the European Defence Industry Programme, the ReArm/'Readiness 2030' plan and SAFE, the Netherlands has stressed three key points. Firstly, it is important not to shut out non-EU allies (in particular, the U.S. as a critical supplier and European dependence on critical technologies). Secondly, additional 'red tape' must be avoided. Thirdly, strong fiscal discipline has to be maintained.

This became a major concern during the decision-making on SAFE. The Netherlands does support SAFE, but it emphasises the need to respect the Stability and Growth Pact, ensuring fiscal discipline by Member States that participate in SAFE. According to the Netherlands, SAFE should neither result in higher budget deficits in individual countries nor in common European debt. Dutch governments and parliamentary majorities have always been firmly against the introduction of Eurobonds, or proposals subsidising Member States, regardless of political costs. The Netherlands participates in ASAP and the European Defence Industry Reinforcement Plan. It does not participate in SAFE. Neither has it requested the European Commission to activate the escape clause in the Stability and Growth Pact, allowing Member States running budget deficits greater than 3% enabling increased defence spending.

Conclusions: Assessing the Dutch EU Security and Defence Perspective

Any future European security architecture will be hard to develop. NATO will remain indispensable for European defence for a long time to come and moreover, the U.S. will remain a dominant world power. A credible EU security and defence policy will have to be based on actual strategies and plans. For now, the EU is indispensable to rationalising the European defence industry and enabling Member States to spend more on defence in the most efficient way. Coalitions of the willing will be helpful in specific situations and provide contributors with credibility and influence. However, they will not provide deterrence against Russia, the main threat to European security. Applying these principles requires nations to start working on the Europeanisation of NATO. What does that actually mean and how can we give actual meaning to a CSDP, beyond the current emphasis on industry and budgetary rules?

In light of this, the Dutch position is not without risk. Holding on to NATO for hard security on the one hand, while keeping the EU in a complementary role on the other, is likely to become more hazardous. The Netherlands risks becoming isolated. The fiscal concerns over ReArm and SAFE diminish Dutch capabilities to influence these initiatives and wider debate on the future of EU security and defence. On the NATO side, the same may happen. The Europeanisation of NATO will require concrete steps and may result in unprecedented change, requiring a more flexible and forward-leaning approach. There is another risk connected to resistance to policy change. The Netherlands may be forced to support and implement change as a result of unexpected events, such as the withdrawal of all U.S. troops from Europe or NATO altogether. Government and parliament have a responsibility to prepare society and individuals for change, as unpopular as that may be.

Nevertheless, there is also reason for optimism. Firstly, there is a broad consensus in Dutch society that the Netherlands has to deal with threats and improve the resilience of Dutch society against (hybrid) threats. Secondly, at the NATO summit in the Hague, the Netherlands has committed to spending 5% GDP on defence and related investments by 2035, hence the defence budget is set to rise steeply. Since 2023, reconstructing the Dutch armed forces has been well underway, refocusing on NATO capability targets. Finally, the coalition agreement of the new government (CDA, D66 and VVD, 30 January 2026) signals change. The Netherlands will support the establishment of a European pillar within NATO and the development of the EU as a geopolitical actor.

Auke Venema is Senior Research Fellow at the Clingendael Institute. His research focuses on security and defence issues, including the development of the European security architecture, EU-NATO relations, international defence cooperation and defence innovation.

Clingendael—the Netherlands Institute of International Relations—is an independent international affairs think tank and academy. Its activities include independent research, training programmes and events for governments, businesses and civil society.

EU Military and Defence Readiness 2030: The View from Albania

Odeta Barbullushi

Albania is a staunch supporter of the EU's military readiness and resilience plans in the face of Russian aggression against Ukraine. It has 100% alignment with the CFSP and contributes to a number of European operations and programmes. However, despite full alignment and compliance with the EU's plans to strengthen its security and defence posture, Albania's position has been one of critical awareness regarding three aspects: firstly, the necessity of including Western Balkans partners in European operations, mechanisms and financial programmes to face the challenge of readiness and resilience in military and security terms; secondly, the need to balance defence spending with spending on the economy and education, innovation and human capital; and thirdly, the need for Europe to become more assertive and unified rather than fragmented *vis-à-vis* others, including the U.S. This three-pronged official approach is also shaped by a medium threat public perception, which corresponds to 'yellow', under the traffic light analogy. In the Albania case, this means a higher sense of uncertainty because of the Russian threat, but seen not only through the prism of national security, but as a wider threat to the Alliance and Europe as a whole.

A Growing Sense of Uncertainty

The Russo-Ukrainian war has opened new opportunities for candidate countries by invigorating their accession prospects as well as paving new paths of enhanced cooperation in security and defence. Albania has capitalised on the so-called Ukraine momentum by accelerating work regarding accession negotiations;

O. Barbullushi (✉)
College of Europe, Tirana, Albania
e-mail: odeta.barbullushi@coleurope.eu

M. Kaeding et al. (eds.), *Security, Defence, and the Future of Europe*,
https://doi.org/10.1007/978-3-032-18279-1_28

doubling up on its diplomatic profile; enhancing its multilateral engagement; and strengthening strategic bilateral relations with EU Member States.

As part of the preparedness plans for a stronger European security and military arm, the White Paper endorsed at the European Council meeting in March 2025 proposes the launching of tailored partnerships with bilateral and multilateral partners across the globe to be enhanced, thereby addressing in a mutually beneficial way a wide range of security challenges, including those in the field of capability development and innovation. Such a proposal clearly paves the way for stronger partnerships with accession countries, particularly with NATO members.

Aimed at strengthening the EU's readiness in defence by 2030, the White Paper outlines seven areas in which European capacities should be strengthened, namely: Air and missile defence; Artillery systems; Ammunition and missiles; Drones and anti-drones systems; Military mobility; AI, quantum, cyber and electronic warfare; together with strategic enablers and critical infrastructure protection, including strategic airlift, air-to-air refuelling, maritime domain awareness and protection of space assets.

Albania views such attempts by the EU to strengthen its military and security arm from three perspectives: firstly, its objective for accelerated integration in the EU by 2030 and enhanced cooperation with the Union; secondly, its strategic partnership with the U.S, which is founded not just on pragmatism, but also on the historical ties between the two countries and the U.S. role in state-building of both Albania and Kosovo; and finally, its being a NATO member and security provider in the region of the Western Balkans. In this context, it is telling that according to the Regional Cooperation Council Security Barometer of 2024, when asked which security mechanism they think it the most important to address the current security challenges, 65% of Albanian respondents stated NATO, but only 20% quoted the EU. This three-vectors foreign and security policy is translated into various initiatives, aimed at strengthening the country's multilateral posture as well as demonstrating its willingness and capacity to contribute to European and transatlantic security.

However, it must be stressed that Albania does not feel particularly threatened by the war in Ukraine from a national perspective. According to the same survey, the low percentage of respondents fearing a war involving their country (36% not at all, 31% not much) demonstrates a low perception of its probability. This leaves another significant 23% of respondents answering that they are worried "a good deal" and a further 7% who are "very much" worried. These findings demonstrate a major shift from the public perceptions on the threat of war involving their country immediately after Russia's invasion of Ukraine. According to the Euronews Barometer streamed live on 14 April 2022, 61.30% of respondents stated that they were "worried that Albania could be involved in the war as a NATO member". However, referring to recent data from the Regional Cooperation Council Security Barometer, a majority of respondents from Albania think that there is a high probability of a war among Western Balkan countries (39%, responding that they are concerned "a good deal", and 14% "very much"). It can be argued that this reflects a deep-seated concern about the role of third actors such as Russia on regional security, as well as different levels of alignment with the 'Euro-Atlantic security community' among the region's countries.

Hence, one can speak of low threat perception regarding Russia, which falls in the 'green' zone under the traffic light system, when one looks at Albania-Russian dynamics. However, when viewed through European optics, the perception is in the 'yellow' zone, which means that Russia is perceived as a country which has and will continue to provoke the EU. Consequently, Europe as a whole and not Albania as an individual country is called upon to respond with a plan and strategy of peace, as the Albanian Prime Minister Edi Rama highlighted on a recent interview for Al Jazeera. This is an important distinction, as Albania's increased security alertness and awareness of the need for a stronger defence posture results from the country's alignment with CFSP, increased cooperation with the EU in the security front and its being an ally country.

Sense and Responsibility: Albania's Strategic Response

Albania has proven to be both a front-runner and a test case for the EU's vision of enhanced cooperation with non-members on security issues. Indeed, Albania continues to be part of the EU Mission in Bosnia and Herzegovina, Operation Althea and since November 2022, it has been a member of the EU Crisis Management Centre. Furthermore, Albania was the first country in the region to sign a bilateral agreement with Frontex in May 2019, allowing for joint actions on Albanian territory, a significant step that paved the way for other countries in the region to sign bilateral agreements with Frontex.

As a candidate, but as yet non-EU member, Albania's response to EU attempts at strengthening the security and defence posture of the Union has been to move in tandem with EU Member States, namely to invest in national industry and strengthen multilateral diplomacy, through enhanced cooperation with and engagement in regional, transatlantic and European platforms and initiatives.

Strengthening Multilateralist Posture and Strategic Partnerships

Albania has positioned itself as a regional champion of multilateralism, despite the differences among Western Balkan countries regarding alignment with the EU CFSP. In February 2024, Tirana hosted the Western Balkans-Ukraine Summit, where, together with Ukraine, it penned a statement that condemned the Russian aggression against Ukraine and committed to further supporting Ukraine. It is also here, in the framework of the Summit, that the Albanian Prime Minister flagged the idea of creating a national military industry. On a bilateral basis, Albania has endeavoured to support Ukraine both diplomatically and politically, as well as in tangible ways, such as offering to host war refugees immediately following the Russian invasion in 2022. It has joined all the EU sanction packages against Russia and in January 2025, co-signed with Ukraine the Agreement on Security Cooperation and long-term support between Ukraine and Albania.

As a NATO member, Albania has striven to present itself no longer as one of the ‘consumers of security’ in the region, but instead as one of the security providers, alongside North Macedonia and Montenegro, the two other NATO Allies in the Western Balkans. As a NATO member, Albania has asked both the Alliance and the EU to invest in completing major infrastructure projects, which would connect Albania’s maritime infrastructure with the EU and non-EU Adriatic countries, which are already NATO members.

On 4 March 2024, Albania inaugurated the transformation of Kuçova Airport into the first NATO tactical airbase in the Western Balkans. In May 2025, Albania hosted the European Political Community Summit, placing security at the heart of the agenda. Indeed, security was the key theme and focus in two out of three panels, combined with competitiveness and democratic resilience. In addition, Albania is the second country in the Western Balkans, alongside North Macedonia, to have signed a Defence and Security Partnership with the EU in December 2024. The first high-level dialogue regarding the Partnership took place during the EU Commission Vice President and High Representative and Kaja Kallas’ visit to Albania in March 2025. It has also been the beneficiary from two rounds of financial support through the European Peace Facility, a total of EUR 28 million.

On the bilateral front, Albania has endeavoured to sign ‘strategic partnerships’ with key EU and NATO Allies. Accordingly, in 2023 Prime Minister Rama signed a statement of Strategic Cooperation with the French President Emmanuel Macron in the following areas: digitalisation and innovation, public administration reform, local government capacity strengthening, security and military industry. Regarding critical infrastructure, ideas about French support to help build the Durres-Prishtina highway were also flagged during the bilateral visit of the French President, following the European Political Community Summit in Tirana during May 2025. In the framework of enhanced partnership regarding security between the two countries, in June 2025 the Albanian Minister of Defense (MoD) visited France and signed a contract with Thales Group, on the basis of which the Albanian Air Force will be equipped with a state-of-the-art radar system for national airspace surveillance.

In addition, Albania has recently pivoted to a process of modernising its military force and creating a basis of military industry. In the words of the Albanian MoD during the bilateral visit in Paris in 2025, the main priorities of the modernisation efforts of the Albanian military forces will be: “Developing a national defence industry, investing in dual-use systems, and training our personnel to operate them effectively”. Since 2024 the Albanian government has established KAYO, the first state-owned company to provide products and services for the Albanian military force, acting as the operating arm of the military sector.

As indicated in the National Security Strategy of 2024, Albania has increasingly focused on increasing investments in strategic areas of defence and security, such as cybersecurity, energy and maritime connectivity. At the moment, defence expenditure has just reached the 2% of GDP target, having raised its defence budget from 1.35% to 1.76% in the last decade, as indicated by the official website of the Ministry of Defence. Reaching the stretching 3.5% target and another 1.5% of GDP on infrastructure-related costs by 2035 is extremely challenging and will certainly have a significant impact on the economy.

Challenges, Dilemmas, and Recommendations

This is Albania's first attempt, as a small NATO country, to have a military industry, after the modernisation and reforms for NATO membership in 2007. There are many issues to resolve, mirroring pan-European challenges indicated in the White Paper, such as fragmented critical infrastructure, the impediments posed by red tape, the lack of finances, as well as limited human capital. These obstacles do not pertain only between the Western Balkans and the EU, but also between the regional countries themselves. At the Youth Charlemagne Prize ceremony event in Tirana in March 2025, the Albanian Prime Minister pointed out the risk of sidelining investment in human capital, education and youth because of increased expenditure in defence and security.

In this connection, Albania should focus on two interrelated initiatives. Firstly, the country should strengthen its human capital, particularly in policy areas such as cybersecurity and cyber defence. This necessity was also underlined by Minister of Defence Vengu in his remarks at the NATO Conference on Cyber Defence in Tirana. Secondly, close internal coordination is required on strategic planning for the increase in defence expenditure as well as defence and security-related infrastructure.

As a further recommendation, the EU needs to communicate as clearly as possible with Member States and candidate countries alike on the planned timeline of boosting defence and security-related expenditure and improve coordination on streamlining expenditure, particularly on critical infrastructure, with members who are also NATO members. Finally, the country must explore how much the EU can help with procurements, facilitation of disbursement of financial instruments for the building of critical infrastructure, as well as the building of capacities and strengthening of human capital. These are some of the questions to which the EU will need to respond by engaging in a joint conversation with the non-EU partner countries. Such dialogue would help to strengthen trust as well as a sense of ownership of the pro-European actors in the region regarding Europe's policies and, more broadly, European security.

Dr. Odeta Barbullushi is Resident Professor at the College of Europe, Tirana campus. Her academic work focuses primarily on processes of transformation, state-building and European integration of countries in Southeast Europe. Prior to joining the College of Europe, she served in the Albanian government for almost a decade, most recently as the Sherpa and Advisor on EU integration and regional cooperation to the Albanian Prime Minister. Dr. Barbullushi is a member of the Balkans in Europe Policy and Advocacy Group (BiEPAG) and the Mediterranean Women Mediators Network (MWMN).

The College of Europe is a post-graduate institute of European studies with three campuses in Bruges, Belgium; Natolin, Poland; and Tirana, Albania. The Tirana Campus was established in 2024 and is currently hosting the second cohort of MA students. The MA Programme in European Transformation and Integration offers in-depth knowledge on EU institutions, the history of the EU and enlargement policy, as well as political and economic transformations in Southeast Europe.

Between Wars and Worries: Why Bosnia and Herzegovina Needs a New Security Compass

Nerma Halilović-Kibrić

Three decades after the Yugoslav wars, Bosnia and Herzegovina still lacks a solid security and defence framework, with outdated 2006 and 2008 documents unable to address hybrid, cyber and geopolitical threats. Political elites exploit the sector for ethno-national agendas, while Russian influence, NATO divisions and an unclear European path exacerbate fragility. Only a new strategy, resilience against disinformation and modernisation of the armed forces can end stagnation and restore Bosnia's credibility in international security. According to the traffic light model of threat perception, Bosnia and Herzegovina currently falls within the 'yellow' zone, reflecting a medium level, where external influence and domestic weaknesses create sustained insecurity, but without any immediate prospect of conflict. Nonetheless, external influence and weak institutions keep Bosnia fragile and reflect Europe's broader dilemma.

Trapped in Two Decades of Outdated Security and Defence Policies: Bosnia and Herzegovina's Lost Direction

Bosnia and Herzegovina's security and defence policy has been drifting for nearly two decades. The 2006 and 2008 post-war documents, focusing on stabilising society and managing surplus military assets, are now outdated and misaligned with today's hybrid threats, cyber risks, energy shocks and geopolitical upheavals. The country's complex constitutional structure further hinders decision-making, leaving it vulnerable to political deadlock.

N. Halilović-Kibrić (✉)
University of Sarajevo, Faculty of Criminal Justice and Security Studies, Sarajevo, Bosnia and Herzegovina
e-mail: nhalilovic@fkn.unsa.ba

M. Kaeding et al. (eds.), *Security, Defence, and the Future of Europe*,
https://doi.org/10.1007/978-3-032-18279-1_29

The 30th anniversary meeting of the Dayton Peace Agreement in 2025 exposed Bosnia's institutional paralysis. International leaders stressed the importance and value of responsibility, sovereignty and integrity; the Dayton meeting should therefore have been both a reminder of peace and an opportunity for a new security vision. Instead, Bosnia once again demonstrated its lack of strategy, ambition and political courage. Political elites often exploit the security sector for ethno-national agendas, stalling reforms while the armed forces face chronic budget shortages; modernisation and training remain neglected. Raising defence spending to at least 1.5% of GDP from the current 0.9% is not a luxury, but a necessity, requiring public spending rationalisation and genuine political will. The European Commission warns in its reports that until depoliticisation takes root and investment increases, the armed forces of Bosnia and Herzegovina will not be ready to meet today's challenges or align with EU standards. The EU's White Paper provides a roadmap for modernisation, but without domestic political will, it remains merely symbolic.

From a Wall of Resistance to Cracks Within: NATO, the EU and Moscow's Shadow

In 2019, the message from the entity of Republika Srpska (RS) was unequivocal: over 80% of its citizens opposed Bosnia's NATO membership. By 2024, though, the picture had shifted. A recent survey by *Koalicija Pod Lupom* revealed that 23.2% now support NATO, while 63.4% remain opposed. Opposition still dominates, but it is no longer monolithic. Meanwhile, within the Federation of Bosnia and Herzegovina, NATO support remains overwhelming: 81.8% want Bosnia and Herzegovina inside the Alliance. This contrast is not new, but the subtle shifts inside RS are. Five years ago, there was virtually no 'grey' zone. NATO was almost an enemy symbol. However, today, 25% of RS citizens openly back Bosnia's NATO path.

While perceptions of NATO continue to evolve, the EU remains the unchallenged aspiration. Membership is supported by a strong majority across both Entities, the only genuine point of consensus in a divided society. Yet the paradox is clear: the EU is seen as a distant future, while NATO is perceived as a decision for tomorrow. These perceptions cannot be separated from external influence. Russia continues to play a decisive role, especially in RS, treating the Western Balkans as a theatre of geopolitical competition. Moscow openly backs RS politics aimed at blocking NATO integration, shaping narratives through media, propaganda and political alliances. The June 2024 opening of Russia's diplomatic office in Banja Luka, celebrated by Sergey Lavrov as a symbol of deepening ties with RS, underscored Moscow's challenge to Bosnia and Herzegovina's sovereignty and its alignment with EU foreign policy. This influence is mirrored in public opinion. A 2024 survey by the Center for Security Studies reveals a deeply divided Bosnia and Herzegovina, with 39% of citizens supporting Ukraine, 38% favouring neutrality and 14% backing Russia. Yet, within RS a striking 63.4% of respondents align with Moscow's position, highlighting the entrenchment of pro-Russian sentiment in the entity. These divided perceptions mirror Bosnia's overall 'yellow' zone threat assessment: while the country does not face an imminent military attack, persistent external interference and internal political fragility sustain a moderate level of perceived insecurity.

However, change is happening. Cracks in the 'wall of resistance' can no longer be ignored. Some RS citizens recognise that in a turbulent geopolitical world, security alliances may matter more than ideological battles. If this trend continues, Bosnia and Herzegovina could soon face a new reality, with NATO becoming less of a taboo and EU membership remaining the broadly accepted destination. The question is whether Bosnia will remain stuck between European integration and Russian influence, or whether those cracks will widen enough to let in a different future?

NATO, the EU and the American Factor: Where Does Bosnia and Herzegovina Stand?

Small and fragile, Bosnia feels the gaps of European engagement more acutely than most. Positioned at the crossroads of Brussels, Washington and Moscow, European security is not abstract; it is a lived reality. Despite the modest scope of its capabilities, Bosnia and Herzegovina holds a noteworthy symbolic significance, as reflected in its participation in missions such as the EU Training Mission in the Central African Republic and in regional frameworks such as the Balkan Medical Forces, which collectively underscore its commitment to multilateral security cooperation. Yet the presence of Operation Althea and NATO as peace guarantors highlights a crucial point: without active European engagement, local institutions struggle to maintain stability. The absence of compulsory military service since 2006, coupled with ongoing debates over establishing a reserve component, further illustrates the challenges Bosnia faces in building robust national defence capabilities and highlights reliance on external actors for security.

Talk of a European army resurfaces from time to time, but Bosnia's experience shows how a limited EU focus on the Western Balkans leaves the country exposed. Russian influence in RS and ongoing disinformation campaigns underscore the risks of neglect. In moments of crisis, Member States invariably turn to Washington. However, America's guarantee has never been unconditional and today, with new global rivalries, the question is how long the U.S. will remain engaged. Ukraine proves the point: without U.S. support, Kyiv's resistance would have collapsed. The same applies to Bosnia: without the American factor, European institutions cannot counter external pressures or prevent domestic political blockades from destabilising the country.

No immediate armed conflict looms, but external influence, weak institutions and hybrid threats leave Bosnia in a state of chronic vulnerability. The country is a lens through which Europe's broader dilemma becomes visible: can the EU truly act as a security pillar in its own backyard, or will it remain absent when it matters most? For now, the answer is grim: strategic autonomy may sound promising on paper, but without active engagement, Bosnia's security depends on others.

Recommendations: From Stagnation to Strategic Vision

Bosnia and Herzegovina faces an urgent need to modernise its security framework and strengthen its capacity to respond to contemporary threats. The first step is adopting a new security and defence strategy that clearly defines its Euro-Atlantic trajectory, aligning national and entity-level policies and thereby reducing the space for political manipulation. Such a strategy must go beyond declarative commitments and instead set measurable goals, timelines and responsibilities for implementation. A transparent and inclusive drafting process, bringing together government institutions, academia and civil society would also help rebuild public trust and demonstrate a shared vision of national security.

Bosnia and Herzegovina's information space remains highly fragmented and vulnerable to manipulation, particularly through foreign-backed media networks and social platforms. Strengthening media literacy, supporting independent journalism and improving communication between security institutions and the public are essential steps. Universities, think tanks and the media sector should jointly develop educational programmes and campaigns that enhance public understanding of hybrid threats. Information has become a strategic domain of conflict and resilience begins with an informed and critically aware society.

At an institutional level, Bosnia must invest in interoperability, preparedness, and capacity-building. This means enhancing the armed forces' operational readiness, improving cyber defence capabilities and introducing comprehensive crisis response mechanisms that integrate civilian and military components. A strong and credible military force is not an instrument of aggression, but a guarantee of sovereignty. Increasing defence spending to at least 1.5% of GDP, modernising equipment and ensuring continual training in line with NATO standards are necessary not only for operational effectiveness, but also for Bosnia's credibility as a reliable regional partner.

Finally, the political leadership must show strategic courage. Security cannot remain hostage to ethno-political bargaining. Bosnia's leaders must prioritise citizens' safety and the country's long-term stability over short-term political gains. As Zbigniew Brzezinski once said: "Geopolitics does not forgive ignorance and does not reward indecision." Every delay incurs strategic costs and widens the gap between Bosnia and its European peers. A comprehensive security reset is therefore no longer an option, but an immediate necessity, one that demands clarity of vision, unity of purpose and sustained political will.

Nerma Halilović-Kibrić is Assistant Professor at the University of Sarajevo, Faculty of Criminal Justice and Security Studies, specialising in Security Culture, Intelligence Methods, Crisis Communication and Hybrid Warfare. She holds a Ph.D. in Security Sciences (2019) and has contributed extensively to the field through publications, research projects and academic supervision.

Her expertise is recognised both nationally and internationally and she has been awarded top honours for her scholarly achievements.

The Faculty of Criminal Justice and Security Studies at the University of Sarajevo, part of the oldest university in Bosnia and Herzegovina, offers education and research in criminalistics, criminology and security studies through three departments. It not only prepares professionals to address contemporary security and justice challenges, but also collaborates with domestic and international institutions.

Georgia's Wartime Shift: Isolated from the West, Left Alone with Russia

Irakli Sirbiladze

Amid the war in Ukraine, Georgia's governing party has undermined the fundamentals of an independent Georgia: its democracy and its ties with the West. Georgians perceive the risk of war with Russia as continuing to be high, 'red' according to the traffic lights system, yet the government's response to the threat shows bandwagoning rather than preparation. Anti-democratic and anti-Western actions of the ruling party leave Georgia isolated from the West and alone with Russia—outcomes at odds with public preferences. In an autocratising Georgia, where elections are no longer free and fair with dissent suppressed, citizens are increasingly becoming the consumers of an elite-driven politics rather than its architects. Such a Georgia is losing vital defence and security cooperation with the West, remaining outside the developing European security architecture and navigating an increasingly unstable world on its own.

The Fundamentals of Georgia Under Revision

Since regaining independence in 1991, Georgia has looked westward in its foreign policy alignment and defence cooperation. All Georgian governments have committed to closer ties with the U.S. as well as integration into NATO and the EU, an aspiration sustained even after Russia's aggression in 2008. Security and defence cooperation also deepened. Georgia's participation in international security missions from Iraq and Afghanistan to Mali and the Central African Republic, regular joint exercises with NATO Member States, as well as bilateral training programmes with the U.S., made the Georgian army better equipped and more aligned with NATO standards. The result was deepening security, political, economic and

I. Sirbiladze (✉)
PMC Research Centre, Tbilisi, Georgia

M. Kaeding et al. (eds.), *Security, Defence, and the Future of Europe*,
https://doi.org/10.1007/978-3-032-18279-1_30

societal ties with the West, albeit without credible guarantees from the U.S. or NATO to defend Georgia against an aggressive Russia.

The traditional foreign and security policy alignment with the West is now under revision. Following the war in Ukraine, major aspects of Georgian-Western relations are crumbling due to the governing party's anti-democratic turn at home and anti-Western stance abroad. In 2024, the U.S. suspended its strategic partnership with Georgia, paused military exercises and sanctioned Georgian authorities, while the Trump administration has so far left this *status quo* unchanged. The EU, which granted Georgia candidate status at the end of 2023, likewise suspended high-level political engagement with Tbilisi and froze military support under the European Peace Facility. While Georgia is taking some measures in its defence policy—such as requiring conscripts to complete their mandatory military service exclusively within the Ministry of Defence and increasing the defence budget in 2025—its security ties with the West are shrinking, putting the country's long-term security at risk.

Georgia's rapid autocratisation has turned politics—including foreign and security policies—into a realm of the ruler rather than the ruled. Throughout 2024 and 2025, the Georgian Dream party has failed to organise free and fair elections, restricted civic space, imprisoned political party leaders as well as peaceful protesters and adopted a law which allows rival political parties to be banned from participating in politics. Restrictions on foreign funding have also undermined the functioning of civil society organisations. Georgia is now an electoral autocracy in which politics has become a top-down, elite-driven exercise rather than a representative reflection of citizens' preferences. This transformation has affected Georgia's foreign policymaking as well. State institutions now convey the foreign policy preferences of the Georgian Dream party and its leader, Bidzina Ivanishvili. A case in point is that although Georgian Dream declaredly prioritised EU accession prior to the 2024 parliamentary elections, it reneged on this promise by announcing a halt to the EU accession process after the elections—a move that triggered widespread protests. All politics in Georgia is now partisan.

Wartime Behaviour: Lying Low Amid High Threat Perception

The Georgian public's threat perception of Russia is certainly 'red' according to the traffic light system. Citizens view Russia as capable of militarily overwhelming Georgia—a perception shared by political elites across the political spectrum. However, preparedness for a potential conflict does not correspond to this high threat perception, as it would require enhancing military capabilities and preparing the broader public for the possibility of war. In contrast, the governing party's level of preparedness, reflecting its own threat perception, falls into the 'green' category: securitisation of the potential adversary is minimal and no meaningful measures have been taken to strengthen defences. Bandwagoning with the threat source—in this case, Russia—is viewed as the most effective means of ensuring survival. By comparison, strengthening defence and military ties with Russia's geopolitical rivals is considered a riskier course of action.

Various public opinion polls show Georgians perceiving Russia as a military threat, whilst acknowledging the need to maintain relations. According to a National Democratic Institute poll, before the war in Ukraine, 71% of Georgians saw Russia as a military threat, a figure that rose to 85% soon afterwards. Another poll by the International Republican Institute shows that, from 2014 to 2023, a significant majority of Georgians believed that Russia's aggression toward Georgia was still ongoing. The same poll indicates that between 2016 and 2021, most Georgians favoured a pro-Western foreign policy course while also supporting continued relations with Russia. Since the 2022 war in Ukraine, though, only 33% of Georgians want relations with Russia to be maintained, while most favour an exclusively pro-EU and pro-Western foreign policy. A June 2025 poll by the Institute of Social Studies and Analysis (ISSA) shows that only 6% of Georgians think Georgian Dream is pursuing integration with the West, while 30% believe that Georgia is pursuing a balanced foreign policy.

As Russia unleashed its war against Ukraine, Georgia's governing party pursued military neutrality and avoided economic or political actions that could provoke Moscow. This reflects the ruling Georgian Dream party's core stance that Georgia must recognise the Russian threat and avoid punching above its weight in dealing with it. According to a National Democratic Institute poll of February–March 2022, most Georgians were satisfied with their leaders' response and half approved the government's decision not to impose economic sanctions on Russia. However, a 2023 study by Caucasus Research Resource Center—Georgia shows that Georgians are not willing to sacrifice Western integration, territories, or independence to avoid Russian military aggression. A June 2025 ISSA poll shows that 47% of Georgians agree that Georgian Dream has kept the country out of a war with Russia, while 45% disagree.

Georgian Dream has, though, moved beyond caution in its relationship with Moscow, further deepening Georgia's economic dependence on and ideological alignment with Russia. The governing party has welcomed Russian immigrants, benefited from Western sanctions on Russia as Georgia's transit value grew and new trade arrangements expanded its role in re-exporting goods to Central Asia, embracing both the restoration of direct flights and Russia's introduction of a visa-free regime for Georgians. Political relations remain formally constrained due to the 2008 war and Russia's recognition of Georgia's territories of Abkhazia and the Tskhinvali Region/South Ossetia. Yet ties between business elites in both countries are growing, there is discursive alignment between the two countries in promoting anti-Western narratives and an official channel of interaction between Georgian and Russian political elites is maintained. A June 2025 poll by ISSA shows that 55% of Georgians view the government's foreign policy orientation as serving the interests of Russia and its allies.

Isolated from the West

Georgia's ties with Russia are growing while those with the West are deteriorating. Since the war in Ukraine, Georgian Dream has eroded democracy at home while promoting anti-Western discourse and actions. This has brought relations with the

EU and the U.S. to their lowest point. The party has spread conspiracy theories, claiming that a so-called deep state directs the EU and U.S. to drag Georgia into war with Russia. An ISSA 2025 poll shows that a majority of the public rejects the idea of deep state influence, while an EU-commissioned 2025 poll shows 74% of Georgians supporting EU membership.

Georgia under Georgian Dream is absent from the new European security awakening, exacerbated by the Trump administration's decision to leave Europe to its own devices on security. Georgia's absence primarily results from the governing party's policies. Growing autocratisation and rampant anti-EU discourse make it impossible to keep Georgia involved in emerging security and defence initiatives. Georgian Dream views the European security awakening as an obstacle to peace rather than a deterrent to Russia. Georgia's alignment rate with the EU's foreign, security and defence policies stands at 40% in 2025, compared to 53% in 2024. At the same time, the EU itself remains ambivalent about its security role and the reach of its developing security umbrella. While defence integration initiatives are important steps toward making the EU an autonomous security actor, it is unlikely that the Union can provide a traditional security guarantee even to its Member States, let alone to enlargement countries. Although ad hoc initiatives such as the 'Coalition of the willing' may fulfil such functions, Georgia is hardly on their agenda.

Georgian Dream's attempt to mend ties with the U.S. is proving futile, threatening the basic security needs of the Georgian state. Georgia's security partnership with the U.S. has been put on hold due to the deterioration of ties between the Biden administration and Georgian Dream. While Georgia still hosted a multinational military exercise in July 2025, relations nevertheless remain low under the Trump administration. Although Georgia is unlikely to secure a credible U.S. security guarantee, it is losing vital security cooperation that could strengthen its defences in an increasingly insecure world.

Recommendations

While the ruling Georgian Dream party pursues an isolationist foreign policy that leaves Georgia at Russia's mercy, future Georgian governments—elected democratically through free and fair elections—should consolidate democracy, mend ties with the EU and U.S. and ensure Georgia's security by strengthening institutional defence and security cooperation with Brussels, Washington and London.

While designing a new European security architecture, mindful of a revisionist Russia and an absent U.S., the EU should address its decision-making bottlenecks to make full use of defence integration projects. Together with the UK, France should prioritise developing joint nuclear deterrence to provide a security umbrella for Europe.

The EU should develop a comprehensive security strategy to incorporate the enlargement states actively, including democratic Georgia, into its emerging security framework. Securing Ukraine, Moldova and Georgia—states key to Russia's imperial ambitions—is vital in deterring future Russian revisionism.

Irakli Sirbiladze is Affiliated Researcher at the PMC Research Centre in Tbilisi and holds an MA degree in International Relations from Queen Mary University of London. His research interests include Georgia's foreign policy, the EU and Eurasia.

Founded in 2010, the PMC Research Centre undertakes studies in the fields of economics, politics, energy, good governance and social security. By combining global and local expertise, the Centre elaborates research-based policy options focused on economic development as well as accountable and transparent democratic governance. Through international cooperation, research and advocacy activities, PMC brings together representatives of academia, civil society organisations, government and industry. The Centre is also a member of TEPSA.

Iceland's Security: A New European Dimension

Baldur Thorhallsson

Iceland's security rests on NATO and U.S. guarantees, but rising threats and President Trump's unpredictability, together with his renewed quest to acquire Greenland, have pushed Reykjavík to diversify its security partnerships. Security and defence cooperation with European states has intensified, with EU-Iceland negotiations on a Security and Defence Partnership awaiting signature and a referendum on resuming EU accession negotiations scheduled for August 2026. On the traffic-light scale of threat perception, Iceland remains on 'yellow'; in other words, credible shelter is available, but critical vulnerabilities remain unresolved.

Strategic Location and Increased Threat

Iceland is the only NATO member without an army, relying instead on alliance guarantees and hosting arrangements at the Security Zone in Keflavík. Rotational Allied air policing missions now punctuate the calendar, with high-end U.S. bombers and naval activity underscoring Keflavík's role in shielding the GIUK gap (stretching between Greenland-Iceland-UK). These moves signal that, while Iceland has no combat forces, its air and maritime space remain pivotal to allied deterrence.

Cyber incidents in Iceland have risen sharply: in 2024, there were a record eight major ransomware attacks against Icelandic institutions. Authorities warned again in 2025 that ransomware had doubled for the fourth year running and that cyberattacks, Distributed Denial of Service attacks and credential theft were the most likely risks facing the country. For a highly digitalised island dependent on subsea cables and real-time data links, this is not a theoretical threat, but a structural vulnerability.

B. Thorhallsson (✉)
University of Iceland, Reykjavik, Iceland
e-mail: baldurt@hi.is

M. Kaeding et al. (eds.), *Security, Defence, and the Future of Europe*,
https://doi.org/10.1007/978-3-032-18279-1_31

From Neighbourly Cooperation to a European Dimension

Reykjavík has responded along three tracks. Firstly, it has deepened practical cooperation with close neighbours. Iceland has enhanced its participation in the Nordic Defence Cooperation and, for the first time, takes part in its military side. Iceland also participates in the UK-led JEF, the high-readiness coalition of 10 Northern European states. For Reykjavík, the JEF provides direct operational ties to capable Nordic, Baltic and British partners, allowing Iceland to contribute politically to rapid-response planning in the North Atlantic, the High North and the Baltic Sea. While Iceland cannot field forces, participation in JEF exercises and decision-making strengthen its role as a security stakeholder and reinforce its strategic partnerships beyond NATO.

Secondly, Iceland has moved to plug into the EU's emerging security instruments. During European Commission President Ursula von der Leyen's visit to Reykjavík in July 2025, the EU and Iceland launched negotiations on a Security and Defence Partnership that covers hybrid threats, cybersecurity, civil protection, secure communications and protection of critical infrastructure. The Commission framed this as deepening ties with a strategic North-Atlantic partner; Reykjavík stresses that the partnership complements, rather than replaces, NATO and the close U.S. relationship. The push towards Europe is reinforced by political uncertainty in Washington. Trump's rhetoric questioning a U.S. commitment to European defence and the value of NATO, along with his aggressive push regarding Greenland (Iceland's geographically closest country), has caused unease in Reykjavík, where policymakers view Nordic and EU partnerships as an insurance policy. A milestone in 2025 was the parliamentary committee's work on security and defence policy, mandated to draft a long-term framework for Iceland's national security. In its September 2025 report, the committee stressed that Iceland's structural vulnerability requires closer integration with both the EU and the Nordic states. It highlighted the importance of deepening collaboration through Nordic Defence Cooperation and Iceland's involvement in JEF. The committee's report is important not only because it provides a rare comprehensive strategy for Iceland's security, but also because it lays the political groundwork for integrating Iceland into European security and defence structures while maintaining NATO and the U.S. as its cornerstone. Political discourse in Iceland, though, will probably continue to grapple with the question of EU membership, particularly with respect to economic implications and issues of national sovereignty.

Thirdly, Iceland has strengthened its security and defence ties with Washington. There are no indications that the Trump administration intends to depart from the bilateral Defence Agreement between the two countries. On the contrary, officials in the Ministry for Foreign Affairs emphasise that the security and defence dialogue between Reykjavík and Washington has never been closer. The U.S. continues to stand firmly by its guarantees, viewing Iceland's strategic location as vital to its own defence.

Pro-NATO and Strong Support for Ukraine

Icelanders remain clearly pro-NATO: an April 2025 national Gallup poll reported roughly 71% support for staying in the Alliance, with under 30% opposed or unsure. At the same time, a large majority of respondents, around 72%, oppose creating a national army, with only 14% in favour. In short, the public backs Allied shelter, but resists militarisation.

Recent polling illustrates that Icelanders are increasingly looking towards Europe: in March 2025, 44.3% supported EU membership (35.6% opposed), while 58% favoured holding a referendum to restart accession negotiations. At the same time, around 74% considered Trump's calls to 'get' Greenland and his wider Arctic ambitions a threat, signalling profound concern about U.S. intentions in the region. These figures show why Iceland's leaders increasingly see European cooperation as essential to diversifying security shelter.

Ukraine has become the litmus test of Iceland's willingness to underwrite European security. Parliament approved a 2024–2028 framework for long-term support to Ukraine, spanning humanitarian, economic and defence-related aid. Reykjavík has financed fuel trucks and winter gear, joined the Czech-led artillery ammunition initiative with about EUR 2 million, trained Ukrainian naval cadets and increased defence-related support by approximately EUR 14.5 million in 2025 alone. These steps enjoy broad parliamentary backing, but they have sparked debate at home, especially over participating in ammunition purchases, given Iceland's lack of a military force.

Iceland has committed to meeting NATO's target of allocating 1.5% of GDP to defence-related infrastructure (civilian defence and resilience) by 2035. The government estimates that it already spends about half of this amount on relevant projects. Currently, Iceland's defence expenditure stands at 0.14% of GDP, well below NATO's 2% benchmark for core defence and the new 3.5% goal for 2035. Owing to its unique status as the only NATO member without a standing army, Iceland was for a long time exempt from any defence spending. A dedicated military budget emerged only after the U.S. closed its Keflavík base in 2006. Since then, expenditure has gradually increased under pressure from allies and in recognition of the need to contribute to collective security.

On the traffic-light scale of threat perception, Iceland remains at 'yellow': credible shelter is available, but critical vulnerabilities remain unresolved.

Recommendations

Deepen EU cooperation as a hedge against U.S. uncertainty. Given Donald Trump's scepticism toward NATO and threats against Greenland, as well as uncertainty surrounding U.S. defence commitments in Europe, Iceland must diversify its shelter. Closer ties with the EU through the new Security and Defence Partnership, cyber initiatives and civil protection cooperation offer insurance against a wavering U.S. For the EU, Iceland adds critical North Atlantic infrastructure and strategic depth.

Develop EU-Iceland cooperation on civil protection and critical infrastructure. Joint investment in monitoring and protecting undersea cables, ports and energy grids would reduce Iceland's vulnerabilities and contribute to Europe's resilience. Iceland's geographic position makes it a natural testbed for dual-use infrastructure that serves both civilian and defence needs.

Anchor Iceland in the EU's Arctic and North Atlantic security policies. By linking its Arctic expertise and hosting role at Keflavík to EU planning, Iceland ensures that the Union's emerging defence dimension has reach into the North Atlantic. For the EU, this strengthens transatlantic deterrence; for Iceland, it adds another pillar of shelter beyond NATO and Washington.

Baldur Thorhallsson, Ph.D., is Professor of Political Science at the Faculty of Political Science, as well as Programme and Research Director at the Centre for Small State Studies at the Institute of International Affairs, University of Iceland in Reykjavik. His research focuses primarily on small state studies, European integration and Iceland's foreign policy. He has published extensively in international journals and written and edited several books on small states.

The Institute of International Affairs (IIA) is a research, teaching and service institute in the field of international relations, European integration and small states at the University of Iceland. IIA is a member of TEPSA.

Kosovo's Security Challenges: Between Progress, Fragility and Uncertainty

Jeta Loshaj

Kosovo's post-independence trajectory shows important progress in the context of consolidating statehood and international integration, but it remains constrained because relations with Serbia have yet to be fully normalised. As a result, Kosovo's integration in the international community is incomplete. Public threat perception, according to the traffic-light system, is 'red' for Serbia's asymmetric actions and hybrid threats, 'yellow' for Russia's hybrid influence and its strategic alignment with Belgrade and 'green' for internal political divisions and the stagnated process of normalising relations with Serbia, which the population views as a lower but persistent risk. NATO, through the Kosovo Force (KFOR) mission, is a major stabilising presence. Nonetheless, the Banjska attack in September 2023 showed how Serbia, which is politically supported by Russia, continues to pose asymmetric and hybrid threats. Addressing these vulnerabilities requires Kosovo to strengthen Euro-Atlantic integration, foster domestic consensus on the normalisation of relations with Serbia and implementation of the existing agreements and project credibility as a rational actor.

To synthesise the complex security landscape, Kosovo's principal security risks can thus be ranked according to their severity. Firstly, Serbia's asymmetric actions and hybrid threats represent the highest risk and the most direct challenge to Kosovo's stability, as they also undermine the integration of Kosovo Serbs within Kosovo's institutions. Secondly, Russia's footprint in Serbia and support for Belgrade and its disinformation activities represent a medium risk, amplifying instability without direct confrontation. Finally, domestic polarisation and political divisions, including those caused by the dialogue for normalisation of relations with Serbia and implementation of the agreements from this process, present a persistent

J. Loshaj (✉)
Kosovar Centre for Security Studies, Prishtina, Kosovo
e-mail: jeta.loshaj@qkss.org

M. Kaeding et al. (eds.), *Security, Defence, and the Future of Europe*,
https://doi.org/10.1007/978-3-032-18279-1_32

low risk. This undermines institutional resilience and limits Kosovo's ability to consolidate its statehood and advance its Euro-Atlantic integration aspirations.

Tracing the National Context

To understand Kosovo's current security landscape, it is important to consider the historical context of the past three decades. In light of the Yugoslav wars, which resulted in the largest mass killing of civilians in Europe since the Second World War, the Srebrenica Genocide, NATO launched a military intervention in March 1999 to stop ethnic cleansing in Kosovo. Kosovo was subsequently placed under UN administration, pending a settlement of its political status. This process resulted in the Comprehensive Proposal for the Kosovo Status Settlement (Ahtisaari Plan), which provided the framework for Kosovo's declaration of independence in 2008.

In 2010, the International Court of Justice confirmed that its declaration of independence did not violate international law, providing important legitimacy to its statehood. International supervision of independence concluded in 2012 and in 2013 Prime Ministers from Kosovo and Serbia signed the First Agreement of Principles Governing the Normalisation of Relations in the framework of EU-led dialogue, while the Stabilisation and Association Agreement between Kosovo and the EU began in 2016. Kosovo has been regarded as a positive example of international intervention and post-conflict state-building. Its close cooperation with the EU, U.S., and other Western partners helped it secure recognition from 120 countries. On 17 February 2026, Kosovo marked 18 years of statehood, throughout which it has made important gains in developing as a liberal democracy.

While Kosovo continues to face challenges that are familiar across the Western Balkans, its situation is also unique; the country is still not recognised by all UN members, including five EU Member States, and Serbia continues to reject the right of Kosovo to exist as an independent state. Serbia's position, supported politically and at times strategically by Russia and China, remains the main security challenge for Kosovo today. Serbia's national security strategy places Kosovo as its single most important challenge. Serbia maintains an aggressive posture towards Kosovo both nominally and at times also through actions, seeking to regain Kosovo through military means, included repeated requests to NATO return up to 1000 Serbian military personnel to Kosovo, which the Alliance rejected. Therefore, when assessing Kosovo's principal security challenges, Serbia is regarded as Kosovo's foremost security threat, a position often reinforced by Serbia's historical and ongoing support from Russia. Serbia's fierce opposition to Kosovo has also led to challenges in the integration of Kosovo Serbs in institutions, which poses a challenge for social cohesion and the democratic functioning of the state.

Before elaborating further on the severity of both external and internal threats to Kosovo, it is important to describe the security establishment in the country. With the end of the war in 1999, NATO deployed a military mission (KFOR) to Kosovo, which is an international peacekeeping force with around 5000 troops. KFOR is a vital security actor in Kosovo and is welcomed by both Kosovo Albanians and

Serbs, as well as other non-majority communities. In the north of Kosovo, where four Serb-majority municipalities are located and Kosovo shares a 380 km border with Serbia, an area often prone to interethnic tensions, KFOR's presence is essential for security and stability.

Internally, Kosovo established the Kosovo Security Force (KSF) in 2018 with a 10-year transition plan to develop a multiethnic, professional and NATO-interoperable defence force. While Kosovo does not have mandatory military service, KSF currently has 4300 troops (via voluntary enlistment) with a target of 7500 personnel by the end of the transition in 2027. Kosovo's Ministry of Defence has also increased defence spending, especially in the aftermath of Russia's full-scale invasion of Ukraine. Kosovo has also focused on bilateral military cooperation, seeking to advance partnerships with the U.S., Turkey, and more recently, Albania and Croatia. With high pro-NATO sentiment and growth in defence investments (EUR 155 million in 2024 and a projected EUR 208 million in 2025), Kosovo is clear about its commitment to eventual NATO membership with 83% of the population in support as well as 89% supporting EU membership. However, the lack of a credible perspective for Kosovo to advance relations with NATO (due to four Member States not recognising Kosovo's independence and relations with Serbia yet to be normalised) continues to expose Kosovo to security vulnerabilities.

Serbia's Hybrid Threats and the Banjska Attack: Kosovo's Main Security Challenge

The first and most significant dimension of Kosovo's security landscape concerns Serbia, which remains the principal external challenge. Serbia represents the highest security threat to Kosovo, both in terms of its intentions and actions, with 76% of citizens perceiving Serbia as the greatest threat to the country's security, followed by Russia. In its national security strategy, Serbia continues to regard Kosovo as occupied territory and has at times engaged in military provocation. In 2023, for example, a Serbian troop build-up along the border with Kosovo prompted the U.S. to issue a public call for withdrawal. On 24 September 2023, a Serbian paramilitary group carried out a terrorist attack resulting in the killing of a Kosovo Police officer and the group taking refuge in the Banjska monastery. The assault, thwarted by Kosovo Police and KFOR, raised serious questions about the level of involvement of the Serbian security apparatus. Both the EU and Kosovo classified the incident as a terrorist attack and the goal seemed to have been the creation of a 'Donbas scenario'. Milan Radoičić, a senior figure in the Serbian List, the main Serbian political party in Kosovo, claimed responsibility for orchestrating the attack, yet remains free in Serbia.

The Banjska terrorist attack stands as one of the most serious security challenges to Kosovo since the March 2004 riots. However, while the attack marked a serious escalation, it should be viewed as an exception rather than a pattern of conventional aggression, as any direct military offensive by Serbia against Kosovo would effectively constitute an attack on NATO, given the presence of KFOR troops in the country. Thus, this reality makes large-scale Serbian military action unlikely, even though hybrid tactics and asymmetric threats remain a persistent risk. Accordingly, from Kosovo's perspective, the Banjska attack, and other security incidents in the north, such as the attack on critical civilian infrastructure in November 2024 are seen as provocations and hybrid warfare tactics from Serbia. This, from Kosovo's perspective is about Serbia's intentions to foster instability in the country and prevent consolidation of authority of Kosovo institutions in Serb-majority areas.

Russia's Influence in the Western Balkans and Its Strategic Alliance with Serbia

The second major security risk for Kosovo stems from Russia's role in sustaining insecurity in the broader Western Balkans. As Serbia's most trusted political and military ally, Russia works closely with Belgrade to undermine the international consensus on Kosovo's independence and weaken its international standing. Moscow has even attempted to use both NATO's intervention in Kosovo and Kosovo's independence as precedents to justify its own actions in the so-called 'Near Abroad'. Through its extensive diplomatic, military, cultural and economic ties with Serbia, Russia sustains a strong presence in the Western Balkans. Unsurprisingly, Russia's invasion of Ukraine in 2022 resulted in growing fears of conflict in the Western Balkans. Disinformation campaigns increased, which fuelled a perception that the Western Balkans could be used by Russia to create a second front for NATO and the EU, to draw resources and attention away from Ukraine.

Kosovo's Internal Political Divisions and the Persistent Challenge of Normalising Relations with Serbia

Apart from these external threats, Kosovo faces internal challenges and this includes the third dimension of risks, which is about domestic political divisions and the lack of normalisation of relations with Serbia. The unresolved dispute with Serbia remains a persistent challenge on many fronts for Kosovo. Most significant is Serbia's categorical refusal to recognise Kosovo's independence. However, part of the problem stems from a lack of consensus in Kosovo about implementing agreements from the dialogue and potential solutions that could lead to normalising relations and mutual recognition. This issue and a lack of full integration within the international community exacerbate this situation have led to heightened political uncertainty. Lack of recognition by five EU Member States and four NATO Allies constrains the capacity of Kosovo to integrate fully into Euro-Atlantic structures. In recent years, the situation has become even further polarised, leaving the country more isolated and prone to instability and even strained relations with Euro-Atlantic allies.

Recommendations

To counter these threats, Kosovo should strengthen security cooperation and deterrence. Prishtina should deepen defence cooperation with NATO and key allies, pursue participation in the Partnership for Peace programme and enhance coordination with KFOR to deter and respond effectively to Serbia's hybrid threats.

Another urgent action to counter malign influence and disinformation would be to establish a national coordination mechanism involving institutions, civil society and media to counter Russian-backed disinformation, build media resilience and align strategic communication with Euro-Atlantic partners.

Finally, Kosovo should build consensus and advance normalisation processes. It is crucial for the country to foster cross-party consensus on dialogue with Serbia, including the implementation of existing agreements, while intensifying diplomatic efforts for wider recognition and closer Euro-Atlantic integration.

Jeta Loshaj is a researcher at the Kosovar Centre for Security Studies (KCSS). She holds an MA in Russian and East European Studies from Indiana University Bloomington and a BA in Public Policy and International Relations from RIT Kosovo. Her experience includes work with the German Parliament, Friedrich Ebert Stiftung and the Council for Inclusive Governance. Jeta's research focuses on Russian influence in the Western Balkans and Kosovo's foreign relations. She has published widely on malign influence, interethnic narratives and Kosovo's NATO integration.

The Kosovar Centre for Security Studies is an independent policy research centre founded in 2008 in Prishtina. It focuses on security sector reform and development in Kosovo and the Western Balkans, promoting good governance, integrity and resilience. For 18 years, KCSS has provided alternative expertise through research, training, advocacy and policy advice. It publishes numerous reports and policy analyses annually. KCSS also organises public events, often in cooperation with regional and international partners.

Liechtenstein: Without Protection, but also Without Worries

Christian Frommelt

What characteristics do you associate with Liechtenstein? This question was posed to its residents in June 2024 as part of the Lie-Barometer survey. The most frequently cited characteristic was safety, followed by home and prosperity. When asked specifically about their assessment of the current situation, 43% of respondents rated safety in Liechtenstein as "very good" and 47% as "fairly good". Only 5% considered safety in Liechtenstein to be "rather poor" or "very poor". There is no doubt that the population feels safe in Liechtenstein. According to the traffic light system of threat perception, Liechtenstein is positioned between 'green' and 'yellow'.

Small and at the Heart of Europe

With just under 40,000 inhabitants and an area of 160 km², Liechtenstein is one of the smallest countries in Europe, bordering the two neutral states of Austria and Switzerland. Its small size and geographical location make Liechtenstein strategically irrelevant in global politics. This may explain why issues of defence and security have not been of great importance in the country's politics to date.

Liechtenstein does not have its own army. Although the constitution obliges every citizen capable of bearing arms to defend the country in times of emergency, Liechtenstein has not had a military in place since 1868. It is also not a member of any defence alliance and has no military protecting power, albeit Switzerland, with which Liechtenstein has close ties through numerous treaties, could best fulfil this role. In fact, Liechtenstein benefits greatly from its cooperation with Switzerland in the area of civil protection, for instance, in the prevention of natural hazards,

C. Frommelt (✉)
University of Liechtenstein, Vaduz, Liechtenstein
e-mail: christian.frommelt@uni.li

M. Kaeding et al. (eds.), *Security, Defence, and the Future of Europe*,
https://doi.org/10.1007/978-3-032-18279-1_33

economic supply and rescue services. However, Switzerland's neutrality precludes it from providing military protection should Liechtenstein be attacked. This puts Liechtenstein in the unique situation of being unable to protect itself and having no protecting power to rely on. Its entire security strategy is therefore based on the idea that Liechtenstein is not relevant enough to be attacked by another state.

Diffuse Self-Image

Liechtenstein declared its neutrality during the Second World War. Unlike Switzerland, though, neutrality in Liechtenstein has no permanent legal basis and thus must be declared in each case of conflict. In this respect, therefore, one can speak of *de facto* neutrality at most.

In light of recent geopolitical developments, the issue of neutrality and, more generally, Liechtenstein's self-image in terms of security policy has been the subject of increased debate. This was also prompted by the handling of international economic sanctions. Liechtenstein has consistently supported the EU's sanctions against Russia. Domestic opposition to this has been very limited and is explained less by sympathy for Russia than by the desire for the strongest possible neutrality and the hope of not exposing the country internationally.

Strong Commitment to International Law

Liechtenstein has been working for many years to strengthen international law at the UN. Among other things, it launched the so-called veto initiative in the UN General Assembly. This initiative aims to strengthen the General Assembly's role in accordance with its mandate under the UN Charter. Liechtenstein has also taken the lead within the Accountability, Coherence, Transparency Group in developing a code of conduct designed to help the Security Council respond more effectively to mass crimes such as genocide.

These examples show that Liechtenstein has recognised the great importance of international law and multilateral cooperation for a peaceful and secure world and that it is prepared to make a disproportionately strong commitment. However, domestically, Liechtenstein's foreign policy activities meet with little response. It is also difficult to say how much Liechtensteiners are concerned with the global security situation and what its position is on plans to strengthen European defence. Security is still taken for granted by citizens, who do not appear to be fully aware of how strongly their country benefits from its neighbours' investments in security.

Change in Political Attitudes

Using the traffic light system, a low threat perception by the Liechtenstein population indicated a setting at 'green'. At a political level, though, the light might currently be turning to 'yellow' as the need for a more serious engagement with national and international security has been recognised. Accordingly, there are concrete plans to develop a security strategy for Liechtenstein. This will not only address military defence, but above all, hybrid threats such as cyberattacks, sabotage, extremism and terrorism. There is also a growing understanding in politics that Liechtenstein must participate in efforts to strengthen the European security architecture so that it is not seen as a free rider.

Liechtenstein is a very wealthy country. However, it remains a small country with a budget that is insignificant by international standards. From a European perspective, Liechtenstein's contribution to the European security architecture will therefore primarily be symbolic. This may explain why there has been little political pressure from the EU or European countries for Liechtenstein to make greater financial commitments. Conversely, though, it would be an opportunity for Liechtenstein to voluntarily engage at the European level in the area of civil protection and promotion of non-military infrastructure in Europe.

Shared values and strong integration in Europe oblige Liechtenstein to assume greater responsibility and pursue a more active security policy. Due to the relative lack of capacity, the focus has to be on financial contributions. However, these contributions do not necessarily have to concentrate on military issues. On the contrary, in any defence alliance, Liechtenstein will always be the weakest link, regardless of whether the threats are hybrid or military. It is therefore understandable that Liechtenstein does not want to expose itself and hence is reluctant to support military projects. Instead, the country should make greater contributions in other areas and, for example, create a Liechtenstein Grant, similar to the Norway Grants in the EEA, which is intended to support economic growth and strengthen civil societies as well as European values. Finally, politicians would be well advised to raise public awareness of the security situation in Europe and to highlight how much Liechtenstein benefits from other countries in security affairs.

Christian Frommelt studied political science in Innsbruck and earned his doctorate at ETH Zurich under Frank Schimmelfennig on the European Free Trade Association states' European policy. He has been Rector at the University of Liechtenstein since 2023.

The University of Liechtenstein is a small, research-oriented university in Vaduz with a focus on business economics, architecture, and business law. It is characterised by close supervision, internationally oriented programmes, and strong ties to the regional economy. Its size allows it to offer a personal study environment with modern teaching methods and practical projects.

Moldova's Secured European Future: Defence, Resilience and the Enlargement Imperative

Iulian Groza and Mihai Mogîldea

Moldova's constitutional neutrality can no longer be equated with passivity. In the context of Russia's war against Ukraine and intensifying hybrid threats, neutrality must evolve into a framework for resilience, credible deterrence and strategic European alignment. We argue that Moldova's transformation—anchored in its National Security Strategy and Security and Defence Partnership with the EU—offers a model for how neutrality and integration can coexist. It calls for embedding defence convergence as a new pillar of EU enlargement and outlines reforms to reinforce Moldova's role as a future security contributor. A traffic light framework that is generally 'yellow' captures Moldova's security landscape—from severe threats posed by Russian aggression and hybrid warfare, through manageable institutional and cyber vulnerabilities, to notable resilience gains in energy independence—together with democratic oversight and EU security cooperation.

From Neutrality to Strategic Resilience

Moldova's neutrality, enshrined in Article 11 of its Constitution, was long seen as a protective shield. However, Russia's aggression against Ukraine, hybrid interference and the illegal presence of Russian troops in Transnistria have stripped neutrality of its protective value. Repeated airspace violations and disinformation campaigns have revealed Moldova's exposure to hostile influence. Neutrality now demands investment in deterrence, cyber capacity, energy independence and institutional resilience.

Moldova's 2023 National Security Strategy redefined neutrality as a strategic responsibility. It identified Russia and its proxies as the most persistent threat to

I. Groza (✉) · M. Mogîldea
Institute for European Policies and Reforms, Chisinau, Republic of Moldova
e-mail: iulian.groza@ipre.md; mihai.mogildea@ipre.md

M. Kaeding et al. (eds.), *Security, Defence, and the Future of Europe*,
https://doi.org/10.1007/978-3-032-18279-1_34

Moldova's sovereignty and set EU membership by 2030 as a strategic objective. Neutrality, in this vision, is not passivity, but preparedness: investing in cyber capacity, energy independence and institutional strength to withstand pressure.

While Moldova does not currently seek NATO membership, its accession process to the EU already functions as a soft security guarantee, given the EU's vital contribution to Moldova's resilience and consolidated aspirations of Moldovans to be safer as part of the enlarged Union family. Through the EU's Strategic Compass, the European Peace Facility, PESCO and the EU's CSDP missions, Moldova is gradually being integrated into Europe's security ecosystem. The 2024 EU-Moldova Security and Defence Partnership Agreement institutionalised cooperation on hybrid threats, early warning and cyber defence, while the EU Partnership Mission in Chişinău offers practical support in resilience-building. In parallel, Moldova has contributed officers to EU missions abroad, underscoring its ambition to be a responsible partner.

Why Moldova Matters

Moldova's stability carries significance well beyond its borders. Situated at the EU-Ukraine frontier, Moldova's resilience is essential for Black Sea security and the Union's eastern border. Moldova's trajectory demonstrates that EU enlargement remains a merit-based process. Reforms deliver tangible progress, while candidate countries advancing steadily can inspire others in the Eastern Partnership and Western Balkans.

A resilient Moldova also weakens Russia's ability to destabilise neighbouring states, including Ukraine and Romania, by undermining hybrid tactics that exploit governance fragility and social cleavages. At the political level, Moldova has become a visible test case for enlargement credibility. Symbolic solidarity, through the Benelux ministers' visit to Chişinău, the presence of Emmanuel Macron, Donald Tusk and Friedrich Merz as well as the EU-Moldova Summit in 2025, illustrates Moldova's new place on the European agenda.

Threat Perceptions: A 'Traffic Light' Framework

To map Moldova's evolving security landscape, a traffic light framework highlights three tiers of perceived threats. In the 'red' zone (high risk), Moldova faces severe risks from Russian aggression and hybrid warfare. According to the polls, 7 in 10 citizens identify Russia as the main threat to national security, citing military presence in Transnistria, election interference and energy coercion.

In the 'yellow' zone (medium risk), challenges include institutional fragility in defence planning, cyber readiness gaps, limited military mobility and limited public trust, especially in the justice sector. These issues are significant, but manageable with sustained reform.

In the 'green' zone (low risk), Moldova has made progress. Energy diversification eliminated dependence on Russian supplies by 2025. Democratic oversight of the security sector has improved and participation in EU defence platforms has enhanced strategic credibility.

The overall rating would be 'yellow' shifting slightly towards 'green' as Moldova strengthens its institutional capacity, societal resilience and strategic partnerships.

Defence Reform in a Time of Hybrid Warfare

Since 2022, Moldova has faced increasing hybrid threats: cyberattacks, disinformation, electoral interference as well as pressure on energy and information infrastructure. Russian troops remain illegally stationed in Transnistria and Kremlin-linked proxies continue to distort democratic processes. The October 2024 constitutional referendum, which narrowly passed with 50.4% support, symbolised both societal support for the European path and the vulnerability of Moldova's information space.

Moldova's parliamentary elections on 28 September 2025 marked a decisive moment for the country's democratic trajectory and European future. The pro-European Party of Action and Solidarity, aligned with President Maia Sandu, won 50.2% of the vote and 55 out of 101 seats, securing a single-party majority and a renewed mandate to advance EU accession. The stakes of this election went far beyond domestic politics: it was a test of whether one of Europe's most vulnerable democracies could resist Russia's hybrid interference and remain firmly on a pro-European course. Moscow deployed a wide-ranging toolkit, from disinformation and cyberattacks to illicit financing, vote buying and election-day bomb threats, yet these efforts failed to derail the process. Notably, support for pro-Russian parties declined to below 30% when considering the overall results, reflecting a significant erosion of their societal influence and an electorate increasingly aligned with Moldova's European aspirations. Moldovan institutions, media, business and civil society demonstrated enhanced societal resilience through a whole-of-society response that improved detection, exposed malign influence networks and countered false narratives. The result underscored not only strong public support for Moldova's European path, but also the growing maturity of its democratic institutions and societal cohesion in the face of external threats.

Amid ongoing regional insecurity and Russia's continued war against Ukraine, an increasing number of Moldovans have come to understand that neutrality alone does not shield the country from external aggression. This awareness is particularly relevant as Moldova remains the target of sustained hybrid warfare, including cyber operations, propaganda and destabilisation efforts. The belief that Moldova could remain safely on the sidelines is eroding, with most citizens (around 66%) aware of persistent threats to its sovereignty and territorial integrity.

According to an Institute for European Policies and Reforms (IPRE) research conducted in 2025, over 60% of Moldovans believe their country should enhance its national defence and security capacities while preserving constitutional neutrality. A similar proportion supports closer security cooperation with the EU, even without pursuing NATO membership. These evolving attitudes reflect a growing societal consensus: for neutrality to remain credible, it must be underpinned by resilience, deterrence and institutional readiness to respond to both hybrid and conventional threats.

Domestically, Moldova has embarked on a strategic transformation, shedding years of ambiguity in favour of a clear commitment to European security integration. The 2023 National Security Strategy marked a turning point, positioning Moldova as an integral part of Europe's evolving security architecture. By 2024, Moldova had achieved 90% alignment with the EU's CFSP. The EU-Moldova Security and Defence Partnership, the first of its kind under the EU's Strategic Compass, institutionalised operational cooperation in early warning systems, cyber defence, hybrid threat response and defence reform. Moldova's participation in CSDP missions has been enhanced and operational ties were further deepened through the deployment of the EU Partnership Mission in Chişinău. The government has launched the CyberCor Institute, established the Centre for Strategic Communication and Countering Disinformation, fully eliminated energy dependence on Russian suppliers by 2025 and reinforced democratic oversight of security institutions.

Yet the gaps remain stark. Defence spending, although tripled over the past 3 years, still accounts for less than 1% of GDP. Airspace surveillance and short-range air defence remain rudimentary, leaving the country exposed to regional spillovers. Military mobility continues to be constrained by infrastructure bottlenecks at border crossings with Romania and Ukraine. Cyber capacities are expanding, albeit not yet fully operationalised, while institutional fragility in defence planning and procurement further slows the pace of reform. Neutrality without resilience risks turning into vulnerability. Moldova's next phase must therefore be to translate strategic intent into tangible capabilities.

It becomes increasingly evident that, unlike Finland and Sweden, Moldova has limited prospects of pursuing NATO accession, at least in the coming years, as neutrality remains a principle supported by the majority of its citizens. Advancing EU accession, therefore, emerges as Moldova's most viable strategic option. While the EU is not a military alliance, for most Moldovans it represents a space of peace, development and security. At the same time, the Union itself is strengthening its defence dimension in response to growing regional and global insecurities, as well as the risk of further war escalation in Europe driven by Russia's actions.

A New Pillar for EU Enlargement: Defence Convergence

The EU enlargement process has traditionally centred on democratic governance and the rule of law. In today's security environment, though, these pillars are insufficient. Candidate countries exposed to hybrid warfare must also demonstrate defence preparedness and resilience. Moldova's trajectory illustrates why defence convergence should become a new pillar of EU enlargement.

Two practical tools would help achieve this. Firstly, a Defence Annex to the Enlargement Questionnaire would allow candid assessment of sensitive domains such as cyber readiness, democratic control of the armed forces, procurement transparency and intelligence protection. Confidentiality would minimise politicisation while establishing a baseline for reforms. Secondly, bilateral Defence Cooperation Roadmaps, inspired by visa liberalisation benchmarks, would set key milestones across airspace surveillance, cyber resilience, infrastructure protection and energy security. Moldova's roadmap could build on the EUR 197 million already provided through the European Peace Facility since 2021.

Embedding defence in enlargement would not only strengthen Moldova, but also reinforce the EU's collective resilience. Candidates should be helped to enter the EU with core instruments that will enhance their security and defence capacities. Moldova's experience shows that neutrality, properly understood, is compatible with the EU's evolving security architecture and can serve as a model for other candidate states.

Recommendations

The first recommendation is to integrate defence and resilience in the enlargement framework. The EU should introduce a dedicated annex under Chap. 31 of the acquis on Foreign, Security and Defence Policy to assess interoperability, cyber readiness, democratic oversight and critical infrastructure resilience. An EU-Moldova Defence Cooperation Roadmap should be launched, with benchmarks on cyber resilience, airspace surveillance, military mobility and energy security, building on the EU-Moldova Security and Defence Partnership and European Peace Facility support.

Furthermore, societal and institutional resilience should be strengthened, scaling up strategic communication, focusing on tangible EU benefits (energy, trade, roaming, mobility) and targeting vulnerable regions such as Gagauzia and rural communities. Independent media, think tanks and watchdogs to counter disinformation should be supported, while promoting digital literacy and safeguarding pluralism. The completion of judicial vetting by 2026 should be endorsed, as well as an improvement in anti-corruption enforcement and ensuring institutional coordination to reinforce the rule of law and public trust.

Hybrid defence and security should be advanced by expanding hybrid defence cooperation, including cybersecurity, intelligence-sharing, sanctions enforcement and monitoring illicit financial flows (including cryptocurrencies). There should be continued engagement with local authorities and civil society in resilience planning to ensure that community-level vulnerabilities are addressed as part of national security.

Iulian Groza is Executive Director of IPRE and a former Deputy Foreign Minister of the Republic of Moldova. His expertise covers European integration, international law and governance reforms in the Eastern Partnership region.

Mihai Mogîldea is Deputy Director of IPRE. He previously held research positions at Collegium Civitas (Warsaw), the Leibniz Institute for East and Southeast European Studies (Regensburg), and the Slovak Foreign Policy Association (Bratislava). His work focuses on foreign policy and security in Eastern Europe.

The Institute for European Policies and Reforms (IPRE) is one of Moldova's leading think-tanks. It promotes European integration, democratic resilience and sustainable governance. IPRE has extensive experience in monitoring the Eastern Partnership, facilitating multi-stakeholder dialogue and advancing reforms that align Moldova with EU standards.

Montenegro's Perspective: Between the Atlantic and the Urals

Danijela Jaćimović, Dženana Đurković, and Nikola Vlahović

Montenegro's role in European security is defined less by its size or military capability than by its alignment, credibility and conviction. As the most advanced Western Balkan state in the EU accession process, Montenegro acts as a bridge between the Union's internal stability and its geopolitical frontier. Its strategic importance lies in demonstrating that even small states can contribute meaningfully to collective security through responsibility, cooperation and foresight.

The country's approach rests on three interlinked pillars: commitment to NATO, pursuit of EU integration and cultivation of regional stability. Applying the traffic light typology of threat perception, Montenegro occupies a space between the 'green' and 'yellow' zones—secure, yet remaining conscious of its vulnerabilities.

Strategic Contribution and Priorities

Montenegro contributes to European security not through divisions or fleets, but through alignment with shared values and strategic objectives. Hence, Montenegro focuses more on modernisation, cyber resilience, training and mobility rather than on heavy weaponry. Its priorities are clear: effective border management, cyber security and resilience against hybrid threats. These goals position Montenegro as a responsible guardian of the EU's future external border.

While NATO remains the cornerstone of Euro-Atlantic defence, its endurance depends on credibility and coherence. From Podgorica's perspective, the development of a European Defence Union, or eventually a European army, is not a contradiction but a complement to NATO. Europe must be capable of acting autonomously where NATO's consensus may falter, particularly within its own neighbourhood.

D. Jaćimović (✉) · D. Đurković · N. Vlahović
Faculty of Economics, University of Montenegro, Podgorica, Montenegro
e-mail: danijelaj@ac.me; dzenana.dj@ucg.ac.me

M. Kaeding et al. (eds.), *Security, Defence, and the Future of Europe*,
https://doi.org/10.1007/978-3-032-18279-1_35

For Montenegro, NATO and the EU represent parallel guarantors of stability, not institutional rivals.

The Transatlantic Dimension

The Atlantic, once a symbol of unbreakable unity, has narrowed in spirit, even as it widens in distance. The U.S. remains indispensable, yet its engagement with Europe has become more selective of late, guided by strategic calculation rather than idealism. Each confrontation between Washington and Moscow risks reinforcing Beijing, the true challenger to the global balance.

Montenegro supports the EU, which advances strategic autonomy while maintaining its transatlantic foundations. The EU's role in supporting Ukraine demonstrates both solidarity and dependence on U.S. leadership. Conversely, the Western Balkans offer a tangible space where the EU can act independently and showcase genuine leadership.

Within this context, Montenegro's dual status as a NATO Ally and the leading EU accession candidate in the Western Balkans grants it both symbolic and strategic significance. Its accession is not merely a national aspiration, but a shared investment in Europe's security architecture.

For success, responsibility must be mutual: the EU must remain committed to enlargement, while Montenegro must continue advancing reforms, political unity and democratic standards. In doing so, Montenegro affirms that even small states can strengthen Europe's credibility and cohesion—reminding us that Europe's strength begins at home.

Financing and Defence Responsibility

Since joining NATO in 2017, Montenegro has been steadily increasing its defence spending, edging closer to the 2% of GDP target and aiming for around 3% by 2026. This shows a clear move from symbolic participation toward a stronger, more strategic commitment. However, pushing spending up even further to 5% of GDP could seriously stretch the country's economy. Because the defence budget comes directly from national funds, any major increase needs to be carefully balanced with other financial and social priorities.

There is also an ongoing debate in Montenegro about whether military service should be mandatory. Discussion is partly influenced by neighbouring countries such as Serbia and Croatia, where reinstating or strengthening conscription is currently being debated. Still, as yet the Montenegrin government has shown little interest in putting this contentious issue on the agenda. Some experts question whether a voluntary system could handle large-scale mobilisation in an emergency, though improvements in training and reserve systems are being considered. For now, the government continues to prioritise voluntary service, supported by reserves and civil preparedness. This approach reflects a practical understanding that national defence is a shared social responsibility, not just a military task.

Public Awareness and Threat Perception

Public opinion in Montenegro mirrors wider European ambivalence. According to the 2024 Centre for Democracy and Human Rights survey, 38.9% of citizens view Russia as the aggressor in Ukraine, 32.6% blame NATO expansion and 28.5% remain undecided. These divisions reveal a society balancing inherited narratives and emerging strategic realities. From a Slavic cultural perspective, where emotional and historical ties to both Ukraine and Russia persist, the war has revived memories of the Yugoslav conflicts, reinforcing a belief that peace is more fragile and more costly than victory.

Applying the traffic light model, Montenegro remains in the 'yellow' zone of cautious awareness, yet grounded in 'green' zone stability derived from alliances and shared democratic values. While not facing imminent military threats, the country remains vigilant about regional instability and hybrid vulnerabilities.

Montenegro understands that modern security extends beyond defending borders, to involve protecting democracy, digital infrastructure and societal trust. Its strategy is pragmatic: to build resilience through partnership, deepen European integration and promote security through cooperation, not confrontation.

Peace and the European Role

For Montenegro, peace through dialogue is the only sustainable path forward. It views the EU as a credible broker in potential peace efforts between Russia and Ukraine—provided that the EU acts with unity and moral authority. The Montenegrin perspective recalls the vision of a Europe stretching 'from the Atlantic to the Urals', a continent where diversity does not preclude solidarity.

This envisioned the EU not as a fortress, but a platform of shared destiny, founded on mutual recognition and economic interdependence. Its success would rely on Germany's leadership and restraint, France's strategic ambition, alongside smaller states' capacity to mediate and innovate.

Montenegro, with its experience of transition and reconciliation, can serve as a regional intermediary, a modest yet meaningful contributor to Europe's peace and security.

Recommendations: What Can Be Done

To enhance regional cooperation and strengthen the EU's common security and defence policy, Montenegro can take three concrete steps. Firstly, the country's contribution should comprise vision, innovation and partnership, rather than military strength.

Secondly, Montenegro should launch a new cooperative platform connecting countries of the Adriatic, Ionian and Black Seas: 'The Balkans on Three Seas'. It should enhance activities such as joint military and civil training programmes, coordinated defence investments and financial cooperation, as well as civic engagement and trust-building across societies.

Thirdly, the country should redefine peace as an active project, emphasising that peace is not a static condition but a continual effort, requiring participation from all European nations.

Danijela Jaćimović is Professor at the Faculty of Economics of the University of Montenegro and a member of the TEPSA Board. Her fields of interest include international relations and European integration.

Dženana Đurković is Teaching Associate and Master's degree student at the Faculty of Economics of the University of Montenegro. Her fields of interest include international relations and monetary economics.

Nikola Vlahović is a member of the YATA Montenegro Research Team. He is a Master's student at the Faculty of Political Science, University of Montenegro and the University of Donja Gorica. His fields of interest include international relations and international security.

The University of Montenegro in Podgorica is a public higher education institution and the oldest in the country. The Faculty of Economics, as one of the most important educational and research institutions in the country, is also a member of TEPSA.

YATA Montenegro is part of the Youth Atlantic Treaty Association, which engages young professionals and students in issues of international security and transatlantic cooperation.

North Macedonia: Cooperation and Partnerships as Fundamentals to Security

Irena Rajchinovska Pandeva

North Macedonia is a small country with great ethnic diversity situated in a turbulent neighbourhood. In the past three decades since its independence, the country has faced a plethora of issues—from political and economic crises to social conflicts. Even though some predicaments were relatively minor in terms of impact whilst others created widespread political and institutional turmoil affecting its stability or severe security issues, each and every event shaped the country's stance and prospects. In addition to its stalled European integration path and complex neighbourly relations (some former, others ongoing), North Macedonia had a lengthy struggle to join NATO but eventually succeeded in 2020. Five years on, the country managed to position itself as a valuable member of the Alliance by actively participating in joint security as part of the Allied interoperability, thus shifting its role from security consumer to security contributor. Employing the traffic light system on threat perception and public opinion polls, North Macedonia is most likely positioned at 'yellow'.

NATO and EU: Strategic Priorities and Main Foreign Policy Goals

Attaining North Macedonia's strategic priorities—EU and NATO membership—has been a constant endeavour pursued by consecutive Macedonian governments for three decades. Its prolonged EU path (identified as a potential candidate for EU membership during the Thessaloniki European Council summit in 2003, applied for EU membership in March 2004, with the decision of the Council to grant the country candidate status reached in December 2005) and ongoing stalemate due to the

I. R. Pandeva (✉)
Iustinianus Primus Law Faculty, Skopje, North Macedonia
e-mail: i.rajchinovskapandeva@pf.ukim.edu.mk

M. Kaeding et al. (eds.), *Security, Defence, and the Future of Europe*,
https://doi.org/10.1007/978-3-032-18279-1_36

Bulgarian veto have caused severe consequences for North Macedonia's progress and reform process. North Macedonia's EU accession is nevertheless still at the top of its political agenda, with a 2024 public opinion analysis undertaken by the Institute for Democracy Societas Civilis—Skopje showing that public support remains high (62%).

Pursuit of NATO membership has also been a lengthy and troublesome process. North Macedonia joined the NATO Partnership for Peace programme in 1995 and the Membership Action Plan in 1999. Hence, cooperation in all relevant aspects, including support for NATO-led operations (for instance in Afghanistan), was established long before it joined the Alliance. The membership process was extended due to a dispute over the country's name raised by Greece. This was finally settled by the signing of the Prespa agreement in 2018, which then opened the path towards full membership in NATO as its 30th member in 2020.

Internally, NATO membership was principally perceived and projected as a guarantee for the nation's territorial integrity, sovereignty and stability. A 2024 public opinion analysis carried out by the International Republican Institute shows that 52% of respondents consider full membership in NATO as the best option for the future of the country, 32% regard North Macedonia's membership as very positive, in addition to 38% who think of it as somewhat positive. The same poll also demonstrated that "only pro-EU and the West" was the best foreign policy course for the country, with 31% of citizens considering it the best option.

Cooperation as a Necessity

In the past three decades, North Macedonia's international posture has been focused on its alignment with the West and fulfilment of its Euro-Atlantic integration aspirations. While the country has already achieved full NATO membership and continues to work towards EU accession, it also maintains existing advances towards new strategic partnerships, which include the U.S. and, more recently, Hungary and the UK (both signed in mid-2025). Some of these cooperation platforms also include extended security collaboration and support; they are of high importance for the development and modernisation of the country, reflecting its standing in an increasingly unstable world.

On the fifth anniversary of North Macedonia's NATO membership in 2025, the country was formally recognised by NATO officials as an Ally that is valuable and reliable, meets the 2% of GDP spending target, contributes to the defence of the Eastern flank, and supports stability in the Western Balkans as well as Ukraine's sovereignty and self-defence. Attestation to North Macedonia's importance was also in evidence a year earlier when the NATO Secretary General appointed Radmila Shekerinska (former Macedonian Minister of Defence) as the next Deputy Secretary General, thus acknowledging the country's progress and strategic significance within the Alliance.

North Macedonia's defence expenditure has increased significantly since the country joined NATO. In 5 years, this has doubled from USD 154 million in 2020 to USD 358 million in 2025 (estimate). Hereafter, North Macedonia's defence expenditure as a percentage of GDP has also been steadily increasing—0.94% in 2018, 1.24% in 2020, 1.89% in 2024 and 2.0% in 2025 (estimated). According to NATO official data, in 2025 North Macedonia's defence expenditure was distributed across the following categories: equipment (32.36%); personnel (41%); infrastructure (1.84%); operation and maintenance and other expenditures (24.80%).

In regard to EU security plans, as North Macedonia is fully aligned with the EU's CFSP, it was the first country in the Western Balkans to sign a defence and partnership agreement with the Union in November 2024. This agreement was presented as a new political framework for dialogue and cooperation on security and defence issues; moreover, it is in line with the bilateral support packages provided by the Council since 2023 that amount to EUR 38 million. This is aimed at strengthening the North Macedonian Army's capacities and European Peace Facility support in the framework of a regional assistance measure for the Balkan Medical Task Force, amounting to EUR 6 million.

With mandatory military service having been abolished in 2006, North Macedonia has a fully professional army based on voluntary recruitment and with a structure that aligns with the country's commitments as a member of NATO. Non-mandatory military service is open to all citizens, provided that certain criteria are met. Despite public debates, the country has no plan as yet to reintroduce mandatory military service, although the current legal framework makes provision for this in cases of national emergency or war.

In terms of the traffic light system for general threat perception, North Macedonia is most likely positioned at 'yellow'. In case of an imminent threat, 'yellow' is also the perceived level given the country's current positioning and mindful of its full membership in NATO and full alignment with the EU's CFSP.

Recommendations

Being a small, landlocked country, North Macedonia's security and stability go hand in hand with its political and economic progress and are of utmost importance for its prosperity. Then again, as a country that is settled at a crossroads, much of North Macedonia's internal stability and security depends on the state of its surroundings, the volatile region it belongs to and increasingly hostile international relations. Hence, the country is compelled and will continue to participate and contribute to all regional, supranational and international efforts to bring and maintain peace as well as cooperation.

North Macedonia's pledge to increase its defence spending to 5% of GDP by 2035 within NATO can be considered as a bold reaction by the Macedonian government; however, the goal seems achievable taking into consideration the past adjustment to membership requirements, fulfilment of the country's obligations, active contribution and most particularly its constant increase of military expenditure, in addition to existing and planned strategic partnerships by the government.

Heightened expectations and projections undertaken at EU level regarding security may be considered as problematic for candidate countries such as North Macedonia, especially in the event of additional burdens to the country's economy. If insufficient funds and support within the ReArm Europe Plan/'Readiness 2030' is therefore likely to occur, then Macedonian participation in the future European security architecture will probably remain within the bounds of its EU accession process, bilateral partnerships and most significantly NATO.

North Macedonia supports EU efforts to regain relevance and reposition itself in order to contribute and provide for international stability and security. Hence, all initiatives in this line should include the EU, especially when taking on a more prominent role in peace negotiations between Russia and Ukraine. The Union was created as a peace project and from today's perspective it is expected that it will act proactively when protecting global peace and ensuring prosperity.

Irena Rajchinovska Pandeva, Prof. dr. Sci.—is Full Professor in Political Science at the Iustinianus Primus Law Faculty, Ss. Cyril and Methodius University in Skopje, North Macedonia. She served as Vice Dean for Science and International Cooperation from 2016 to 2024. Currently she is Head of the Institute for political science, media and communications at the Faculty and member of its Executive board. From 2020 until 2023 she was a member of the TEPSA Board.

The Iustinianus Primus Law Faculty is the oldest higher education institution in North Macedonia offering programmes in law, political science and media. It is part of the Ss. Cyril and Methodius University in Skopje.

Why Staying Outside the EU Weakens Norwegian Security

Pernille Rieker

Norway's security outlook has changed profoundly since Russia invaded Ukraine and Donald Trump returned to the White House. Once confident with the U.S. guarantee of security and its NATO anchor, Norway now faces a more uncertain transatlantic environment while remaining outside the EU. As Russia reasserts itself in the High North, concerns have grown about hybrid operations and potential attacks on critical infrastructure—especially Norway's offshore installations and gas production, now vital to Europe's energy security. While Norway spends more and cooperates more closely with Brussels, it still lacks a voice where key decisions are made. In this new European reality, it could be argued that Norway's threat perception corresponds to 'yellow', under the traffic light system: it prepares seriously for potential conflict and hybrid threats, but does not expect a direct attack. Remaining outside of the EU now weakens rather than safeguards Norwegian security.

Introduction

Norway stands at a strategic crossroads. The war in Ukraine, renewed great-power rivalry and Donald Trump's return to the White House have fundamentally changed Europe's security environment. For Norwegians, these shifts pose a double challenge: on the one hand, the country must protect its national sovereignty in the High North and safeguard society against hybrid attacks as the American security guarantee becomes less certain; and on the other hand, it must find a way to recalibrate the EU relationship at a time when the Union is emerging as a central actor in European security. Meanwhile, most Norwegians still remain reluctant to become full members.

P. Rieker (✉)
ARENA – Centre for European Studies at the University of Oslo, Oslo, Norway
e-mail: pernille.rieker@arena.uio.no

M. Kaeding et al. (eds.), *Security, Defence, and the Future of Europe*,
https://doi.org/10.1007/978-3-032-18279-1_37

Although Norway is not an EU Member State, it is deeply integrated through the EEA, Schengen and more than 100 sectoral agreements. Around 75% of Norwegian exports go to the EU and new initiatives in areas such as cybersecurity, preparedness and defence industry cooperation directly shape Norwegian politics. Yet, Norway has no seat at the table where these decisions are made.

Paradoxically, this situation has long been accepted by most Norwegians, but in these changing times, it is becoming increasingly difficult to sustain. In recent years, Norway has struggled to secure access to key EU initiatives, from secure satellite communication (IRIS^2) to the Health Emergency Preparedness and Response Authority. Even in areas where Norway contributes, such as the European Union Military Assistance Mission in support of Ukraine or joint procurement of ammunition (ASAP), participation is *ad hoc* and lacks real influence over design and priorities. The May 2024 security and defence partnership agreement between Norway and the EU was a step forward, yet it remains largely symbolic. Norway may be invited to meetings, but only at the goodwill of EU Member States.

Between NATO Dependence and EU Integration

While NATO remains indispensable for territorial defence, the EU has proven able to mobilise tools that NATO lacks: sanctions, industrial policy, crisis management and hybrid threat responses. While NATO deters and reassures, the EU delivers resilience by countering cyberattacks, regulating critical infrastructure and reducing energy dependence on Russia. For Norway, these dimensions are increasingly tangible. Its offshore energy infrastructure and undersea cables have become potential targets, underscoring how national and European security are intertwined. The war in Ukraine and the Baltic Sea incidents have heightened awareness that energy security is no longer only an economic issue but part of Norway's total defence. For Norway, which has long defined its role through NATO, this dual structure requires a rethink. Relying on NATO alone is no longer sufficient. As the U.S. to some extent signals retreat, Brussels is becoming the arena where much of our future security architecture is defined.

Paradoxically, while Norway is becoming ever more entangled with EU security and defence policy, all is quiet on the domestic politics front. Since the referenda in 1972 and 1994, EU membership has been treated as a taboo subject. This institutionalised silence means that while Sweden and Denmark openly debate the EU's role in security, Norway presents itself as a passive rule-taker. Yet public opinion has become more fluid. Support for full membership has risen from the high twenties a few years ago to the mid-thirties, and at times around 40 percent, in more recent polls, while the share of undecided voters has also at times increased markedly. This indicates that citizens sense what politicians avoid saying, namely that the line between NATO and the EU is blurring and hence Norway risks being marginalised in the institutions shaping Europe's collective response. However, without a parliamentary majority for membership, the *status quo* remains.

Rising Budgets, Shrinking Influence

The EU itself has changed profoundly over recent years. It has securitised areas ranging from trade to digitalisation and adopted strategies on space, cyber and economic security. This trend towards a more integrated, resilient Europe is unlikely to reverse, despite the rise of populist parties. The most plausible trajectory is continued 'differentiated integration': deeper cooperation in some areas, looser arrangements in others. For outsiders such as Norway, though, this creates structural barriers. Sector-spanning policies no longer fit neatly into the existing European Economic Area (EEA) or bilateral agreements. Participation depends increasingly on whether EU members perceive it as useful.

Since 2022, Norway has significantly raised its defence budget, reaching 3.3% of GDP in 2025, including military support to Ukraine. NATO's June 2025 decision, Norway has committed to moving towards a total of 5% of GDP by 2035. Much of this increase prioritises fixing critical shortfalls in today's forces, boosting personnel and investing heavily in the Navy, Army and Home Guard. Conscription has long existed formally in Norway, but gender-neutral conscription was introduced in practice from 2016. Today, around one in six young Norwegians are called up for service each year and support for conscription has grown markedly since Russia's full-scale invasion of Ukraine. Military service is widely seen as part of a broader 'total defence' concept that combines civil and military preparedness.

Norway has had relatively positive experiences with the European Defence Fund, where Norwegian companies have participated actively, although without decision-making power. However, access to newer EU financing instruments such as SAFE under the 'Readiness 2030' plan, or the proposed European Competitiveness Fund, remains uncertain. As illustrated by negotiations over IRIS² as well as the Health Emergency Preparedness and Response Authority, structural barriers still limit predictability and long-term industrial alignment for non-members, reducing Norway's influence even as cooperation deepens.

On peace talks, the Norwegian debate is clear: premature negotiations with Moscow would reward aggression. Sustained military support is seen as the only way to bring Russia to the table on acceptable terms. Following the surge in energy revenues after the Russian invasion of Ukraine, Norway has faced domestic debates about how to use this extraordinary income responsibly. The government has channelled a significant share into support for Ukraine, committing more than EUR 7 billion (the Nansen Support Programme) for military, humanitarian and reconstruction assistance between 2023 and 2027. Public opinion has remained largely supportive and cross-party consensus has held that Norway's energy windfall must be used to bolster European security and Ukraine's defence. At the same time, there is broad recognition that the EU must prepare the diplomatic architecture of any future settlement—through reconstruction funding, monitoring and security guarantees and that Norway should align itself closely with this effort.

Norway's Threat Perception: 'Yellow'

Measured against the traffic-light typology used in this volume, Norway's current security outlook corresponds to 'yellow'—signalling a medium threat perception. Russia's growing assertiveness in the High North and increased hybrid activity have prompted significant investment in deterrence and resilience. Defence spending has risen sharply and civil preparedness has been strengthened. Yet, Norway does not view a direct military attack as imminent. Russia is perceived as a threat to regional stability rather than an immediate aggressor. The government's strategy, therefore, focuses on deterrence through NATO, closer cooperation with EU partners and strengthening total defence rather than preparing for full-scale war.

Recommendations

Norway cannot change geography: it is a country, dependent on its neighbours and allies, but it can change how it engages. At a time when Europe is rearming, integrating and redefining security, Norway's strategic silence is no longer sustainable. Safeguarding both security and democracy requires an honest debate about Norway's place in Europe—including whether full EU membership has become the only way to ensure a voice in shaping the future of European defence.

Pernille Rieker is Director of ARENA – Centre for European Studies at the University of Oslo and Research Professor at NUPI (part time). Her research focuses on European integration and security, as well as Norway's relationship with the EU and NATO. ARENA – Centre for European Studies at the University of Oslo is a leading research centre dedicated to the study of European integration, governance and democracy. Established in 1994, it combines academic excellence with policy relevance and contributes to public debate on Europe's role in a changing world.

Security on the Sidelines: Serbia's Public Perceptions of European Defence and Strategic Autonomy

Maja Bjeloš

As Europe reshapes its security architecture in response to growing geopolitical tensions, Serbia stands apart in an unexpected way. Unlike its EU-aspiring neighbours moving toward closer strategic ties, Serbia's public remains deeply sceptical of NATO and the EU's defence ambitions. This scepticism is less about current threats and more rooted in historical trauma and domestic narratives, revealing how enduring perceptions of sovereignty and global power continue to shape security attitudes on the continent's periphery.

In terms of the traffic light analogy, Serbia falls within the 'green' category, indicating a low perception of external military threat. Although memories of the Yugoslav wars and NATO intervention remain present, for the foreseeable future Serbia does not anticipate aggression from any neighbouring states or historic rivals. However, mirroring broader global and regional dynamics, the country has undertaken efforts to rearm and modernise its military capabilities.

Diplomacy Over Deterrence: Serbia's Preference for Peace and Non-Alignment

The 'Security Radar 2025: Europe—Lost in Geopolitics' survey reveals a Serbian public deeply committed to diplomacy, with 79% of respondents favouring peaceful conflict resolution over militarisation. This preference aligns with widespread support for a multi-vector foreign policy that balances relations with various powers, alongside strong endorsement of international institutions such as the UN and the Organisation for Security and Co-operation in Europe (OSCE). However, Serbia's relationship with NATO remains fraught: nearly 80% of citizens reject any

M. Bjeloš (✉)
Belgrade Centre for Security Policy (BCSP), Belgrade, Serbia
e-mail: maja.bjelos@bezbednost.org

M. Kaeding et al. (eds.), *Security, Defence, and the Future of Europe*,
https://doi.org/10.1007/978-3-032-18279-1_38

expansion of the Alliance's role, viewing NATO enlargement as a direct threat. This deep mistrust traces back to the lasting scars of the 1999 bombing campaign and Serbia's bitter perception of NATO's involvement in Kosovo's 2008 independence. For this reason, the doctrine of military neutrality, established by a 2007 parliamentary declaration, continues to enjoy strong public backing and shapes Serbia's cautious stance on defence integration.

Serbian attitudes toward the EU reflect similar disenchantment. 65% of citizens believe that EU policies conflict with their national interests, while support for the Union's deeper involvement in global security is split almost evenly, with a slight tilt toward opposition. Despite Serbia's candidate status, many doubt the EU's credibility as a security provider. Confidence in the Union's ability to uphold democratic values has waned, undermined by its muted response to democratic backsliding in the region and unclear signals about enlargement.

The U.S. fares worse still in Serbian public opinion, notwithstanding official attempts to cast Donald Trump in a positive light within pro-government media outlets. Viewed by 70% of respondents as the greatest threat to European peace, the U.S. occupies a uniquely negative place in the national psyche. Military cooperation continues quietly behind the scenes, but public legitimacy for these ties is scarce. In sharp contrast, Serbia's populace shows strong support for strategic partnerships with Russia and China, with 66% viewing these countries as vital counterweights to Western dominance and reliable allies on the global stage.

Serbia has significantly increased defence spending, exceeding NATO's pre-Trump era 2% of GDP threshold. Even after NATO set a new target of 5% of GDP for defence spending, Serbia, with a projected 2.52% of GDP allocated for defence in 2025, will outspend more than many EU and NATO Member States. In contrast to state defence spending, Serbs express nuanced priorities. While not rejecting military investment outright, a clear majority (67%) insists that welfare and socio-economic development must take precedence over military build-up. Most also favour funding any increase in defence budgets through special levies on the wealthy rather than by cutting essential services such as education, healthcare, or pensions. In this context, the EU's proposals for joint borrowing or relaxed fiscal rules under its 'White Paper on European Defence—Readiness 2030' are unlikely to find popular support unless accompanied by strong social and economic guarantees.

The military remains the most trusted institution in Serbia and investments in defence are often perceived as a populist tool used to boost the political ratings of ruling party leaders and project state power. Although the Serbian Armed Forces are a professional force, the political establishment has in recent years floated the idea of reintroducing conscription, which was abolished in 2011. Compulsory military service, though, lacks public support—particularly among younger generations. The issue is frequently revived in public discourse not as a response to genuine geopolitical security threats, but as a means of diverting attention from ongoing political crises and addressing the human resource shortages caused by thousands of officers and soldiers departing from the army.

Serbia's Distinct Reading of Security Threats

Applying a 'green' categorisation to Serbia's threat perception underscores the country's distinct security mindset. Most Serbs do not perceive themselves as direct targets of military aggression. Instead, they identify domestic factors—such as authoritarian governance, pervasive corruption and organised crime—as the primary sources of insecurity. Although 86% of Serbian citizens cite war as one of their main personal concerns, this fear is rooted in perceptions of global instability, rather than directed toward neighbouring countries or regional militarisation. Nevertheless, the regime continues to instrumentalise ethno-nationalist narratives, securitising Albanians and Croats as 'enemies' to reinforce internal cohesion and distract from domestic challenges.

Serbia's views on the war in Ukraine diverge sharply from those common in EU capitals. A majority oppose providing military assistance to Ukraine, favouring humanitarian and economic support. This partly explains the government's efforts to obscure arms exports to Ukraine—estimated at over EUR 800 million—by channelling them through third-party intermediaries. Under the influence of state-sponsored media that promote pro-Russian narratives, many Serbs view the conflict as a proxy war between Russia and the West rather than a clear case of Russian aggression, with only 26% assigning blame to Russia—a figure that ranks among the lowest in Europe outside Russia itself. Public opinion in Serbia aligns with calls for diplomatic resolution and intensified peace talks, emphasising Serbia's preference for neutrality over geopolitical alignment.

The EU's potential role as a mediator in future peace efforts is welcomed by many Serbs, provided the focus remains on de-escalation and diplomacy rather than coercion or militarisation. Public sentiment suggests the EU could rebuild credibility by championing inclusive and transparent negotiations and strengthening international legal frameworks, rather than pursuing strategies that heighten conflict.

Broader security concerns—terrorism, extremism, climate change—are widely recognised in Serbia, but are consistently filtered through a lens of national vulnerability and sovereignty. Serbian public opinion is shaped by a lasting sense of national exceptionalism and perceived marginalisation in global affairs. Serbian society thus exhibits a conflicted foreign policy identity: while an overwhelming 86% of Serbs want the government to prioritise internal development, a substantial 60% believe Serbia should also promote its values abroad to enhance its international standing, reflecting a tension between inward focus and regional ambition.

Recommendations

Serbia remains unlikely to embrace the EU's concept of defence and strategic autonomy in its current form. Deep-rooted public scepticism toward military alliances, large defence budgets and adversarial postures reflects a societal preference for sovereignty, non-alignment and a multipolar world order, in which diplomacy occupies a central place in Serbia's strategic culture. As Europe advances its defence integration to counter Russia, Serbia's position on the sidelines offers a powerful reminder that genuine security requires not just deterrence and investment, but also attention to the good governance, accountability, trust and historical narratives that shape national identity.

To rebuild trust and re-engage Serbian society, EU policy-makers should prioritise diplomacy and peacebuilding over militarisation, aligning with Serbia's strong public support for peaceful conflict resolution. Credibility can be restored through a consistent commitment to democratic standards, fighting against corruption and tangibly supporting civil society and media freedom in the region.

Defence-related initiatives should be paired with robust welfare measures and communicated in ways that demonstrate tangible benefits for citizens, acknowledging the public's prioritisation for socio-economic development over military expenditure. Flexible cooperation formats—such as joint efforts in disaster response, cyber resilience, counter hybrid threats, or peacekeeping—could serve as entry points for practical collaboration. The EU should also invest in strategic communication and public education that fosters critical thinking and counters disinformation, encourages historical reconciliation and demonstrates the tangible benefits of European partnerships at a local level.

Maja Bjeloš is a Senior Researcher at the Belgrade Centre for Security Policy (BCSP), a leading independent think tank in the Western Balkans focused on security, foreign policy and democracy.

The Belgrade Centre for Security Policy monitors public opinion, conducts strategic research and promotes regional stability as well as EU integration.

Switzerland: Variations on the Theme of Neutrality

Frank Schimmelfennig

Neutrality continues to enjoy overwhelming support in Switzerland, but its meaning is contested. Political conflict divides the advocates of broader international cooperation and the defenders of strict neutrality. However, both public opinion and military spending suggest that the Swiss traffic light threat perception remains 'green'.

From Safe to Sorry?

Located in the centre of Europe, surrounded by friendly EU and NATO countries and pursuing the oldest policy of permanent military neutrality in the world, Switzerland must seem to be the least likely place in Europe to be galvanised by the geopolitical threats and uncertainties that encumber the continent. Indeed, while Swiss voters are experiencing a heightened sense of insecurity when compared to the past, 86% feel "very safe" or "rather safe" according to the 'Security 2025' public opinion study. With 0.72% of GDP in 2024, Switzerland is bottom of the league in terms of European defence expenditure relative to the size of its economy. Still, Russia's invasion of Ukraine and doubts about the U.S. commitment to European security have provoked political demands for strategic (re)orientation. Across the political spectrum, there is agreement that the Swiss army is neither in good shape nor on a clear path to improvement.

F. Schimmelfennig (✉)
ETH Zurich, Zurich, Switzerland
e-mail: frank.schimmelfennig@eup.gess.ethz.ch

M. Kaeding et al. (eds.), *Security, Defence, and the Future of Europe*,
https://doi.org/10.1007/978-3-032-18279-1_39

Two Tales of Neutrality

Neutrality is a deeply entrenched and highly popular political norm in Switzerland. According to the 'Security 2025' report, 87% of voters are in favour of maintaining neutrality in the current international environment. At the same time, neutrality is a flexible norm that has been reinterpreted under varying historical circumstances. The political right, represented by the Swiss People's Party, the largest party in parliament, favours a strict interpretation. It is sceptical of Switzerland's alignment with EU sanctions against Russia and international defence cooperation. Correspondingly, it demands a focus on autonomous territorial defence capacity across the entire spectrum of military capabilities. By contrast, the centre-left counts on enhanced international military cooperation with the EU and NATO. Voters are similarly split; a narrow majority (53%) approves of Switzerland moving closer to NATO.

Some small steps have been taken in this direction, which are compatible with neutrality according to the Swiss government. In 2023, Switzerland agreed an Individually Tailored Partnership Programme with NATO; in 2025, it joined two PESCO projects on military mobility and cyber defence training with the EU and started to participate in the Patriot missile project run by NATO's Support and Procurement Agency.

Limits of Autonomy and Cooperation

Swiss defence policy veers between nationalist and internationalist orientations, producing uneasy compromises along the way. Swiss authorities have pledged to raise defence spending to 1% of GDP by 2032. However, it is not clear how this minor rise will be financed. In addition, after an unforeseen price increase, Switzerland might not buy all 36 F-35 fighter jets from the US as previously intended; moreover, public opinion has turned against the deal altogether. Switzerland's limited and uncertain investments are neither sufficient to reach the goal of providing comprehensive military capabilities for an autonomous defence posture, nor will they make Switzerland a credible partner for international military cooperation when NATO countries commit themselves to a goal of 3.5% of GDP on defence spending. They will do little to correct the perception that Switzerland continues to be free riding on the deterrence and defence efforts of EU and NATO members.

In addition, neutrality-based export restrictions in the Ukraine conflict have undermined the trust of EU and NATO partners and their willingness to cooperate with Swiss firms in arms production. However, the Swiss army and defence industry rely on international cooperation for the procurement of many crucial weapons systems and, as with Norway, Switzerland is interested in signing a Security and Defence Partnership to strengthen its defence capabilities.

Moreover, Switzerland seeks interoperability with NATO forces, cooperates technologically and takes part in training exercises. However, participation in NATO exercises, in particular collective defence (Article 5) exercises with ground troops, is highly contested domestically. At the same time, there are limits to what NATO gains from the involvement of a country that is ambiguous about its own contribution to collective defence in the event of an attack.

Finally, it is of major concern to the Swiss People's Party that Switzerland is losing its traditional role as mediator and provider of good services when it leaves the path of strict neutrality. Indeed, in the Russian perspective, Switzerland ceased to be a symbol of neutrality once it had aligned itself with EU sanctions. A peace conference organised by the Swiss government in 2024 did not foresee Russian participation and hence little or nothing was gained. Diplomatic efforts to manage the conflict have moved elsewhere.

Recommendations

Autonomous territorial defence is a delusional goal based on scenarios of the past century. Switzerland and the EU share values of liberal democracy and a peaceful, rules-based international order that is threatened by all great powers, including the erstwhile American security guarantor. Furthermore, their economies and infrastructures are highly interdependent. In this situation, Switzerland should see itself co-producing European security as a collective good. This general recommendation entails specific recommendations oriented towards mitigating the tensions in Swiss defence policy, without sacrificing formal neutrality.

Firstly, Switzerland should raise its defence spending in line with the level of NATO countries. Secondly, the country needs to reform its rules for arms exports to enable a stable and mutually fruitful European cooperation in defence. Thirdly, Switzerland should cooperate with the EU and NATO on the joint defence of digital and energy infrastructures as well as the European airspace, which are common European spaces rather than national territories. Participation in the European Sky Shield Initiative is certainly a good start.

Frank Schimmelfennig is Professor of European Politics at ETH Zurich. He is also a member of the Swiss National Research Council and Chairman of the Scientific Board of Institut für Europäische Politik Berlin.

The Centre for Comparative and International Studies (CIS) is a joint research and teaching centre for political scientists at the ETH Zurich and the University of Zurich. CIS is the Swiss member of TEPSA.

Between Necessity and Norms: Turkey's Integration into Europe's Emerging Security Architecture

Alper Kaliber

Turkey's geostrategic location and expanding defence industry make it a key player in Europe's security and defence initiatives. Yet, authoritarian backsliding and diverging EU Member State positions limit its scope for sustainable cooperation. This chapter argues that pragmatic but values-informed engagement is essential for anchoring Turkey within Europe's evolving security architecture. Public opinion surveys reveal a traffic light pattern in Turkish threat perceptions: 'red'-level geopolitical anxieties focused on Israel; 'yellow'-level economic and political concerns linked to the U.S. and domestic instability; and 'green'-level relations with European partners reflecting low perceived risk and shared institutional ties, with the exceptions of Greece and the Republic of Cyprus, which stand at the 'yellow' level.

Introduction

Over the past decade, the EU has been shaken by successive and overlapping crises: the Eurozone debt turmoil; the Syrian civil war and ensuing migration flows; Brexit; the COVID-19 pandemic; and, most recently, Russia's full-scale invasion of Ukraine. Each of these crises has disrupted Europe's strategic environment, exposed institutional vulnerabilities within the Union and compelled Member States to reconsider their collective security arrangements. These developments accelerated calls for the EU to assume greater responsibility for its own defence and foreign policy. The launch of initiatives such as the ReArm Europe Plan and SAFE in 2025 exemplifies the EU's ambition to strengthen its defence industrial base and consolidate its role as an autonomous security actor.

Within this shifting landscape, Turkey's geostrategic relevance has gained renewed salience. Situated at the crossroads of Europe, the Middle East and Eurasia,

A. Kaliber (✉)
Istanbul, Istanbul, Turkey

M. Kaeding et al. (eds.), *Security, Defence, and the Future of Europe*,
https://doi.org/10.1007/978-3-032-18279-1_40

Turkey controls access to the Black Sea through the Turkish Straits, while exerting growing influence across the Eastern Mediterranean and the wider Middle East. Its territory functions as a vital corridor for the transit of Caspian and Middle Eastern hydrocarbons to European markets, linking energy security with geopolitics. This geographic centrality, combined with NATO-trained armed forces and a rapidly expanding defence industry, enables Turkey to position itself as an indispensable, if sometimes ambivalent, component of Europe's emerging security architecture.

Ankara has actively sought to leverage this position. Turkish leaders often argue that the war in Ukraine has elevated Ankara's strategic weight. By maintaining simultaneous engagement with both Kyiv and Moscow, Turkey has projected itself as a balancing actor capable of sustaining dialogue with adversarial parties. Yet from a European perspective, Turkey's claims to the role of mediator remain contested. Although Ankara has participated in 'Coalitions of the willing' and signalled readiness to monitor ceasefire arrangements, it has notably refrained from aligning with the EU's sanctions regime against Russia. This selective approach has fostered doubts among European capitals about Turkey's reliability as a long-term partner.

At a societal level, the Turkish media extensively covered the war in Ukraine for various reasons, including the geographical proximity of the conflict to Turkish territory, Turkey's long-standing political and economic ties with both Ukraine and Russia, the strategic importance of the Turkish Straits in controlling access to the Black Sea and the overlapping yet often conflicting interests of Turkey and Russia in the Caucasus region. Despite this close engagement, Turkish public opinion has largely perceived the war as distant from Turkey's immediate security concerns. While most citizens view Russia's invasion of Ukraine as an unjust act of aggression, the conflict has not generated the same sense of alarm or existential threat that it has in many European countries. Unlike much of Europe, the Turkish public generally does not interpret the war as a challenge to Europe's—or Turkey's—core political and normative values, but rather as a regional power struggle unfolding within a broader context of global instability.

This sense of distance from the conflict is consistent with broader patterns in Turkish threat perceptions. Various public surveys yield remarkably consistent results. According to the 2025 Pew Research Center Global Attitudes Survey, Israel is most frequently identified as Turkey's greatest threat (43%)—a 'red'-level perception, reflecting views of Israel's superior military capabilities and adversarial intent amid persistent regional tensions. The U.S. (30%) follows as a 'yellow'-level threat, perceived mainly in economic and political rather than military terms, linked to U.S. influence over Turkey's economy and foreign policy. EU Member States, by contrast, rarely appear as threats and, when mentioned, are categorised in 'green'—indicating low-level concerns rooted in diplomatic rather than military tensions. The notable exceptions are Greece and the Republic of Cyprus, designated as 'yellow'-level threats owing to their long-standing disputes and potential for conflict with Turkey in the Aegean and Eastern Mediterranean. According to the Security Radar 2025 survey by the Friedrich-Ebert-Stiftung, Turks view economic instability—especially inflation and financial crises—as their most pressing threat, followed by wars and conflicts.

Defence-Industrial Complex and Strategic Autonomy

A key factor underpinning Turkey's geostrategic resurgence is the growth of its defence-industrial base, which has become both a symbol and an instrument for Ankara's pursuit of strategic autonomy. Turkey has been investing heavily in developing a self-sufficient military-industrial complex, reducing dependence on foreign suppliers while expanding its ability to project influence abroad. According to the Stockholm International Peace Research Institute, Turkish defence expenditure in 2024 amounted to USD 25 billion, roughly 1.9% of GDP, placing the country 17th in the global ranking of military spenders. Turkey's defence exports reached USD 7.15 billion last year, directed mainly to Ukraine, EU and NATO members, Gulf countries (notably the United Arab Emirates and Qatar) as well as Caucasus and Middle East and North African states such as Azerbaijan, Tunisia and Uzbekistan. Unmanned aerial vehicles have emerged as the flagship product of this growing export portfolio.

Defence production is deeply woven into Ankara's national narrative, feeding into domestic legitimacy and bolstering Turkey's bargaining power abroad. By cultivating its own industrial base, Turkey signals its ambition to transition from a consumer of Western technologies to a competitive producer in the global arms market. Simultaneously, it employs arms exports as tools of foreign policy, nurturing ties with governments in Africa, Asia and the Middle East, together with presenting itself as both a regional power and a strategic partner to Europe. Yet, unlike in many European countries, Turkey's conscription system has changed little since the Republic's founding, aside from a slight reduction in service length. Military service continues to be compulsory for men, reflecting the persistence of traditional notions of citizenship, masculinity and national duty within its defence paradigm.

NATO, the EU and Strategic Autonomy

Turkey's role reveals the tension between NATO cohesion and the EU's pursuit of strategic autonomy. Ankara is indispensable to NATO's Southeastern flank, yet its assertive regional policies and procurement of Russian S-400 missile systems have complicated trust within the Alliance. Nevertheless, its ability to engage flexibly with Washington, Moscow and regional actors enhances its diplomatic leverage.

For the EU, Turkey embodies both opportunity and risk. On the one hand, its geography and military capacity can serve as a force multiplier in stabilising the Black Sea and Middle East regions. On the other hand, its independent orientation creates uncertainty. The EU's strategic autonomy agenda requires both cooperation with NATO and selective partnerships with non-EU actors. Turkey fits uneasily into this equation: too important to exclude, yet too unpredictable to integrate fully.

However, despite longstanding political frictions, Ankara has engaged in various EU-led security and defence mechanisms. Brussels has labelled Turkey a 'like-minded partner', allowing it to contribute to selected projects. In 2025, Turkey joined the SAFE initiative, which seeks to reinforce Europe's defence industrial base. Although non-EU members cannot directly access SAFE funds, candidate countries may contribute up to 35% of a defence product, granting Turkish firms valuable entry points into European procurement schemes.

Turkey also participates in the ESSI, launched in 2022 to enhance air and missile defence through joint procurement. Additionally, Turkey remains active in the EU Battlegroups, multinational rapid-reaction units under the CSDP. These engagements are both practical and symbolic: they facilitate interoperability and crisis management, while signalling Turkey's continuing claim to relevance in Europe's security order.

Turkey's growing defence-industrial base offers the EU tangible opportunities. Unmanned aerial vehicles, land systems and naval technologies produced in Turkey could complement European capabilities. If integrated effectively through frameworks such as SAFE and PESCO, joint procurement could generate economies of scale, improve interoperability and strengthen Europe's collective security.

Barriers to Deeper Integration

Two enduring challenges limit Turkey's deeper integration. Firstly, for more than two decades, Ankara has curtailed fundamental rights and freedoms, criminalised dissent and instrumentalised the judiciary against the opposition. This entrenched authoritarianism undermines institutional checks and balances. If the EU engages with Turkey while ignoring these deficits, it risks eroding its own normative credibility. Cooperation thus becomes largely transactional, driven by short-term calculations rather than shared long-term commitments, yielding arrangements that may be operationally effective yet politically fragile.

Secondly, while some EU Member States, including Poland, Spain and Italy, advocate pragmatic engagement with Turkey, others, such as Germany, Sweden and Finland, adopt a more cautious approach that balances strategic utility with governance concerns. Meanwhile, Greece, Cyprus and France regard Turkey primarily as a strategic rival, particularly in the Eastern Mediterranean. These divisions seriously hinder the EU's ability to develop a coherent, forward-looking strategy toward Ankara.

Recommendations

The EU should apply a calibrated approach to security cooperation reflecting Turkey's perceived threat level and reliability as a partner. To move forward, the EU should: encourage industrial cooperation under clear governance standards; expand cooperation with Turkey on security matters through structured participation in SAFE and PESCO, while addressing rule of law and human rights concerns; do not view Turkey's aspirations for strategic autonomy as inherently opposed to those of the EU, but remain cautious regarding its growing misalignment with the EU foreign policy; maintain dialogue on migration, counter-terrorism as well as climate and energy security; encourage Turkey's participation in capability development projects where mutual interests align; enable Turkey's constructive contributions to crisis management in Europe; and enhance societal dialogue, supporting academic, students', industrial and civil society networks to strengthen epistemic communities that promote cooperative security thinking.

Alper Kaliber is a Senior Fellow at Istanbul Policy Center (IPC). Before joining the IPC, he worked as a visiting scholar at the Federal University of ABC in São Paulo, Brazil. Between 2014 and 2024, he served as a faculty member at Altinbas University, where he coordinated several Jean Monnet modules and chairs. His research focuses on European security, European integration, international security studies, EU–Turkey relations and the Cyprus conflict.

The Istanbul Policy Centre at Sabanci University is a global policy research institution addressing issues such as foreign policy, democratisation, local governance, climate change, transatlantic relations and conflict resolution. Since 2001, the IPC has provided decision makers, opinion leaders and stakeholders with objective analyses and innovative policy recommendations.

The UK: Between the 'Special Relationship' with the U.S. and Stronger Defence Cooperation with Europe

Marion Messmer

The UK has a self-image as a security policy leader in Europe. However, as other European states have increased defence spending, the UK can no longer simply rely on distinguishing itself through the size of its own financial commitment. The UK could instead leverage the strength of its industry to help build more independent European capabilities to ensure the continent's future security. Since the start of the war in Ukraine, the UK has operated on a 'yellow' threat perception: Russia is seen as an adversary that could plan an attack against NATO in the next few years. The UK government has adjusted defence spending and capability investments accordingly. This threat perception is likely to last so long as the Russian invasion of Ukraine continues.

The UK's Role in European Security and Defence

The UK has long seen itself as a European security and defence leader. As with most European countries, it reduced its investment in security after the end of the Cold War, but nevertheless remained one of the top spenders in NATO until other states boosted their own defence spending following Russia's invasion of Ukraine. The UK has reliably exceeded 2% of GDP on defence spending annually since 2014, with a commitment of around 2.2% annually, qualifying in 2021 as 4th largest spender in NATO. This was in part due to the UK's nuclear arsenal which requires a large proportion of the defence budget for maintenance and modernisation. However, as other NATO members have significantly increased their defence spending, the UK increase has been more moderate by comparison. Despite spending 2.4% of GDP in 2025, the UK has fallen to 12th place in the NATO defence

M. Messmer (✉)
Chatham House, London, UK
e-mail: MMessmer@Chathamhouse.org

M. Kaeding et al. (eds.), *Security, Defence, and the Future of Europe*,
https://doi.org/10.1007/978-3-032-18279-1_41

spending league table, which raises questions about its ability to claim leadership in NATO without offering additional evidence of what exactly is being contributed to the Alliance.

The UK has a strong relationship with Ukraine, having provided support since Russia first invaded Crimea in 2014. When Russia's full-scale invasion began in 2022, the UK could leverage its pre-existing relationships with the Ukrainian government and military to provide additional assistance quickly. Public opinion stands consistently behind the government's support for Ukraine. Ipsos polling from September 2022—February 2025 shows that only 11–17% of the British public oppose supporting Ukraine. Support has consistently been above 53% over the course of the Russian invasion. Along similar lines, a YouGov poll from June 2025 showed that 49% of Britons supported a further increase in defence spending, 22% thought it should remain the same and 11% thought it ought to decrease.

Despite the increased threat perception, British armed forces struggle to recruit as many new recruits as required to fulfil national goals and NATO plans. This has reignited a debate on whether the UK ought to introduce conscription. For the time being, though, there is no concrete plan to do so and the Ministry of Defence would need to put together a workable policy proposal to be able to move ahead with conscription, which was previously abandoned in 1960. While Ipsos polling from May 2025 suggests that 28% of Britons would like to see an increase in the number of British Army personnel, only 35% indicated a personal willingness to defend their country if it became necessary.

Since Brexit, rather than investing in the EU's security potential, the UK has spent more of its political and diplomatic capital on NATO and minilateral arrangements to strengthen European security. This included becoming the framework nation for NATO's enhanced forward presence in Estonia, as well as setting up the JEF to provide additional security on NATO's north-eastern flank. It has also displayed leadership with regard to establishing the 'Coalition of the willing', a grouping of 33 states which have pledged enhanced support for Ukraine, given that the U.S. has distanced itself since the start of Trump's second term. Another UK strength is its relatively strong intelligence and technology sector. As the U.S. is becoming a less reliable ally, the UK could step up to work with other European states in developing independent European capabilities, especially in intelligence, surveillance and reconnaissance—an area in which European NATO members have tended to rely on the U.S.

An Intertwined Relationship with the U.S.

Since the Second World War, the UK has based a good deal of its security policy on its close relationship with the U.S. This has been a sensible strategy for a long time, but the isolationism of the second Trump administration and its sometimes-contradictory foreign policy messaging have increased UK concerns about U.S. longer-term reliability.

To some extent, the UK's reliance on the U.S. is hard to disentangle. Nuclear capabilities are intertwined with those of the U.S. in a way that is particularly difficult to resolve. For instance, the UK relies on the U.S. for maintenance and updates of its Trident missiles. While the U.S. cannot interfere with the UK's nuclear launch decisions, there are concerns that if the relationship were to break down, the U.S. might refuse to service Trident missiles. As a result, this would degrade the UK's nuclear capabilities in the medium term.

Despite, or perhaps because of, these concerns, earlier in 2025, the Strategic Defence Review recommended that the UK buy some F-35As—fighter jets that are certified to carry U.S. nuclear weapons. The UK has since joined NATO's nuclear sharing arrangement, which implies that there are now U.S. nuclear bombs stationed in the UK. In a crisis, they would be delivered by British pilots, but only on a U.S. launch order. The UK was part of a similar sharing arrangement during the Cold War but is the first NATO Ally to return to such an arrangement now that the security environment has worsened again.

This move effectively strengthens U.S. signalling about its commitment to extended deterrence and Article 5 at a time when this has been questioned. It also highlights the UK government's difficult strategy trying to balance between European partners and the U.S. While the UK government so far has been able to find common ground with the Trump administration at a time when others have struggled to do so, it is a difficult tightrope to balance on.

Defence Spending and Public Expenditure

As the EU has become an important actor for defence industry coordination and financing, the UK is struggling with how to allow its industry to benefit from these arrangements. The UK defence industry has a history of cooperation with its European counterparts and is a government priority. However, there are concerns that this is an area in which it might be disadvantaged after Brexit. It also remains a challenge that the Labour government frames defence spending as needing to benefit the domestic economy. While this is understandable given the challenging economic environment this government has inherited, it risks weakening procurement decisions because it sets contradictory incentives.

Recommendations

The UK should focus on procuring the necessary equipment to improve European defence and NATO interoperability. That means domestic economic benefits ought to be a second priority. For each procurement, the government needs to weigh up whether speed of procurement, or investment in building a European capability, is the more important requirement and then invest accordingly. This might mean that some spending benefits non-European, non-NATO partners such as the Republic of

Korea or Israel, whereas in other cases it will lead to a slower procurement pipeline but will establish production capacity in Europe.

Investment in the UK's defence industry should continue, which furthermore must be able to cooperate as seamlessly as possible with industrial counterparts in the EU. Membership in the EU SAFE programme is a positive example of the UK participating in EU action. Defence company MBDA, set up to be deliberately pan-European, is another positive example of how the UK government can work with other European governments to strengthen the industrial base.

The UK government should further diversify its foreign and security policy relationships away from a primary reliance on the 'Special Relationship' with the U.S. This includes investing more in European defence relationships, as well as looking to partners such as Japan and the Republic of Korea that have faced similar security challenges and could provide a model for the UK.

Marion Messmer is the programme director the International Security Programme at Chatham House, who holds a PhD in Security Studies from Kings College in London. She is an expert in European security and defence, arms control, nuclear weapons policy issues and Russia-NATO relations. Before joining Chatham House, Marion was Co-Director of BASIC.

The Royal Institute of International Affairs (Chatham House) is an independent British policy institute and a trusted forum for debate and dialogue. Established in 1920, it sits at the forefront of international affairs research.

Ukraine's Lessons for Europe

Oleksiy Melnyk and Mykola Sungurovskyi

The likelihood of war spreading beyond Ukrainian borders is real, but not inevitable. In order to deter Russia—the only military threat to Europe—European leaders should ensure that their countries are not only prepared to accept this new reality, but are also ready to face the challenge both technically and mentally. In view of the current situation facing the country, the threat perception assessment according to the traffic light system positions it squarely in the 'red' zone.

Russia: The Only Military Threat to Europe

Russia is correctly identified as the only military threat to Europe today. However, Russia is not alone and Vladimir Putin would not be so confident in his belief that he can defeat Ukraine militarily and undermine the rules-based international order without active sponsors such as China, Iran, North Korea, as well as other international and domestic enablers of his aggressive policies.

Ukraine's victory is the key to securing Europe's future. Otherwise, not only will Russia be encouraged and rewarded for maintaining its aggressive policy, but others may also try to follow the same path in resolving disputes within their neighbourhoods. It goes without saying that any significant military crisis elsewhere in the world will critically aggravate the already existing non-military threats for Europe (such as migration, disruption of trade and energy supply). Unfortunately, Ukraine missed the opportunity to defeat Russia on the battlefield during its attempted counteroffensive in 2023, but whatever Ukraine's future victory will look like, Russia should not be allowed to walk away victorious and unpunished.

O. Melnyk (✉) · M. Sungurovskyi
Razumkov Centre, Kyiv, Ukraine
e-mail: melnyk@razumkov.org.ua; sungurovsky@razumkov.ua

M. Kaeding et al. (eds.), *Security, Defence, and the Future of Europe*,
https://doi.org/10.1007/978-3-032-18279-1_42

Russia's aggressive actions were recognised by NATO and the EU as "the most significant and direct threat to Allies' security" not long before the outbreak of Russia's full-scale war against Ukraine in 2022. It took Western leaders almost 15 years to respond to Putin's "declaration of war", proclaimed in his speech at the Munich Security Conference in 2007. It is better late than never, but nevertheless the West wasted a critical amount of time and numerous opportunities to deter Russia at the outset of this crisis. Has Europe woken up yet? A Ukrainian soldier, who was asked this question by an international journalist, said: "Yes, Europe is awake, but still drinking coffee and dressed in pyjamas."

Russia is *the* long-term threat. As long as power in Russia remains in the hands of the *Siloviki* (KGB successors), it would be disastrously naive to hope for its democratic transformation even after Putin. There is no real political opposition in Russia and this is unlikely to change in the foreseeable future. Most Russians seem to be very enthusiastic about supporting the idea of imperial greatness and invincibility under a strong-handed ruler. According to the Levada-Centre, 87% of Russians approve of Putin's policies and the rest live in fear, guided by deeply rooted instincts of self-preservation. The case of Dmitriy Medvedev (President of Russia in 2008–2012 and one of the most radical anti-West Russian officials now) should serve as an example of a KGB 'special operation', when a kind of liberal official is appointed to be President in order to create the illusion of a democratic transformation in Russia among Western leaders. If another Medvedev becomes President, it will simply mean that Russia needs breathing space to attract Western investors and technologies. This political trick will last for no more than one election cycle until the beginning of the next geopolitical cycle of 'rising from the kneeling position' under the leadership of another Putin.

The Russian society at large is also one of the most critical enablers of Moscow's aggressive policies.

Ukraine's Lessons for Europe

Travelling nowadays between Ukraine and EU countries is a significant journey not only physically in terms of distance, but also mentally across different worlds. For Ukrainians, this is a kind of time-travel from the current wartime reality both into the settled past and much longed-for future of peace and stability. Despite physically experiencing peaceful surroundings, the journey has not been made mentally given that grim reality must be faced again back home once a trip is over. One cannot change the past, but should try to shape the future by learning and taking into account its lessons. Ukraine's experiences, both positive and negative, can help other nations not necessarily to avoid worst-case scenarios, but better prepare for them. One of the main purposes of this chapter is to make a moderate contribution to numerous publications of lessons learned and recommendations that have eternal value, or may become outdated quickly because of the extreme dynamics of war.

There are already some joint initiatives for collecting, analysing and disseminating Ukraine's experience, such as the NATO-Ukraine Joint Analysis, Training and

Education Centre, but they are mostly focused on military-related know-how. However, there is much more to be done concerning civilian matters and individuals' experience, which need to be systematically analysed and communicated with governments and citizens of European countries.

The most important lesson is to be aware and vigilant. One's adversary does not necessarily share the notion that 'nothing good ever comes of violence', especially with Russia's current international behaviour being steered by President Putin and apparently widely supported by the population. Before 2014, the majority of Ukrainians tended to believe that a Russian-Ukrainian war was not possible, despite a centuries-long record of oppression, hostilities and coerced brotherhood. For those in the minority who argued that Moscow would not hesitate to use military force to conquer Ukraine if other non-military means fail, there were plenty of counter-arguments. Those arguments and cost-benefit calculations were convincingly rational, coherent and logical, such as international law, bilateral agreements as well as mutual economic and trade dependence. Putin's logic was different!

As soon as the first step to accepting the reality of an existing military threat is made, the next is "*Si vis pacem, para bellum*" (If you want peace, prepare for war). Peace-time politicians quite often see the risk of losing the next scheduled elections as being much higher than losing a war, which they prefer to consider as an unthinkable scenario. Saving on defence allows governments to secure popular support, because it is much more beneficial to sell an infrastructure megaproject to their voters than an investment in a multi-year defence modernisation programme. Ukraine used to spend about 1% of its GDP on defence for many years before 2014. The rapid increase in defence and security spending up to 5% in 2015–2022 enabled various necessary transformations in the security sector and defence industry, thereby creating a capability to drive back the first waves of Russian attacks and survive for the initial months of the war until international military support began to arrive. Ukraine was also much better prepared for the full-scale invasion in February 2022, having about 420,000 people with real combat experience gained in the period of 2014–2022. However, there is still debate about whether there was a proper balance of defence *versus* healthcare and education. The cost to Ukraine for wounded veterans, families of soldiers killed and those missing in action in 2023 is USD 172 million a day and still rising. Ukraine's defence spending has reached 31% of GDP—the world highest defence burden. The point is that saving on defence may cost 10 times more in financial terms, let alone the war damage estimated at hundreds of billions and the human cost, which is impossible to measure in financial terms.

An investment in defence hardware and infrastructure is important, but it will be of little value if there are no operators. One of the biggest Russian advantages on the battlefield is the manpower. It is not only about numbers, but also about the freedom of the Russian political and military leadership to expend them in hundreds on a daily basis and the ability to recruit new soldiers by using vast financial incentives or unrestricted repressive state instruments. As mentioned above, in February 2022 Ukraine had a manpower of nearly 420,000 veterans in active service and in reserve to meet Russian aggression. Additionally, during the first few months, the number of citizens with or without military training willing to take arms was much higher than the Ukrainian Defence Forces were able to digest (equip, arm and train). However, with every month of the protracted war and the growing number of losses, there were fewer and fewer volunteers to fulfil the permanent needs and by mid-2023 mobilisation/conscription became the primary source of new recruits. Various initiatives such as using commercial recruitment agencies, individual units' recruitment campaigns and offering special contracts for men aged 18–24 or for foreign citizens are important, but supplementary.

Lastly, it is vital to consider Ukrainians' vision of their country's future security, based on experience and perceptions. According to a September 2025 public opinion survey by the Razumkov Centre, 42.2% of respondents consider NATO membership as the best way to ensure Ukraine's security, despite only 24.5% believing that all NATO Members will immediately come to help in case of military attack. Furthermore, 25.3% are sure that Members will not risk the lives of their citizens for the security of Allies. At the same time, Ukrainians are particularly confident in the EU's compliance with guarantees, given to Ukraine: 61.9% believe that the EU will adhere to guarantees and be able to protect Ukraine; another 33.6% are confident in the EU's adherence, but doubtful of its ability to defend.

Recommendations

Russia must be forced to learn the lesson that 'nothing comes from violence and nothing ever could'. Deterring Russia's aggressive policy will not solve all the European security problems, but if Russia walks away victorious and unpunished, a possible military attack against Europe, as well as the probability of major military crises in other parts of the world, will increase dramatically and the already existing non-military threats to Europe will be severely aggravated.

European politicians should take the Russian threat seriously and properly communicate their concerns to their societies, raising awareness of the hard defence and security risks as well as threats. Furthermore, they should establish permanent monitoring of public opinion, measurable indicators of verbal and practical readiness to support government policies for increasing security and defence spending, even at the expense of social benefits. It is time to make preparations in all domains and let the enemy know.

Finally, this is more of a cautionary observation than a recommendation. War is far too serious a matter to be exploited for political manoeuvring. If defeating domestic political opponents becomes a higher priority than confronting or preventing war, then one risks losing the very foundation of democracy—free elections—especially in territories that may fall under occupation.

Oleksiy Melnyk, Co-director, Foreign Relations and International Security Programmes at Razumkov Centre. He joined the Centre in 2001 after 21 years of military service, including participation in UN peacekeeping. In 2005–2007, he served as the First Assistant to the Minister of Defence of Ukraine. His main areas of research are international security, conflict management, national security and defence governance as well as reforms.

Mykola Sungurovskyi is the Director of Military Programmes at Razumkov Centre. His main areas of research are national security, strategic planning and defence reforms. Before joining the Razumkov Centre in 1999, he spent almost 30 years in the military and his last position was as Department Director at the Analytical Service of Ukraine's National Security and Defence Council.

Razumkov Centre is a not-for-profit, non-partisan and non-governmental think tank that conducts research in the areas of internal politics, economic and social development, energy, economics, foreign policy together with national and international security. The Centre also has an in-house Sociological Service.

Co-funded by
the European Union